IMAGES of America

CROOK COUNTY

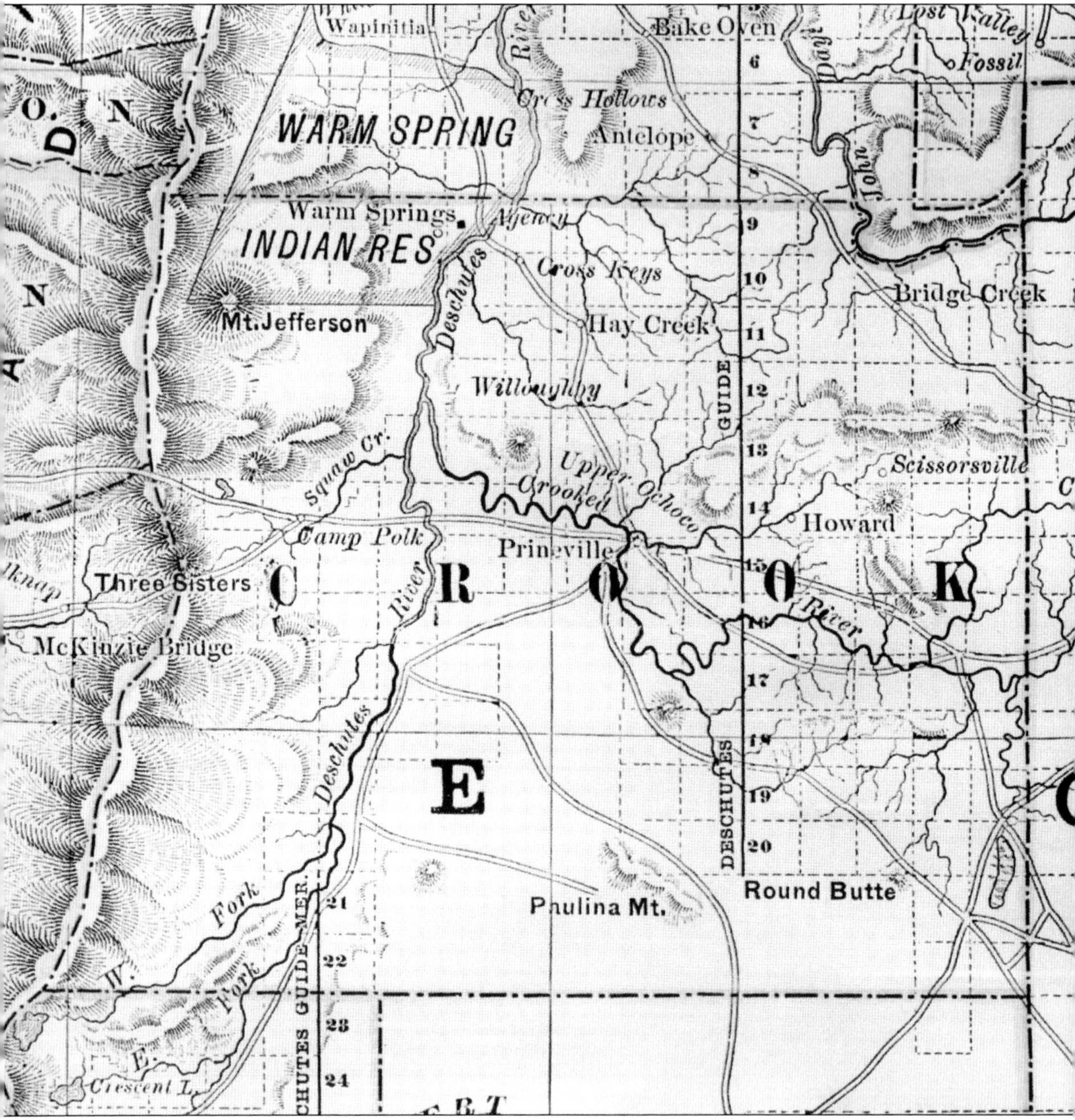

Prior to 1882, all of central Oregon was part of Wasco County with the county seat in The Dalles. A growing population on the frontier of central Oregon and the need for more local government led to legislative actions to create Crook County from Wasco County in October 1882. This is a map of the newly created county as it appeared in 1883.

On the Cover: These loggers are standing with their spouses next to a load of ponderosa pine logs on a wagon pulled by oxen near Ochoco Creek about 18 miles east of Prineville around 1890. Logging and sawmill operations were among the first industries in Crook County, as homesteaders needed lumber to build their homes.

IMAGES
of America

CROOK COUNTY

Steve Lent

ARCADIA
PUBLISHING

ISBN 978-1-4671-3059-2

Published by Arcadia Publishing
Charleston, South Carolina

Printed in the United States of America

Library of Congress Control Number: 2013935430

For all general information, please contact Arcadia Publishing:
Telephone 843-853-2070
Fax 843-853-0044
E-mail sales@arcadiapublishing.com
For customer service and orders:
Toll-Free 1-888-313-2665

Visit us on the Internet at www.arcadiapublishing.com

To the memory of my great-grandparents George and Mitty Bible Stege and John B. and Viola Harris Lent, pioneers of eastern Oregon.

Contents

Acknowledgments

Numerous people have assisted in providing photographs to the archives of the Bowman Museum in Prineville, Oregon. Crook County has a rich historical heritage, and several pioneer families remain in the region and have shared their family histories and photographs and have aided in the historical accuracy of this book. There are too many to recognize all of them, but their efforts are much appreciated.

Eloise Brummer on the Bowman Museum staff has proofread the document and has shared family stories. I am always indebted to my "history buddy" Frances Juris as she continually shares her knowledge and enthusiasm for local history at the young age of 95. The board of the Crook County Historical Society and Gordon Gillespie, executive director of the Bowman Museum, have provided encouragement and allowed access to the numerous photograph archives of the museum.

The researchers of the Crook County Genealogical Society have assisted with information and insights; special thanks go to Mary Mayfield, Vicky Nelsen, Loiselle Dahill, and Ruth Cholin.

Unless otherwise noted, all of the images in this book appear courtesy of the Crook County Historical Society and the Bowman Museum.

INTRODUCTION

The interior of Oregon was among the last frontiers to be settled in the state. Gold was not discovered in the region in large quantities, and marauding Indians discouraged early settlement. During the Civil War, regular military troops were withdrawn back East to fight, so Oregon volunteers provided protection. However, the numerous problems with raiding Indian bands discouraged settlers from entering the region. The conclusion of the Civil War allowed regular troops to return West, and campaigns were conducted to remove the threat to settlement.

The entire region of central Oregon was included in Wasco County with the county seat in The Dalles. Some scattered settlers established themselves along the old Dalles–Canyon City Wagon Road in the northern part of central Oregon, but the first settlement in central Oregon was not until 1867, when Elisha Barnes came to explore the possibilities of the area. He returned to the Willamette Valley and convinced some of his neighbors to join him in settling in the fertile Ochoco Valley with its lush grasslands. George Barnes, Ewen Johnson, Edward White, Billy Smith, David Wayne Claypool, and Raymond Burkhart came to begin the settlement of the region near the confluence of Mill Creek and Ochoco Creek about seven miles east of present Prineville. This small group of men met with hardships and was raided by a band of Indians. They were forced to return to the valley but returned the following year and brought their families.

Francis Barney Prine settled in the lush Crooked River valley in 1868 below the lava rimrocks, and the post office of Prine, which later became Prineville, was established. Soon, numerous other adventuresome settlers came to the region and began to settle on the rangelands. George Barnes had claimed that the vicinity was a "stockman's paradise," and livestock could be grazed year-round without putting up hay. The first settlers began squatting on the best rangeland. The region was not fully surveyed until the late 1870s, so many could not establish homesteads until the land was surveyed.

Prineville served as the main commercial center for the early settlers and became the main community of the region. Prineville was incorporated in 1880 and was the only incorporated community in central Oregon for several years. Outlying areas began to develop supply points for settlers, and numerous post offices were established in the homes of local homesteaders. None of the post office sites became major communities, but the communities of Paulina, Powell Butte, and Post began to thrive. Other outlying sites such as Bend, Redmond, Sisters, and Madras began to develop after the turn of the 20th century.

A tragic event occurred near Grizzly Mountain north of Prineville in 1882 when a neighbor in a property dispute killed two settlers. Since the county seat was in The Dalles, there was no major local law enforcement. The man who shot his neighbors was captured and held in a hotel in Prineville, as there was no jail in the community. A group of local men decided that it would take too long to wait for justice from The Dalles and formed a group known as the Committee of Vigilance, or the vigilantes. They took justice into their own hands and killed the suspect as well as a hired hand of the man and began the vigilante era in the region. Several deaths were attributed to the vigilantes during a four-year period of violence. Concerns over the vigilante justice led local legislator B.F. Nichols to introduce legislation to create a new county to meet the needs of central Oregon. After much intrigue, Crook County was created from Wasco County on October 24, 1882. Prineville was appointed the county seat until local elections could be held to select the permanent county seat. The new county was named for Gen. George Crook, who had been involved in command of efforts to contain Indian depredations in eastern Oregon.

The first election for the county was held in 1884, and with the establishment of local government, the vigilante era came to an end. Prineville became the permanent county seat. The region began to thrive as a livestock center, and large herds of cattle and bands of sheep ranged on the grasslands. Eventually, this led to another violent era in central Oregon that became known as the Sheep and Cattle War. Sheep men and cattlemen vied for the same rangelands, and bitter disputes erupted. Cattlemen took the initiative and created "sheepshooter's" organizations and established boundaries of cattle ranges. This resulted in the killing of numerous sheep by cattlemen, and this dispute lasted until the establishment of the national forest reserves in 1905. At that time, administrative control of public lands was initiated, and allotments for grazing were established.

Much of Crook County includes numerous acres of national forestland and general land office lands that became Taylor Grazing Act lands, which finally became the Bureau of Land Management. Vast areas of the county land are under federal jurisdiction.

Numerous small sawmills were established to provide for local lumber needs, and the large stands of ponderosa pine provided the natural resources necessary to operate the mills. Major sawmill production was not established until the late 1930s.

The arrival of the railroad lines into central Oregon in 1911 resulted in the major community of Prineville being bypassed by the rail lines, which passed through the developing communities of Madras, Redmond, and Bend. Bend began to be the major commercial center of the region after the railroads arrived. Soon, outlying areas to the north and west of Prineville began to express interest in having their own local government. In 1914, Jefferson County was created from Crook County, and in 1916, Deschutes County was created from Crook County, leaving a much smaller land base for the county but leaving it among the largest in Oregon.

Prineville became concerned that the community would become a ghost town without a connection to the railroad, so a bond issue was passed to connect a rail line from Prineville to the Oregon Trunk Railroad just north of Redmond. Eventually, the railroad became very profitable when large lumber mills were established in Prineville. Crook County had a lumber boom from post–World War II until the late 1960s, and five major mills were operating in Prineville. However, timber supplies began to diminish, and by 2001, all major mills were out of business. Farming and ranching were the other major business activities. Local entrepreneur Les Schwab began a tire business in Prineville in 1952, and his business acumen resulted in the franchising of numerous stores and the establishment of a tire empire headquartered in Prineville until 2010, when corporate headquarters was moved to Bend.

One

Exploration and Early Settlement

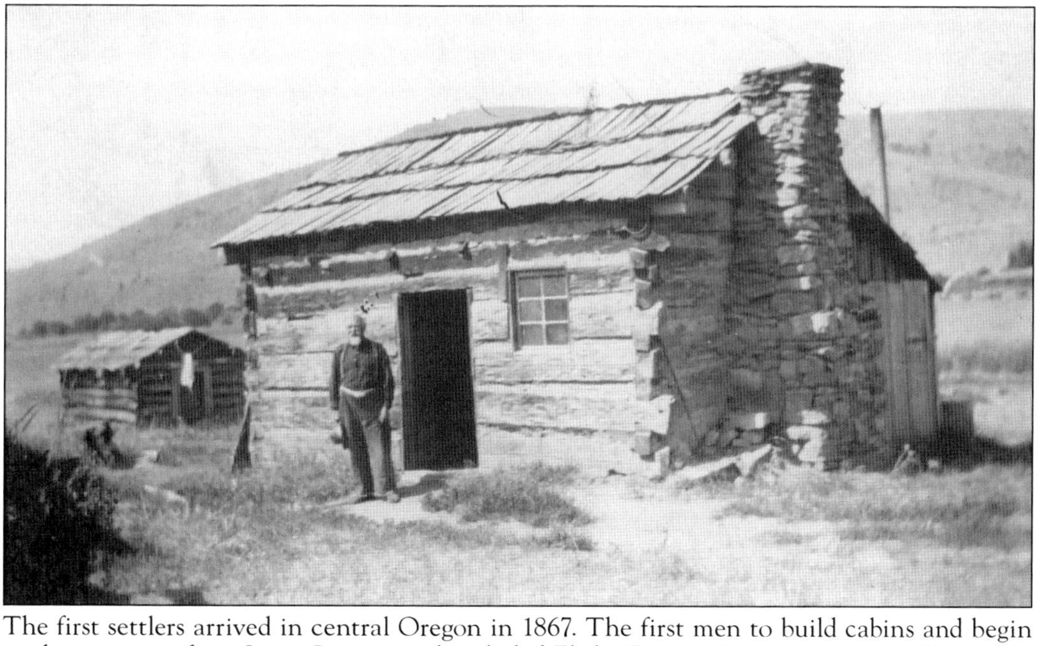

The first settlers arrived in central Oregon in 1867. The first men to build cabins and begin settlement were from Linn County and included Elisha Barnes, George Barnes, Billy Smith, Edward White, Raymond Burkhart, Ewen Johnson, and David Wayne Claypool. This is a photograph of Billy Smith in front of his cabin near the confluence of Mill Creek with Ochoco Creek about 1870.

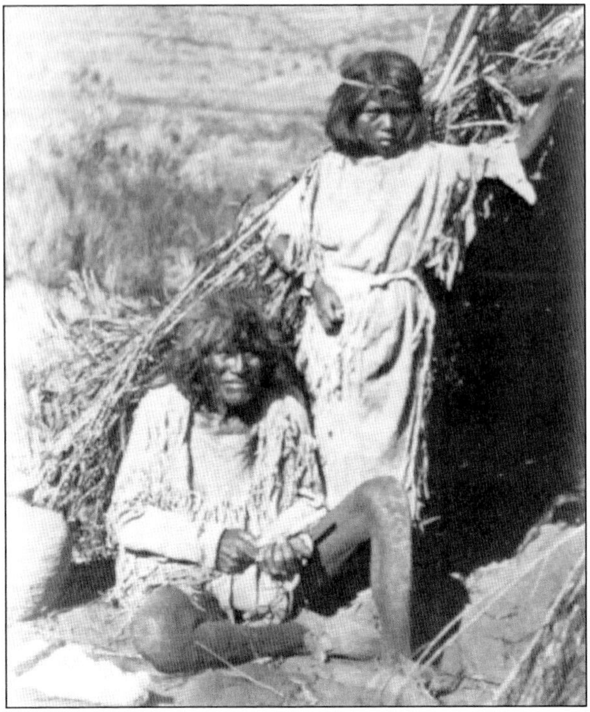

Northern Paiute Indians occupied central Oregon prior to the arrival of Euro-Americans. This is an early photograph of Northern Paiutes in front of a typical sagebrush-and-juniper-constructed wigwam. The bands of Northern Paiute roamed the region and were hunters and gatherers; they commonly lived in small family units.

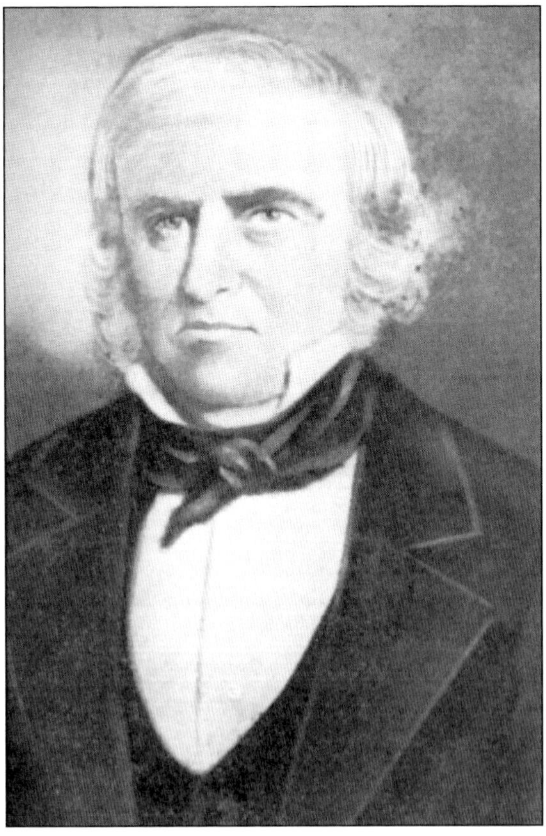

Peter Skene Ogden is believed to be the first Euro-American to traverse the region of Crook County. A brigade leader for the Hudson Bay Company, he was seeking fur-bearing animals in the Great Basin. He first traveled through the region in the winter of 1824–1825 en route to the Snake River. His party of trappers left Fort Nez Perce near present Walla Walla and ascended up the Deschutes River and Crooked River, passing near the sites of present-day Prineville and Paulina.

A recently discovered engraved rock was found on the southeastern slope of Maury Mountain on a rimrock ridge; the engraving features a cross and the date 1831. Prior to this finding, there were no known visitors to the region at that time or earlier. It is believed that it must have been left behind when John Work's Snake River expedition passed through the region. John Work (pictured) was the successor of Peter Skene Ogden and was in charge of the Snake River expeditions in 1830–1831.

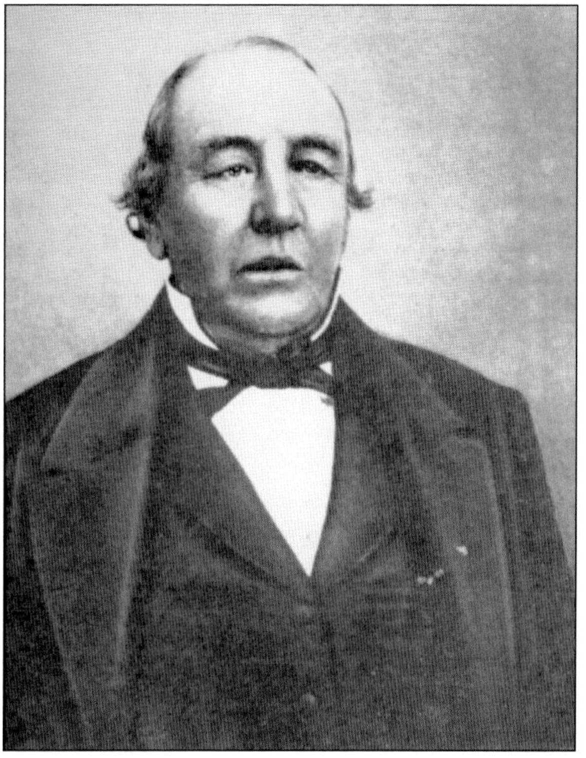

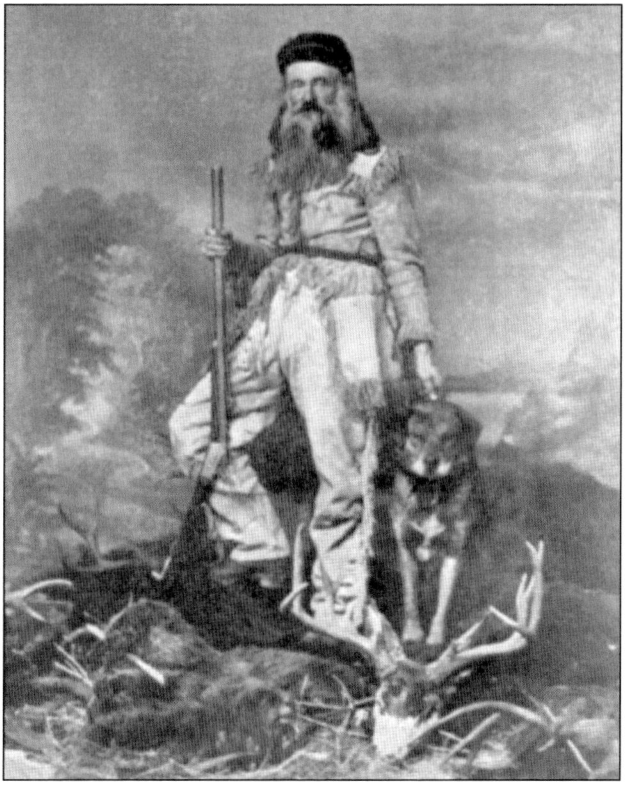

In September 1845, Stephen Meek, who had trapped beaver in the region, convinced a large group of travelers on the Oregon Trail that he knew of a shortcut to the Willamette Valley through the interior of Oregon. He was hired to lead them through the harsh environment of the region, and the group left the main Oregon Trail at the mouth of the Malheur River near present Vale, Oregon. The group became lost and endured many hardships and deaths as they passed through central Oregon and present Crook County. The infamous Lost Meek Wagon Train was one of the most tragic cutoffs on the Oregon Trail.

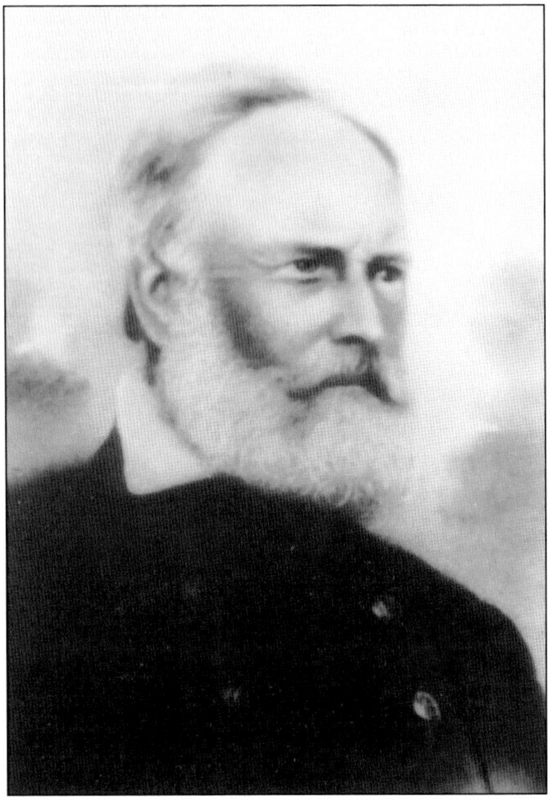

Maj. Enoch Steen passed through central Oregon and present Crook County in 1860. His mission was to establish a military wagon route to southeastern Oregon from Fort Vancouver. He passed through the present site of Prineville and followed along the Crooked River and established a camp known as Camp Separation on the northeast slope of Maury Mountain. He was following a similar route taken earlier by Captain Wallen. He then headed southeast to the Harney Valley region.

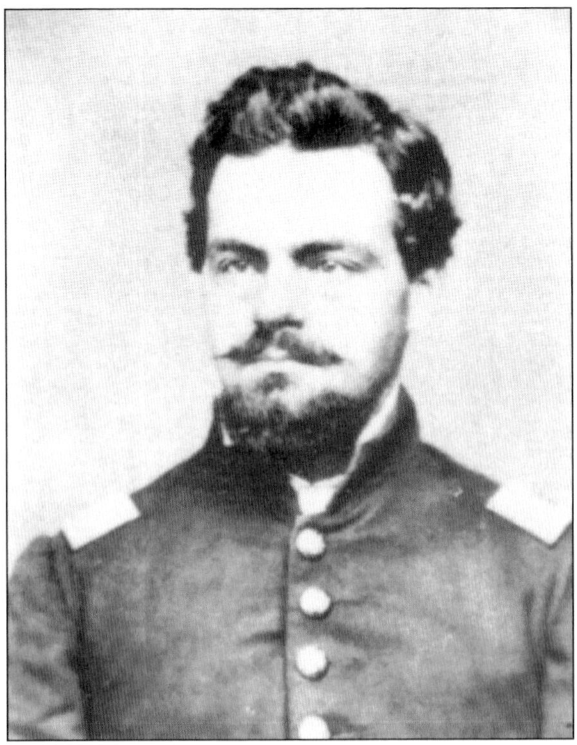

Capt. John Drake led a company of 1st Oregon Cavalry volunteers on an expedition up the Crooked River and into eastern Oregon in 1864. Regular troops were involved in the Civil War, and volunteers were mustered into service to protect settlers and wagon routes from the interior of the state to eastern Oregon. His unit was camped at the confluence of Crooked River and the North Fork of Crooked River when scouts discovered a camp of raiding Indians at the head of a valley, about five miles northeast of his camp. He sent Lt. John McCall and Lt. Stephen Watson to engage the Indians in battle.

Northern Paiute Indian leader Paulina had led several raids on wagons and early settlers and was widely feared for his aggressive activities. The region had been the realm of his people prior to the arrival of the Euro-Americans. His raiding ways from 1861 to 1867 attracted the attention of the military. He was involved in a battle in upper Rabbit Valley northwest of the present town of Paulina on May 20, 1864. He was killed near Trout Creek just north of Ashwood in 1867.

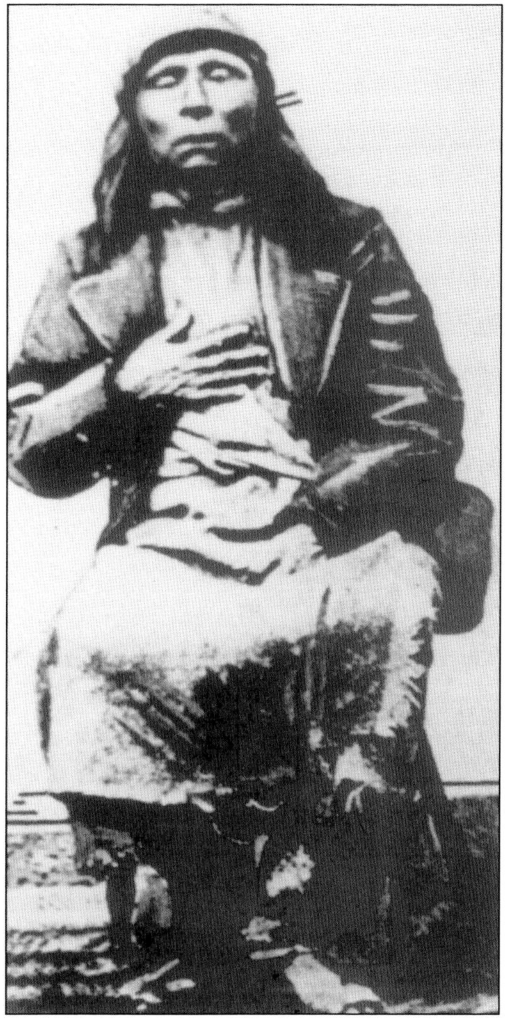

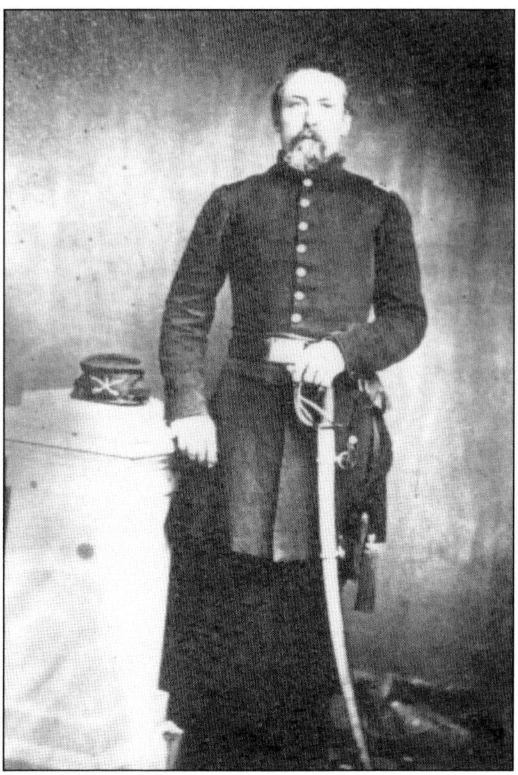

Lt. Stephen Watson was under Capt. John Drake's command in the 1st Oregon Cavalry. Early on the morning of May 20, 1964, Warson, Lt. John McCall, and Warm Springs scout leader Stock Whitley, with companies of soldiers and scouts, made a charge on Paulina's camp at the upper reaches of Rabbit Valley. Watson was killed in the initial action as well as three soldiers in his company, and Stock Whitley was fatally wounded. The skirmish was brief but deadly for the soldiers. Paulina and his band escaped but lost most of their provisions and supplies.

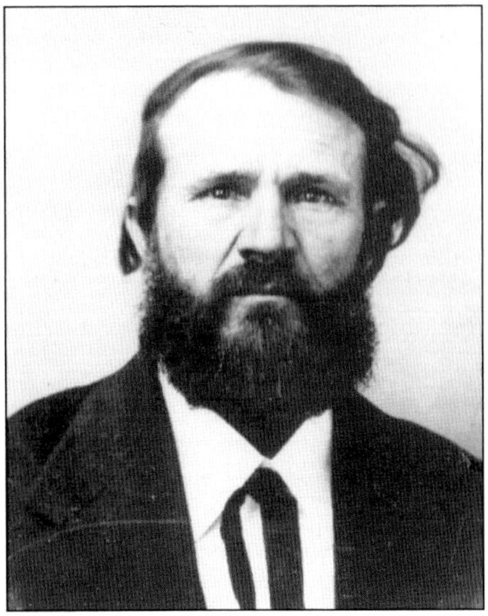

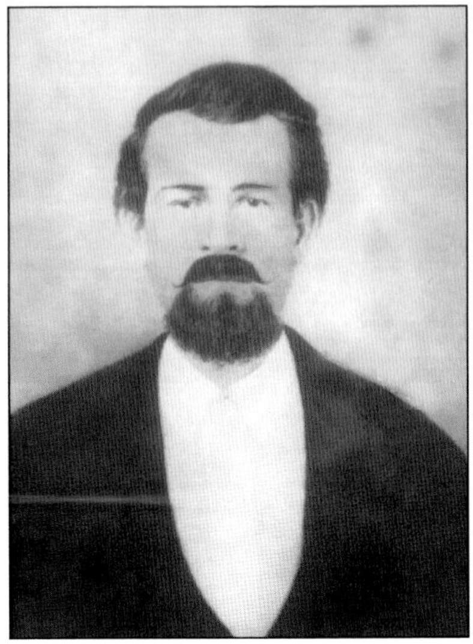

Elisha Barnes (left) and his son George Barnes (right) were among the first Euro-Americans to settle in central Oregon. Elisha Barnes had come to the Ochoco Valley in 1867 to scout out the possibilities of farming and ranching and liked what he saw. He returned to the Willamette Valley and convinced some of his neighbors to join him in settling the region. George Barnes accompanied five other men who crossed the Cascade Mountains and built a cabin near the confluence of Ochoco Creek and Mill Creek. Elisha Barnes later would become the first mayor of Prineville when the community was incorporated in 1871, and George Barnes became the first lawyer in central Oregon.

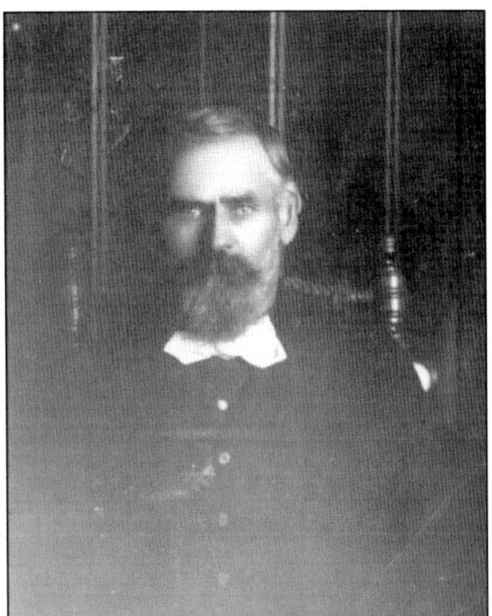

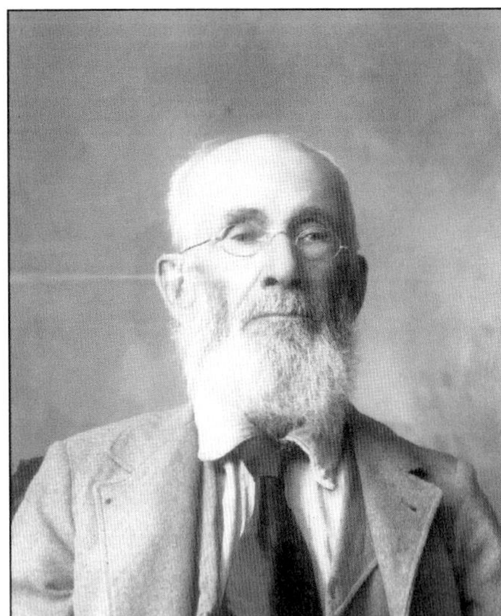

David Wayne Claypool (left) and Edward White (right) accompanied George Barnes in settling the Ochoco region. Both men were from the Scio vicinity of Linn County. Together the men built a log cabin and began preparing land for ranching and farming. Indians raided the group and burned the cabin. The men had fortunately been away clearing land and escaped harm, but they were forced to walk to the Warm Springs Indian Reservation several miles northwest on the Deschutes River for assistance, as their horses had been stolen. They crossed back over the Cascade Mountains but returned to the Ochoco Valley with their families in 1868.

This is a photograph of Ewen and Nancy Johnson several years after they settled in central Oregon. Ewen Johnson was in one of the first groups of settlers in the Ochoco Valley. He had helped build the first log cabin and was forced to return to the valley after the Indian raid. He brought his wife, Nancy, with him when he returned the following year. She was among the first Euro-American women to settle in the region.

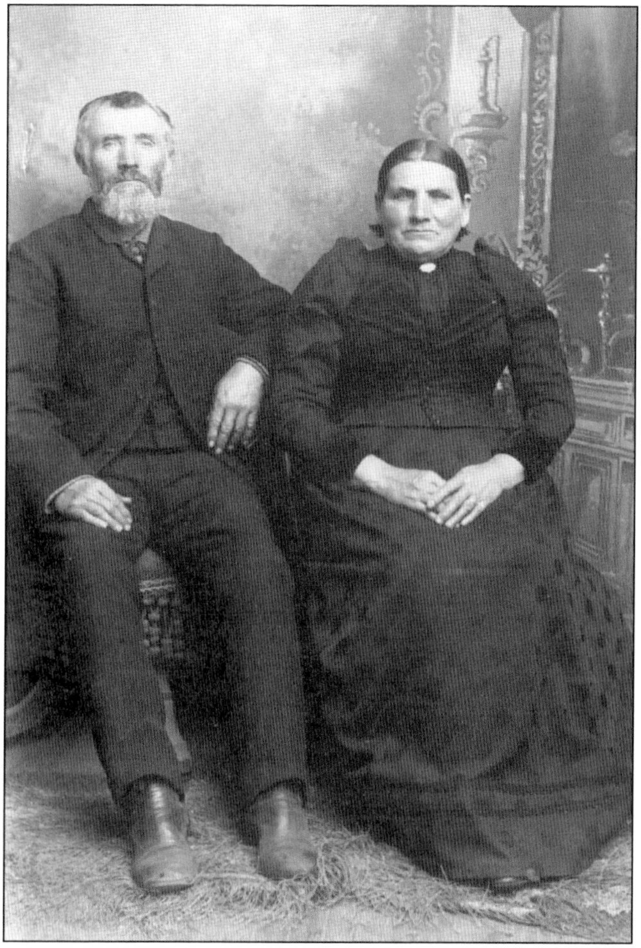

Ewen and Nancy Johnson established a ranch near the confluence of Mill Creek and Ochoco Creek and operated it for many years. This is their ranch house. From left to right are son Jake Johnson, Ewen Johnson, Nancy Johnson, and their son Jehu Johnson. Johnson Creek to the east of present Prineville is named for Ewen and Nancy Johnson. The Mill Creek Cemetery was established on land donated by the family. Nancy and Ewen are buried in the Mill Creek Cemetery.

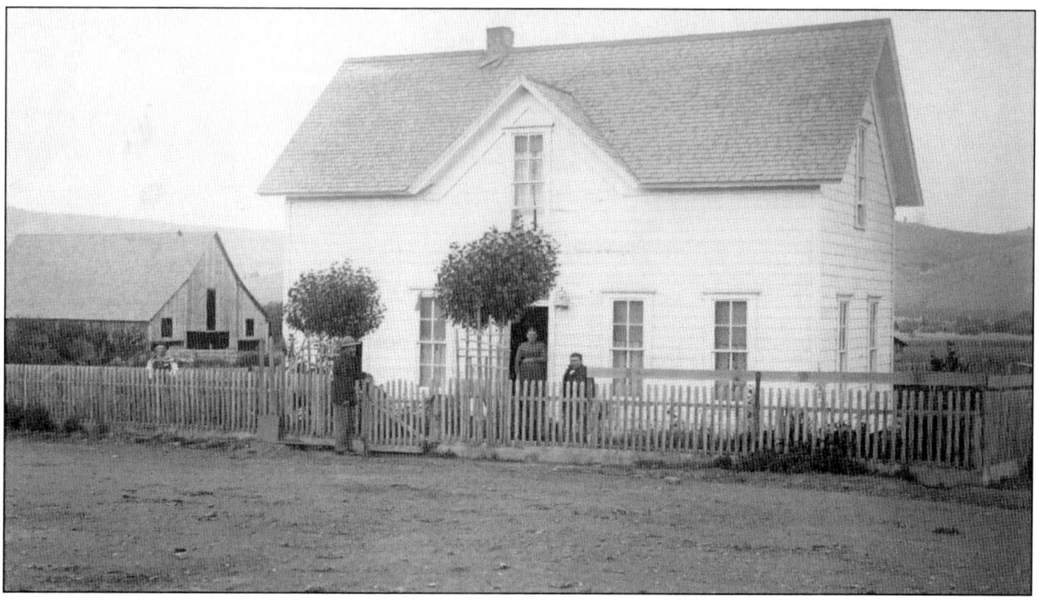

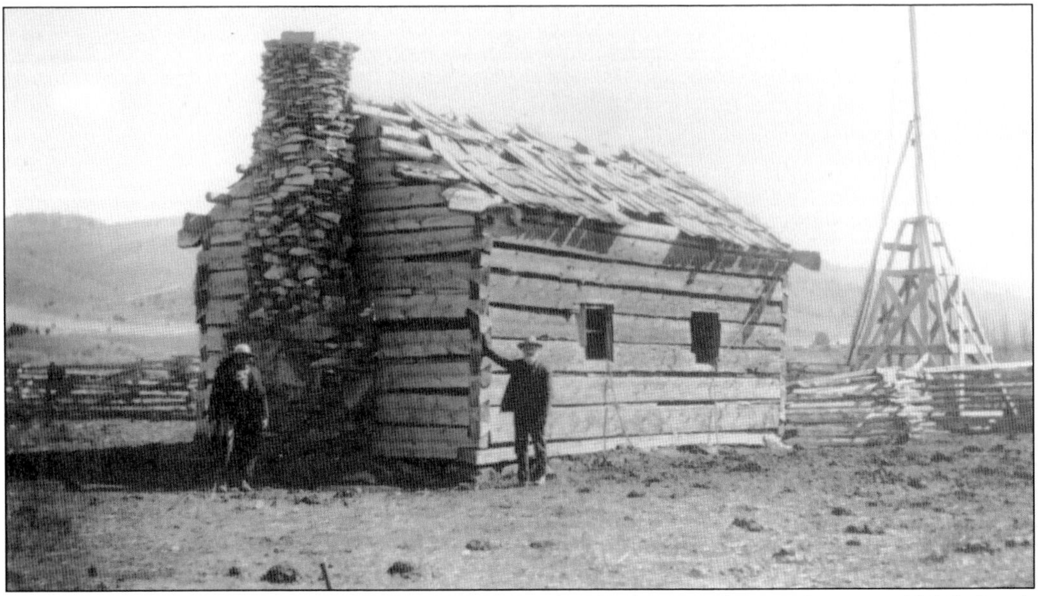

The first school in central Oregon was this log cabin built near the confluence of Mill Creek with Ochoco Creek in 1868. The building was made from hand-hewn logs, and planks were whip sawed to make the floor. All furniture and apparatus in the school were homemade. The first teacher was William Pickett. Standing by the building is Jehu Johnson on the left, and his father, Ewen Johnson, on the right.

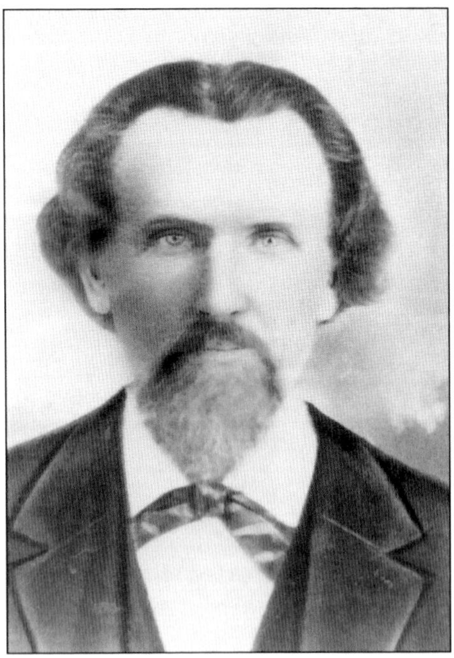

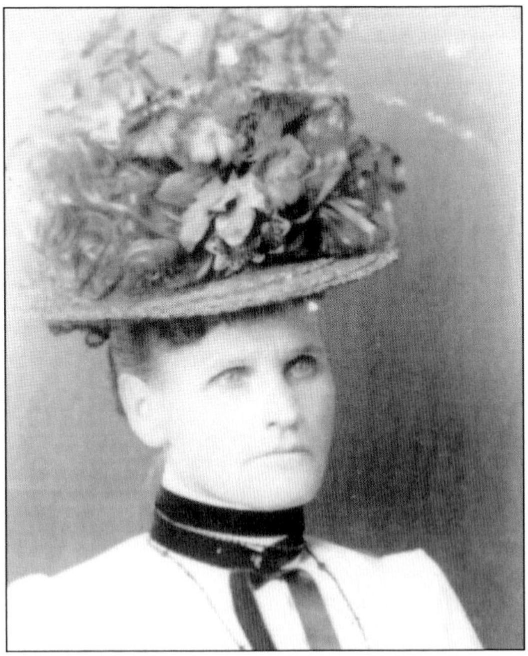

Francis Barney Prine (left) came to settle in the Crooked River Valley in 1868. He built a log cabin along the banks of the Crooked River and established a blacksmith shop and dispensed liquor. The post office of Prine was named for him, and the community later became Prineville. His wife, Elizabeth (right), was among the first Euro-American women to settle in the valley. Barney and Elizabeth later divorced, and Barney left the region.

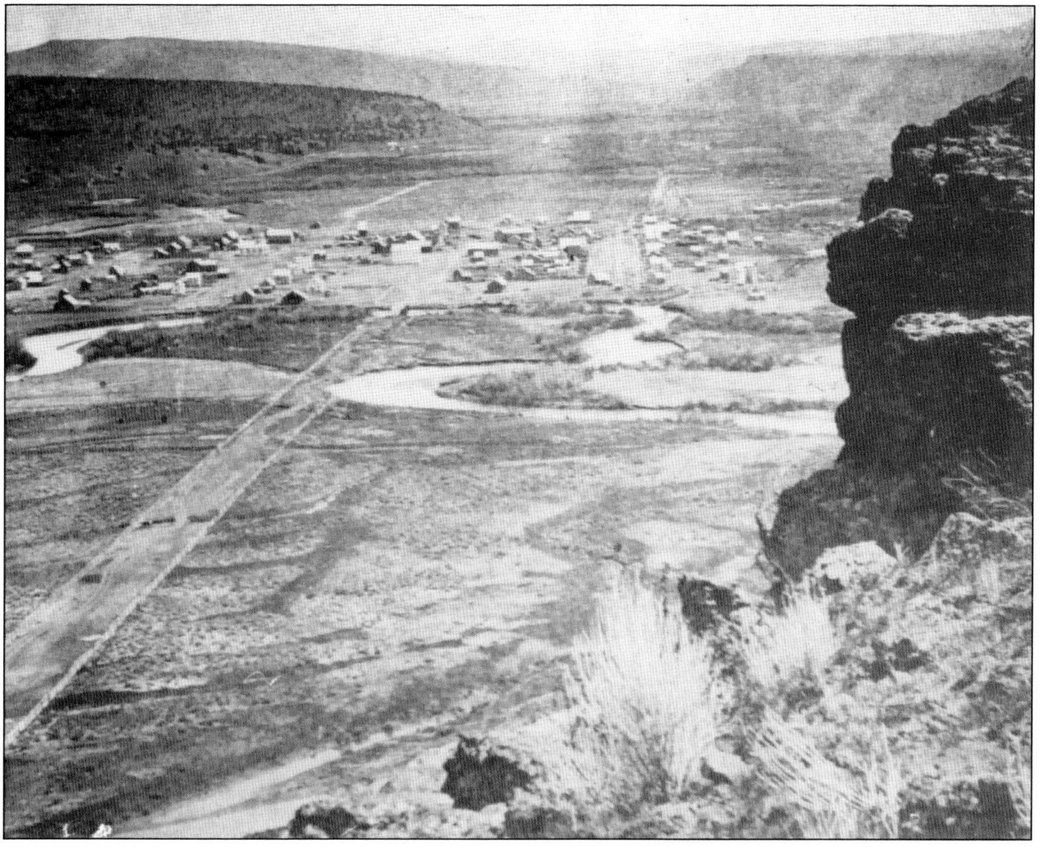

This is the first known photograph of Prineville, taken from a rimrock to the west of the community in 1881. The road approaching the town from the lower left is Second Street, which was the main thoroughfare into town from the west. The Crooked River meandered through the valley and flowed near the center of the present community. Prineville was the main community in central Oregon from 1868 until 1911.

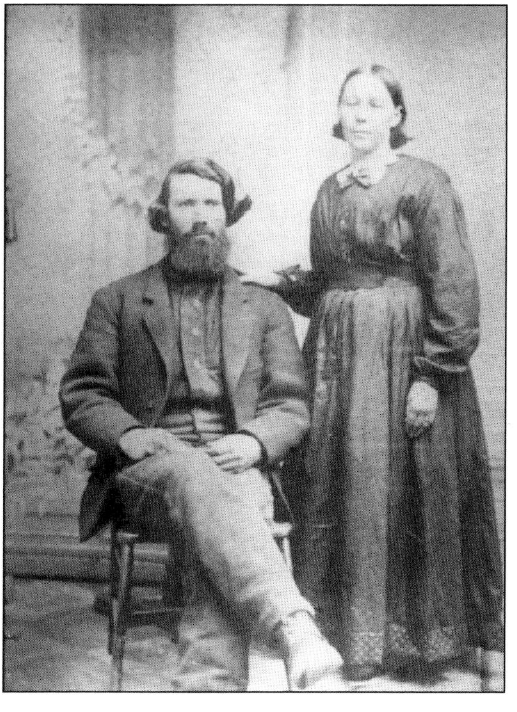

William and Mary Marks settled along upper Ochoco Creek in 1868. Marks Creek, which is a main tributary to Ochoco Creek, was named for them, as their homestead was located near the confluence of the two creeks. William had originally come with his brother Bluford to find a place to establish himself in the region and later brought Mary to the homestead site when he had built a cabin.

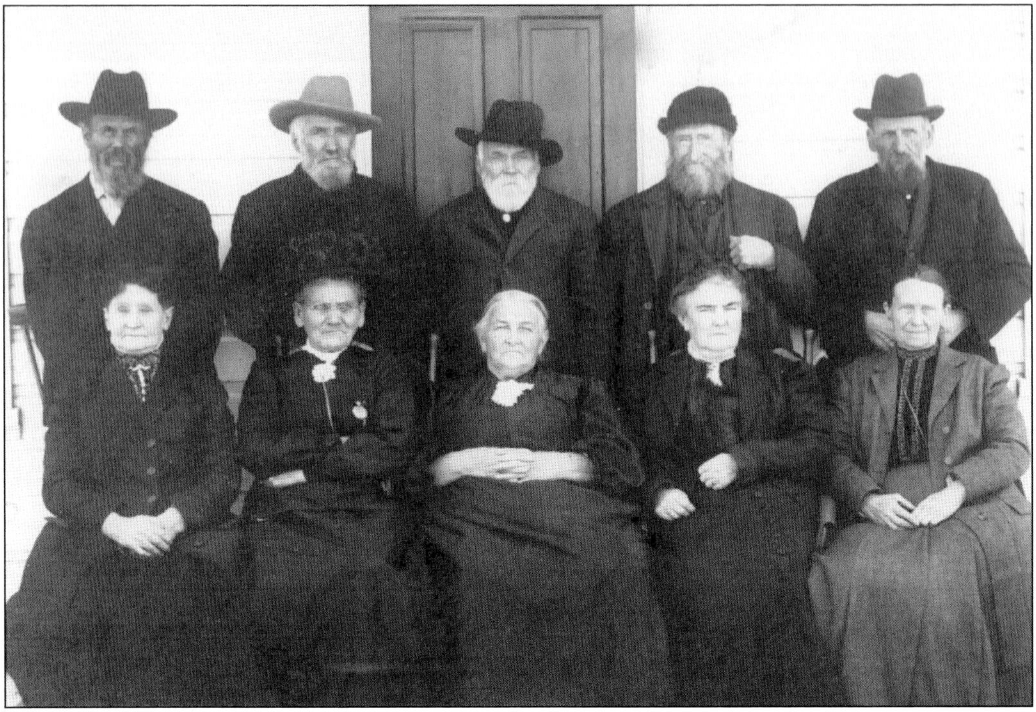

This is a pioneer reunion photograph of some of the early settlers in Crook County. Pictured around 1901 are, from left to right, (sitting) Mary Vanderpool, Nancy Johnson, Lavina Templeton, Ellen Gulliford, and Nancy Zell; (standing) Jim Vanderpool, Ewen Johnson, James Lawson, Joseph Hunsaker, and Abe Zell.

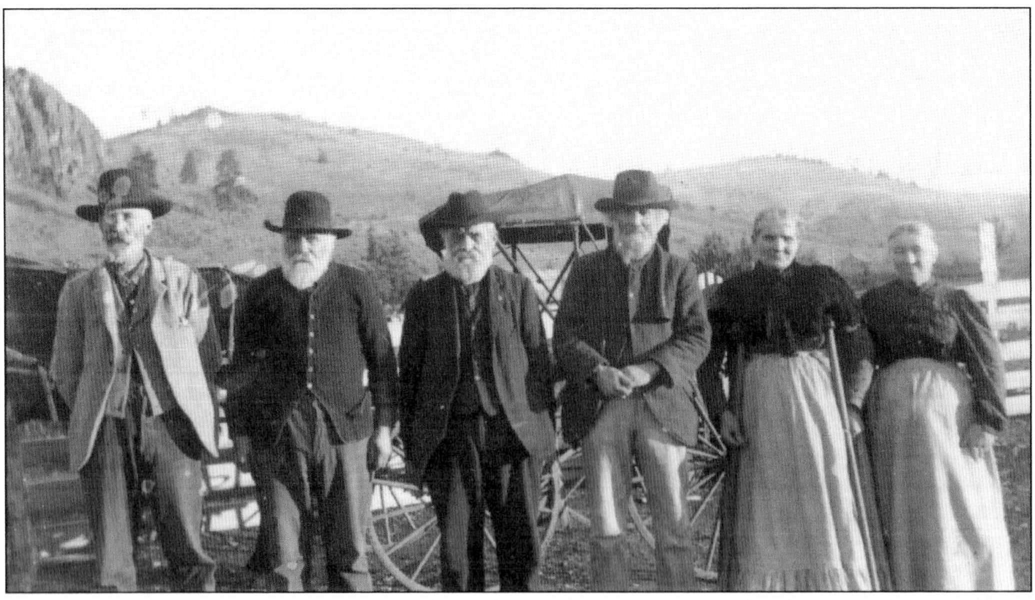

This group of early pioneers settled in the Mill Creek vicinity several miles east of Prineville in the late 1870s. From left to right are Henry P. Evans, James Lawson, a brother of James Lawson, Ewen Johnson, Nancy Johnson, and Emily Evans. This photograph was taken about 1900 along Mill Creek.

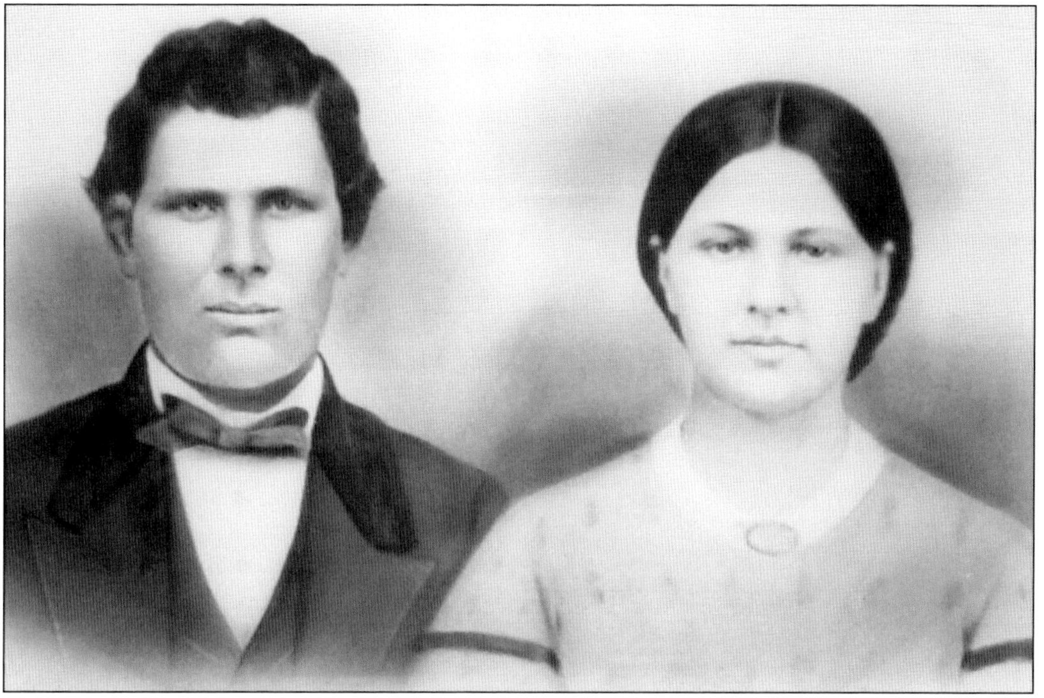

Enoch and Almeda Roberts Demaris came to central Oregon in 1876 and settled on upper Mill Creek. Enoch served in the Civil War and was severely wounded. After their marriage, they moved West by wagon train. Enoch died from complications of his Civil War wound in 1878. Almeda lived on for many years. Many of their children and grandchildren became prominent in the emerging lumber industry of the region.

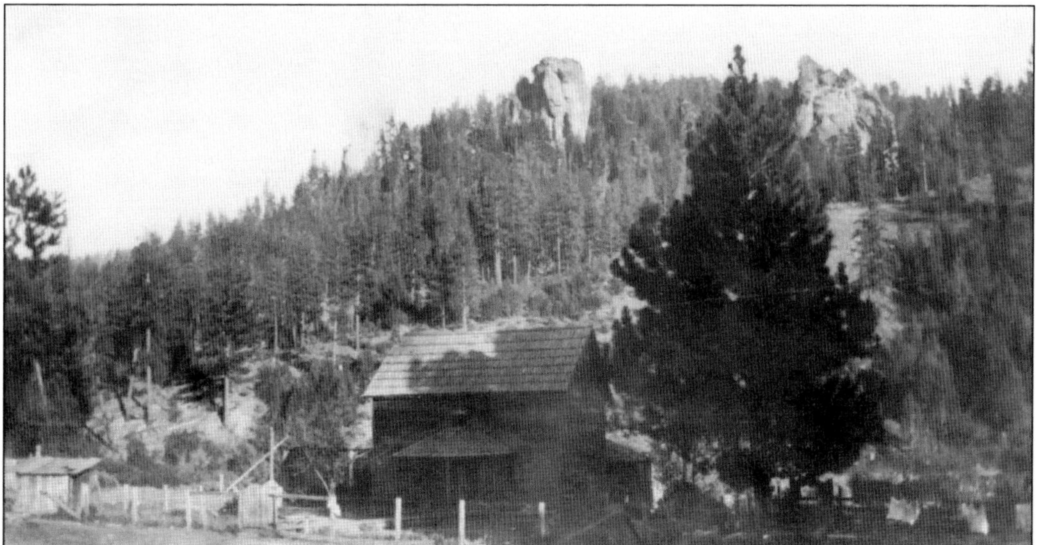

This is a view of the homestead cabin of John and Cynthia Jane Demaris on Mill Creek just below Steins Pillar, which is in the background. John was the son of Enoch and Almeda Demaris and began a mill operation on Mill Creek in partnership with William Birdsong around the turn of the 20th century.

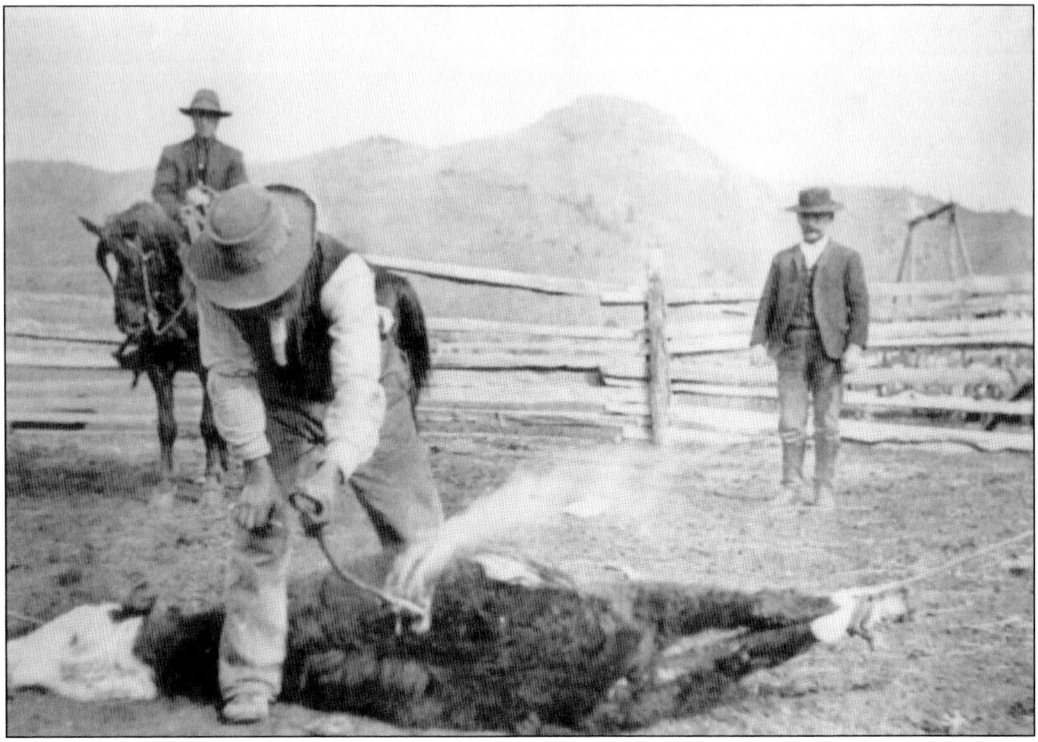

This is a view of branding a calf at the Ewen Johnson Ranch on Mill Creek about 1880. From left to right are Gilbert Lawson on horse, Charlie Lister branding, and Jake Johnson standing to the right. The lush grasslands of the region attracted settlers to engage in the livestock business. Most of the earliest settlers raised sheep or cattle.

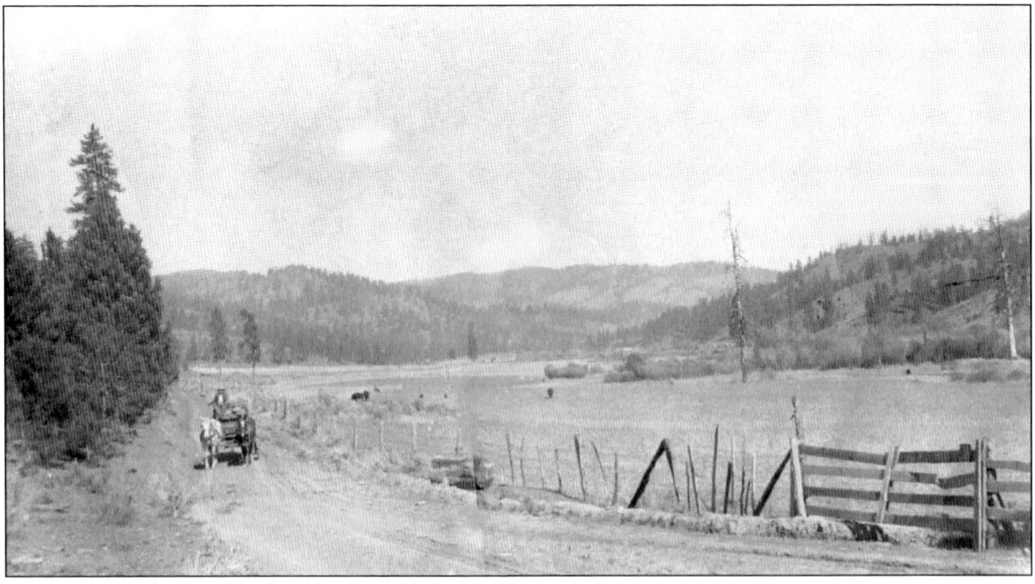

This is an early view, looking north, of the Mill Creek drainage. A wagon road traversed up the creek valley. The meadowland provided excellent forage for livestock. Mill Creek and McKay Creek valleys are referred to as the "Cradle of Central Oregon Settlement."

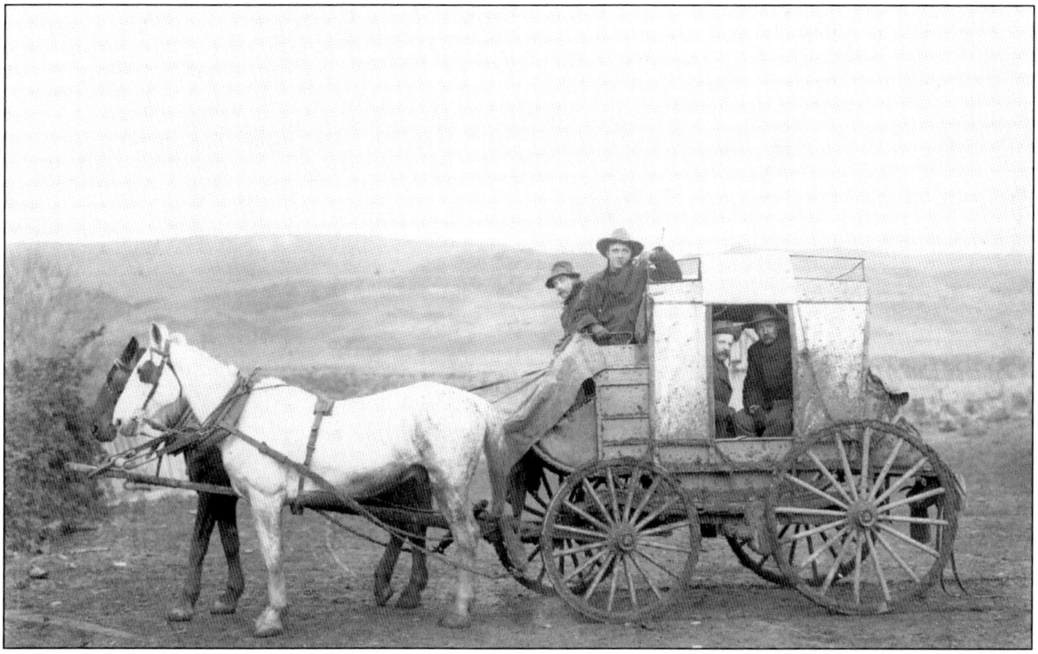

Stagecoach operations to central Oregon began early as settlers came to the region. This is an early stage from The Dalles to Prineville. It was a rugged trip for passengers, and they were frequently required to get out and help push the stage out of mud or snow. This stage shows signs of passing through a muddy trail.

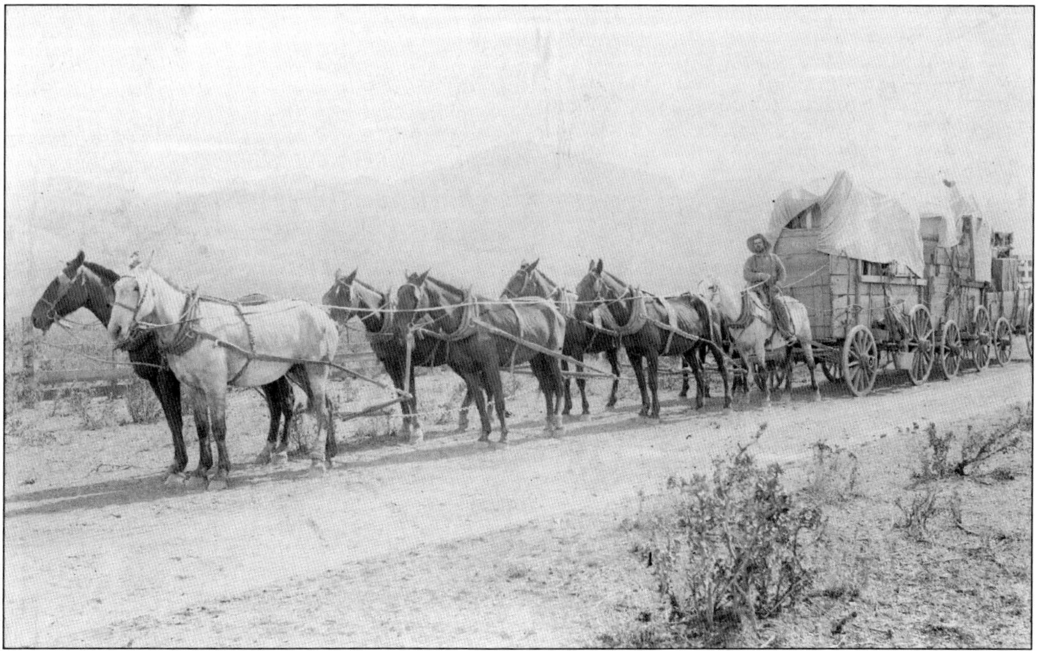

Freight wagons provided the transport of necessary commodities for the growing population of Crook County. Most freight traveled from The Dalles to Prineville. Outlying areas then had freight shipped via Prineville. Stephen Yancey operates this horse-drawn freight wagon. He and his brother Jesse operated the Yancey Brothers Freight.

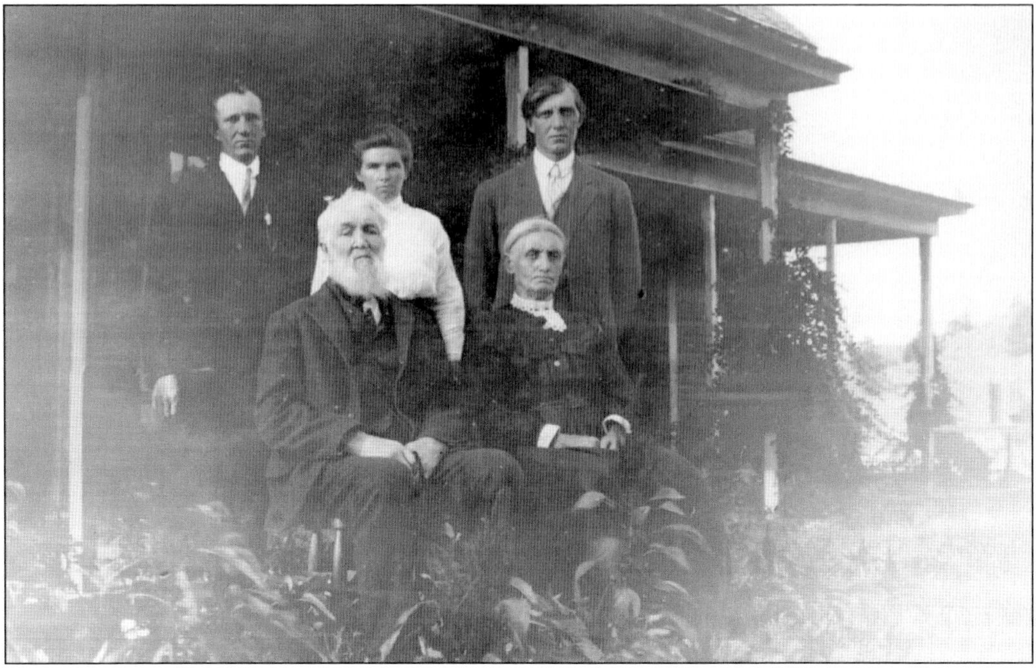

Samuel Logan followed his brother Thomas to settle along Camp Creek in southern Crook County in 1883. Thomas established the 96 Ranch in 1870. After he had built a cabin, Samuel brought his family to his claim adjacent to his brother's 96 Ranch. They developed one of the prominent cattle ranches in the area. Pictured are, from left to right, (sitting) Samuel Logan and Elmira Fisher Logan; (standing) Fisher Logan, Rose Logan, and Allen Morgan Logan.

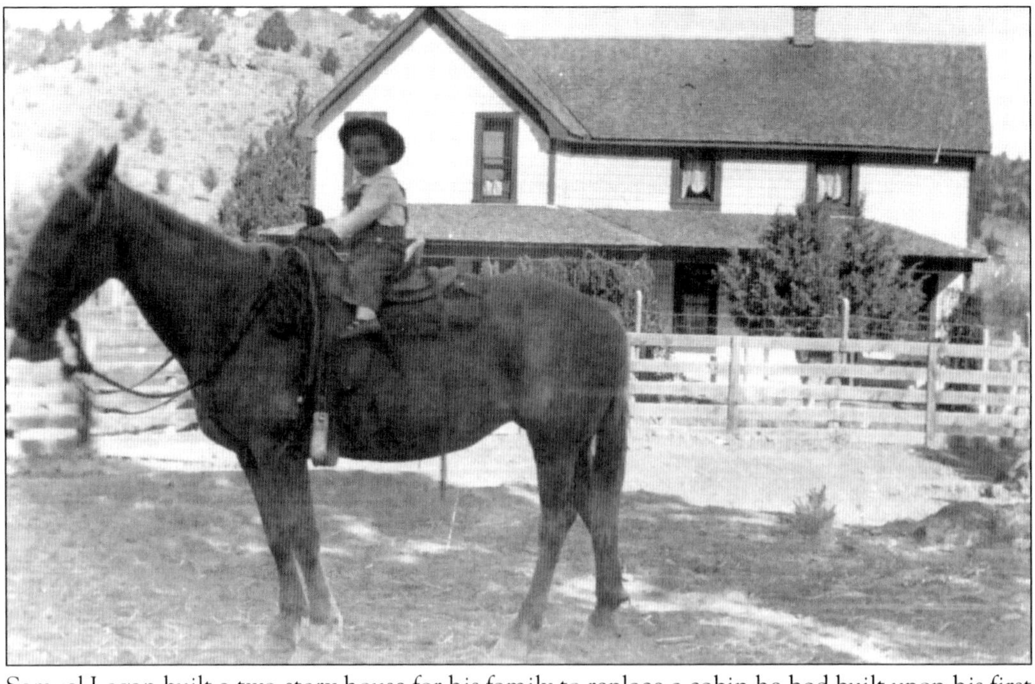

Samuel Logan built a two-story house for his family to replace a cabin he had built upon his first arrival at Camp Creek. This is the Logan house in 1886; young Fisher Logan is on the horse.

Nine-year-old Andrew Noble came to the Upper Country of Crook County with his father, William, in 1870. They spent the winter along Beaver Creek about 12 miles northeast of present Paulina. William moved his family to his homestead at the confluence of Sugar Creek and Beaver Creek. William moved back to the Willamette Valley in the late 1880s, leaving Andrew and his mother to run the ranch. Andrew married Varina Skelton in 1892, and this is their wedding photograph.

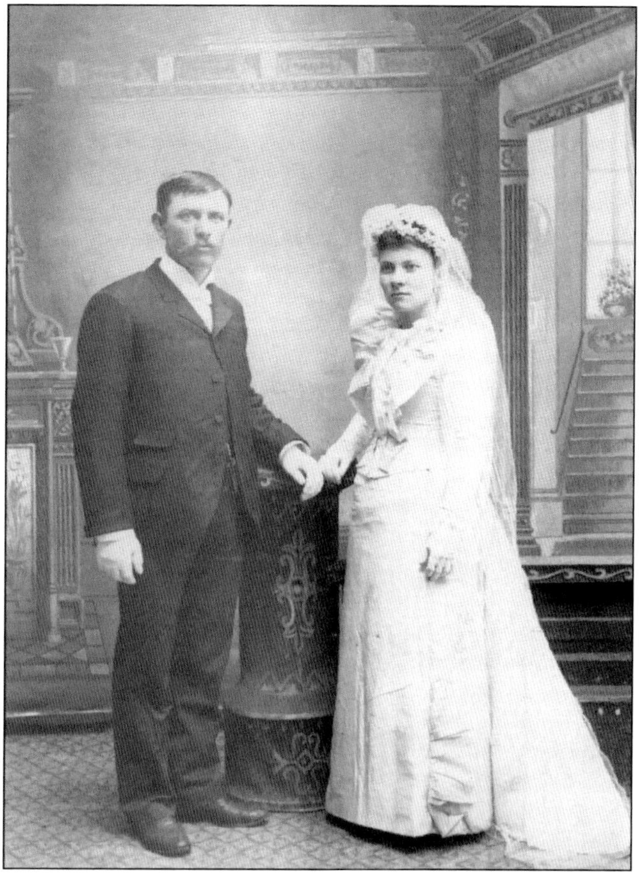

Sugar Creek Ranch was located at the confluence of Sugar Creek and Beaver Creek. William and Andrew Noble established this ranch in 1870. Andrew Noble operated the ranch until 1911, when they sold the ranch and moved into Prineville. The ranch was among the first established in the Beaver Creek country.

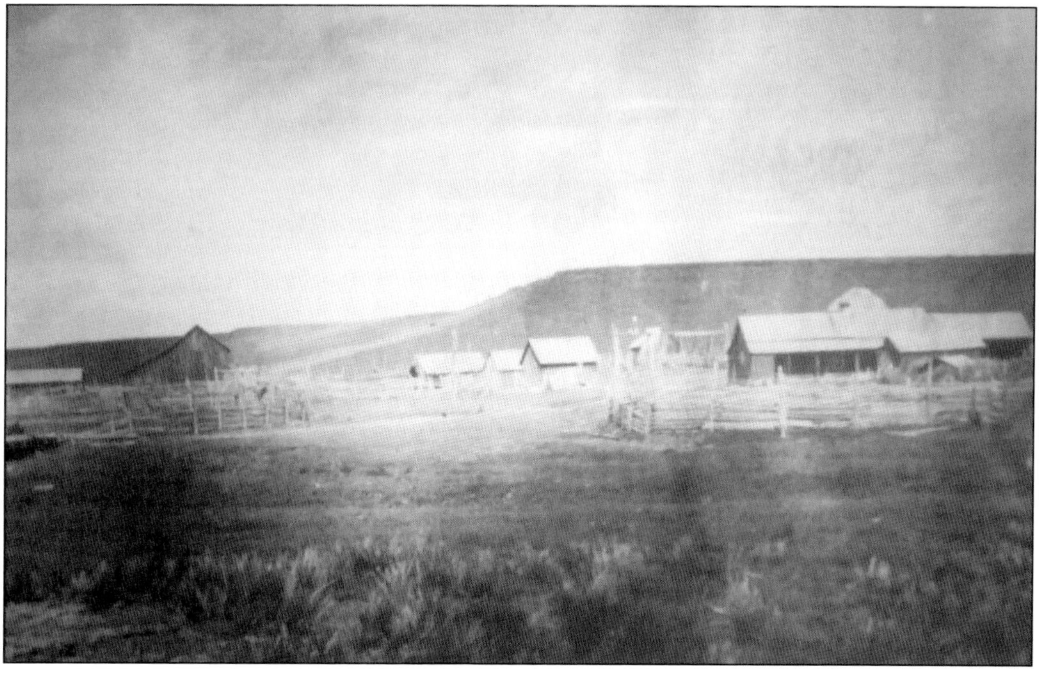

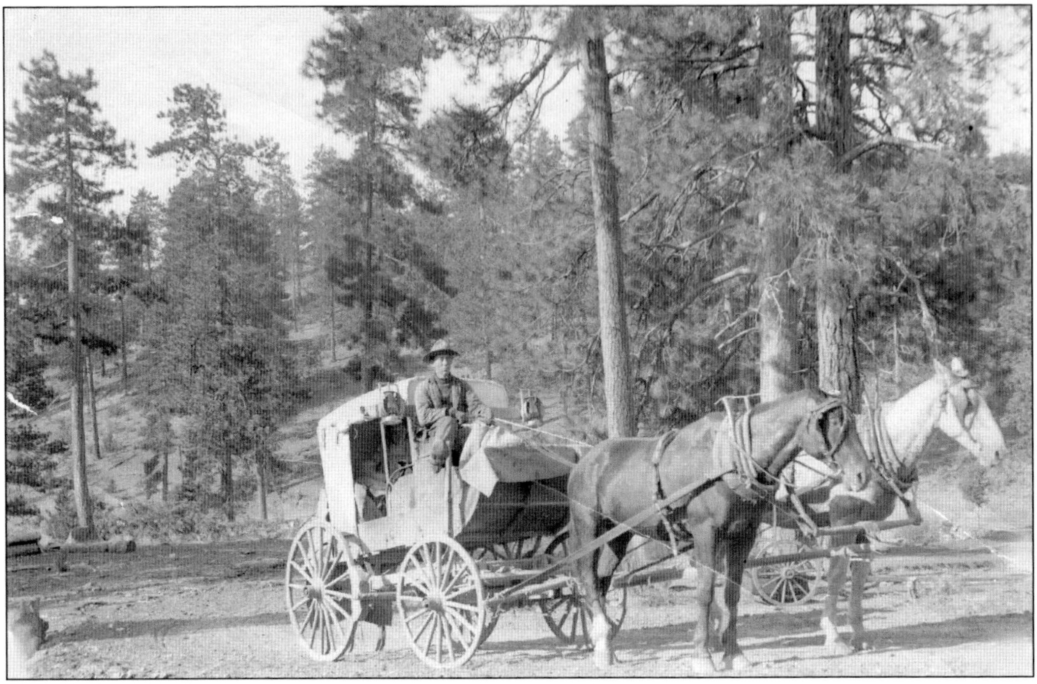

Aaron Pike is driving a stagecoach from The Dalles to Prineville around 1900. The route followed Cow Canyon to Trout Creek, then on to Hay Creek Ranch, crossing over a pass near Grizzly Mountain, and then to Prineville. This stage is on the Grizzly Mountain route through the pine trees.

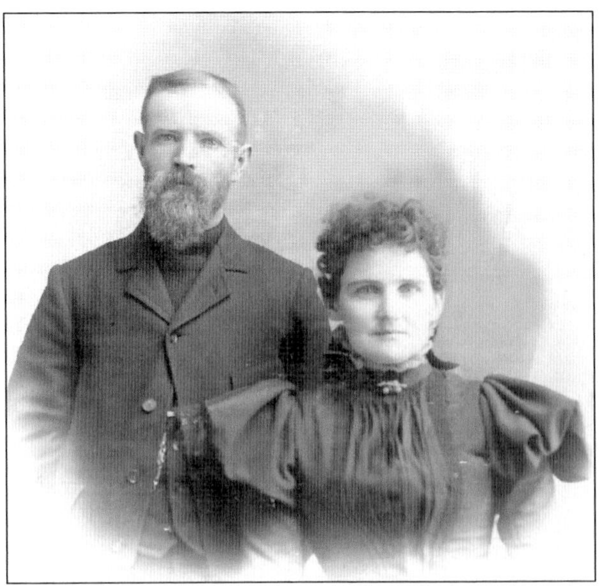

Sidney and Frances Day Stearns were prominent ranchers. Sid Stearns was among the earliest settlers in central Oregon. He first came to settle along the banks of the Deschutes River at the site of present Bend in 1883. In 1887, he married Frances Day, and they began their married life in the cabin along the Deschutes River. That claim was relinquished, and they established a ranch on the meadows near present LaPine. Later, they moved their headquarters ranch to Crooked River about five miles south of Prineville. After Sid's death in 1923, his sons Cecil and Harry along with their mother, Frances, continued to operate the ranch until the family eventually sold it.

Two

Turbulent Times on the Frontier

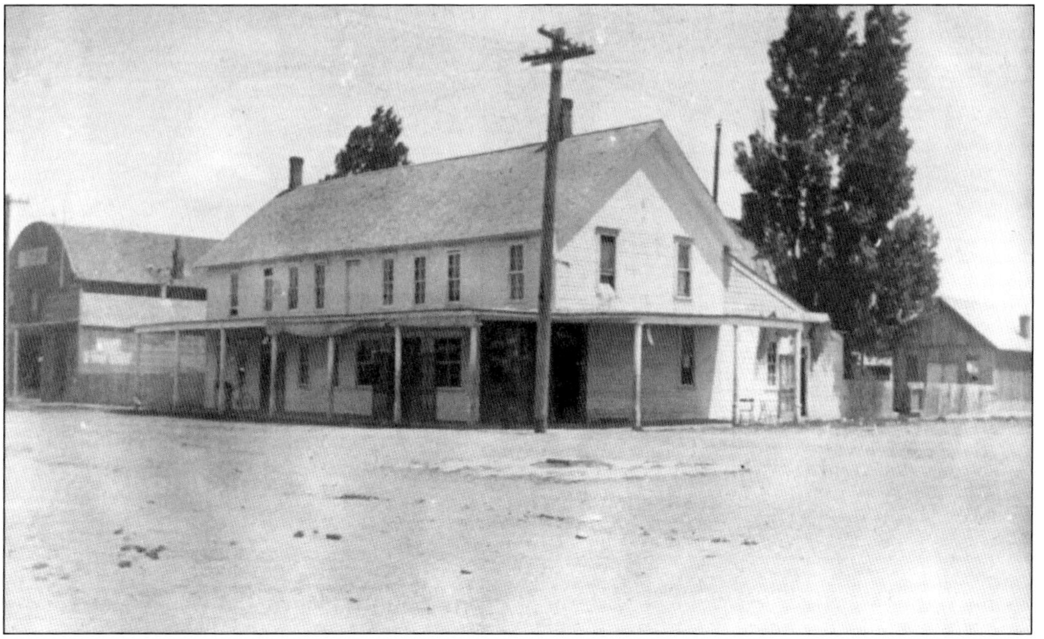

A tragic event occurred near Grizzly Mountain north of Prineville in 1882 when a neighbor in a property dispute killed two men. The suspected killer, Lucius Langdon, was captured, but there was no jail in Prineville, so the prisoner was held in custody at the Jackson Hotel, shown in this photograph. The vigilante era of justice in central Oregon began when masked riders rode into the hotel and killed the prisoner. The building was used as a hotel until 1905, when it was replaced with a stone structure.

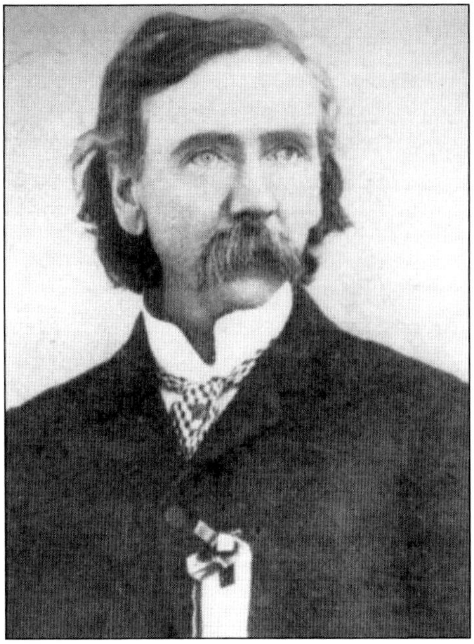

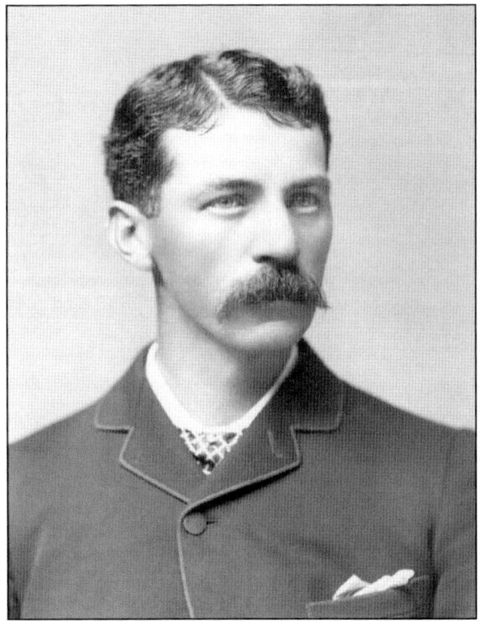

William Thompson (left) was a prominent rancher who lived on Hay Creek north of Prineville in 1882 and became active in local affairs. Thompson was alleged to be the leader of the vigilante group that took justice into its own hands for a period of two years from 1882 to 1884. James Blakely (right) was a rancher on Willow Creek north of Prineville. He assisted in capturing Lucius Langdon, who was a suspect in the murder of two neighbors near Grizzly Mountain. He opposed the vigilantes after they killed Langdon in the Jackson Hotel. He was part of an organization known as the Moonlighters that met to plan strategies against the vigilantes. Blakely became the first elected sheriff of Crook County when the first elections were held in 1884. Many years later, Blakely accused Thompson of being the leader of the vigilantes.

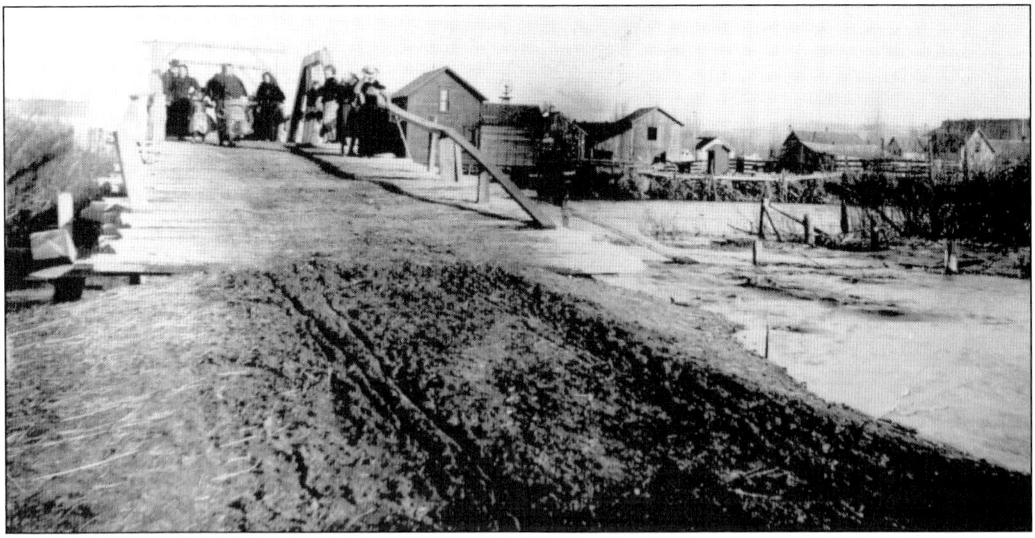

The first bridge across the Crooked River into Prineville was constructed around 1877 on Second Street. The wooden structure was made of heavy timbers. After the vigilantes killed Lucius Langdon, they rounded up his hired hand who happened to be in Prineville and dragged him to the bridge where he was hanged from the timbers. This photograph was taken about 1885.

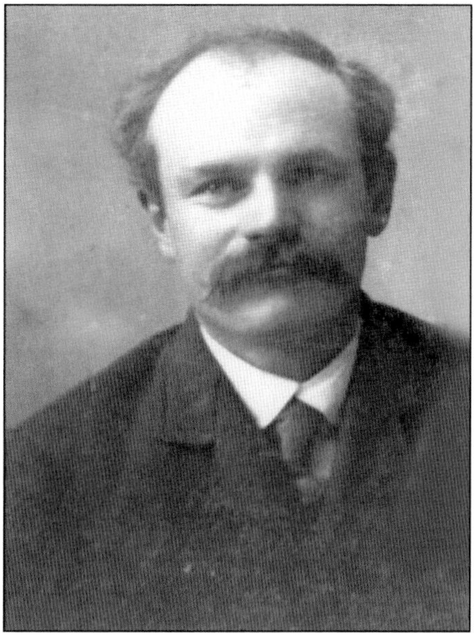

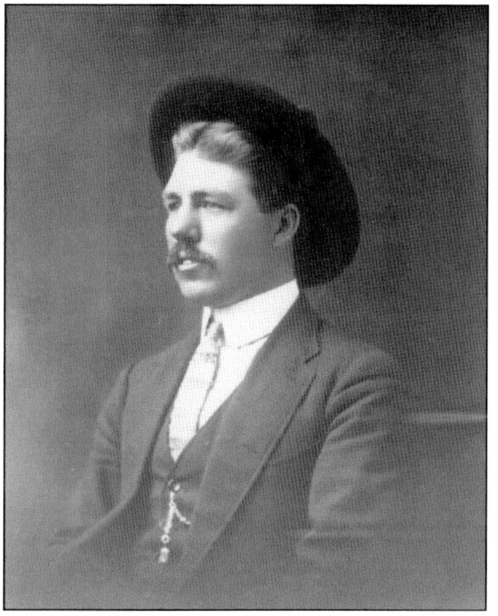

Al Swartz (left) had kept horses on the Crooked River south of Prineville at a site now known as Swartz Canyon. He was vocal about his opposition to the vigilantes. The vigilantes accused him of stealing horses, and he was mysteriously shot in the back and killed while playing cards in a Prineville saloon on the night of December 22, 1882. The same night two young men associated with Swartz were found hanging from a juniper outside of Prineville. William Thompson killed Frank Mogan (right) in Kelly's Saloon in Prineville on December 18, 1883. Mogan was shot in the back of the head, and Thompson was found responsible for the death, but no action was taken. A judgment against Thompson was granted to Mogan's widow for $3,600, but Thompson managed to avoid making any payment.

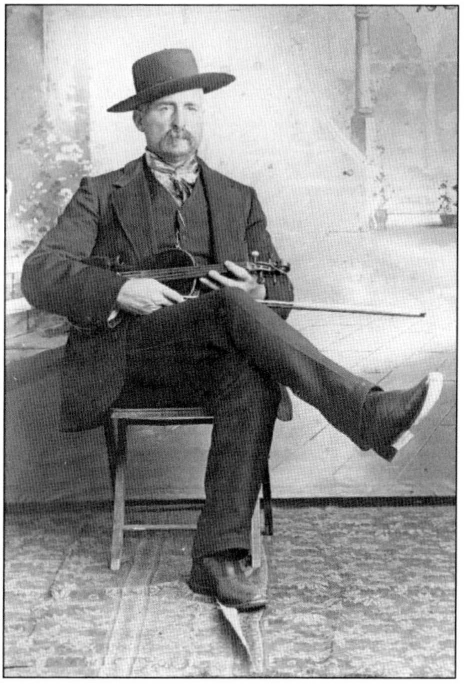

Tillman "Till" Glaze came to Prineville in 1877. He had been involved in a deadly feud in Dallas, Oregon, and killed two members of a family in self-defense. He decided to start anew and brought his family to Prineville and settled. He operated a local saloon and was a well-known musician. He attempted to remain neutral during the vigilante era but was a good friend of Jim Blakely, who opposed the vigilantes. Till was killed in a gunfight in Burns, Oregon, in 1894.

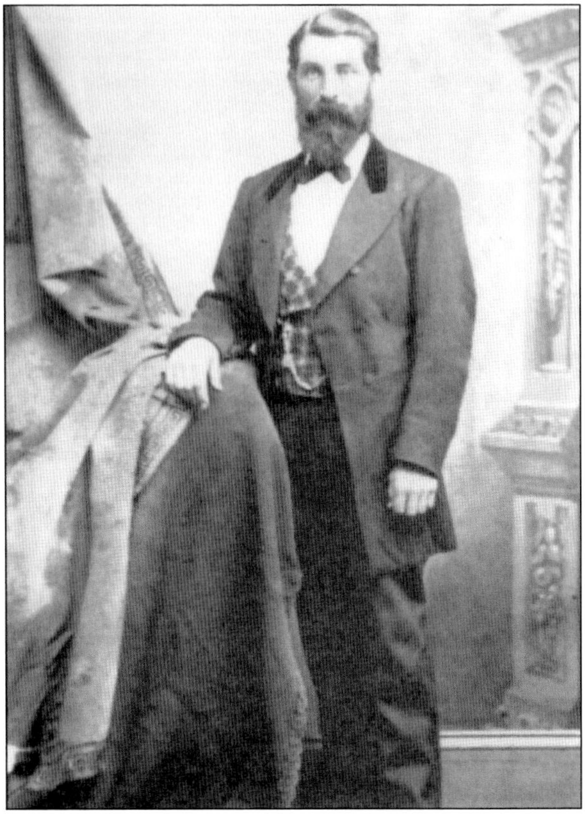

Hank Vaughn came to Prineville in 1881 with a reputation for being a gunfighter. Shortly after coming to town, he was involved in a gambling argument in the Singer Saloon with Charlie Long, and a gun duel resulted. Both were shot several times, but both survived. Hank moved on to the Pendleton country and met an untimely end on June 16, 1893, when his horse fell on him while he was riding intoxicated on the streets of the town.

The Singer Saloon was located in Prineville on the east side of Main Street near the corner of Second Street. Till Glaze purchased the saloon in 1878. This was the site of the gunfight between Hank Vaughn and Charlie Long in December 1881. The Singer Saloon is on the left, and the Prineville Stage Stop is on the right. The saloon building was destroyed by fire in 1917.

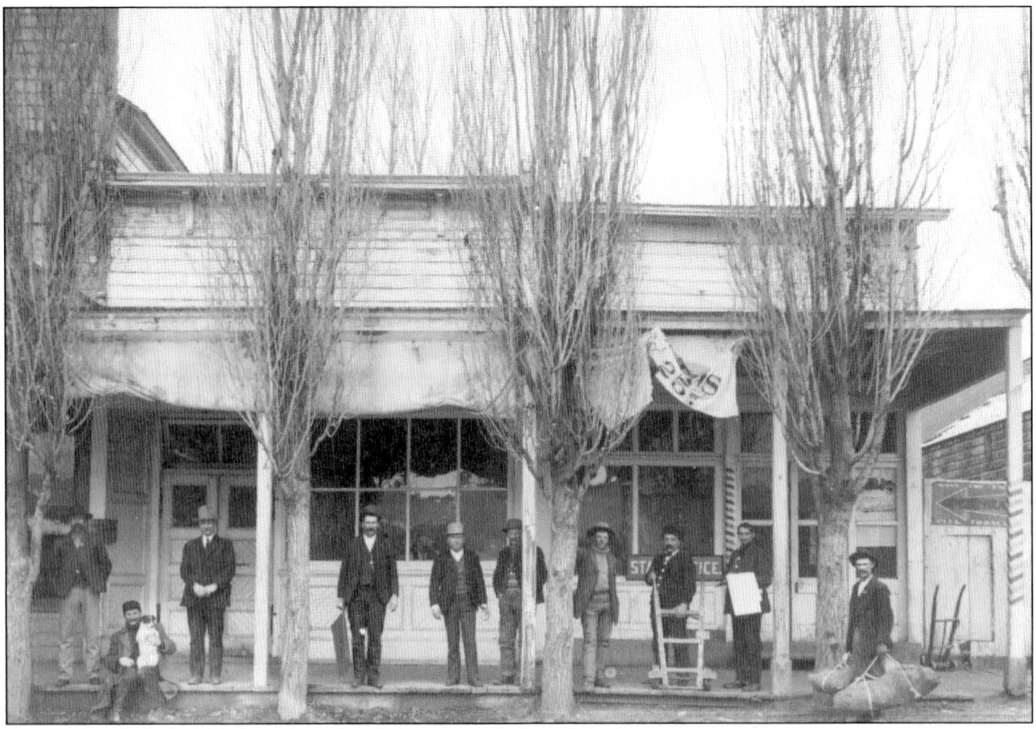

Benjamin Franklin "B.F." Nichols came to central Oregon from Polk County, Oregon, in 1878. He established the first drugstore in Prineville and became active in local affairs. He was elected to represent the Prineville district of southern Wasco County in the Oregon state legislature in 1882. Nichols introduced legislation to create Crook County from Wasco County, which became official on October 24, 1882. Nichols became known as the "Father of Crook County." The reign of the vigilantes ended shortly after the first elections were held in the new county in late 1884.

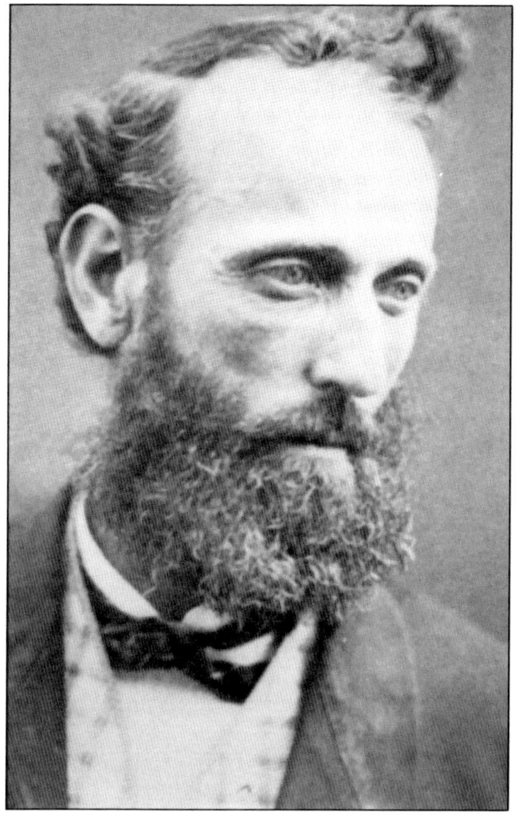

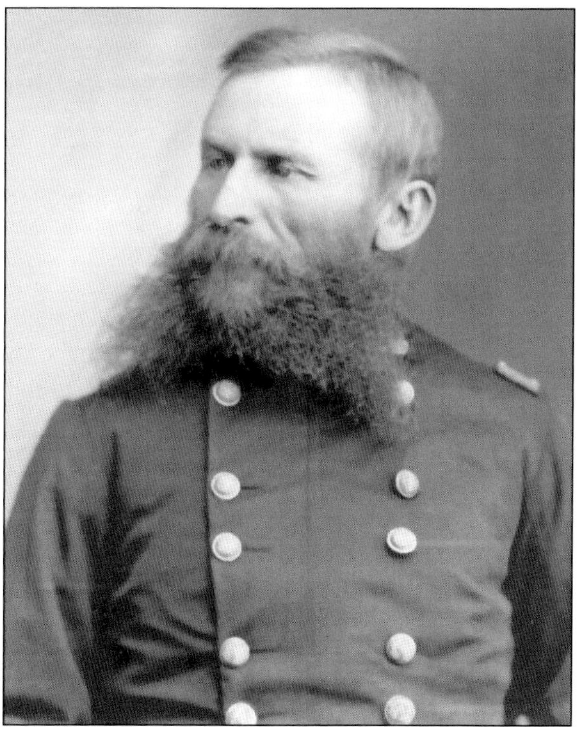

Crook County was named for Gen. George Crook. He had spent the early part of his military career in Oregon before the Civil War. During the Civil War, he rose to the rank of brigadier general. He returned West to head the Department of the Columbia, which included central Oregon. He was involved in skirmishes with Native Americans in the Oregon country and other areas of the West.

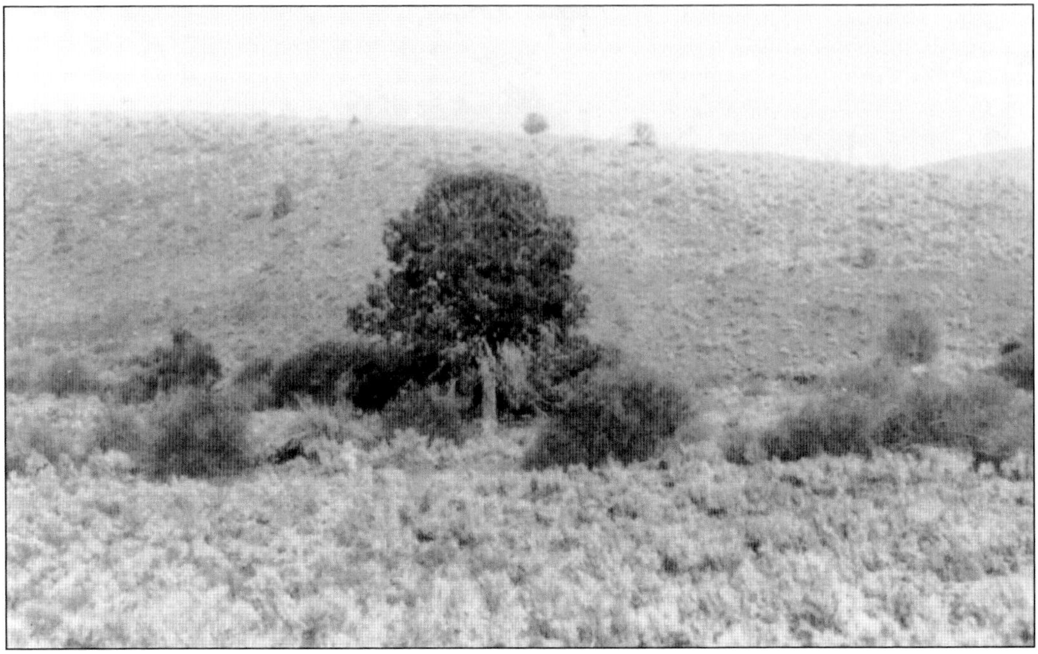

This is the infamous "Sheepshooter Tree," located on Wolf Creek northeast of Paulina. The tree was just upstream from the Mills Ranch. Paulina area cattle ranchers met under this tree to determine strategies for removing sheep from what they thought was traditional cattle range. Not all cattlemen participated in what became known as the Sheepshooter's Organization.

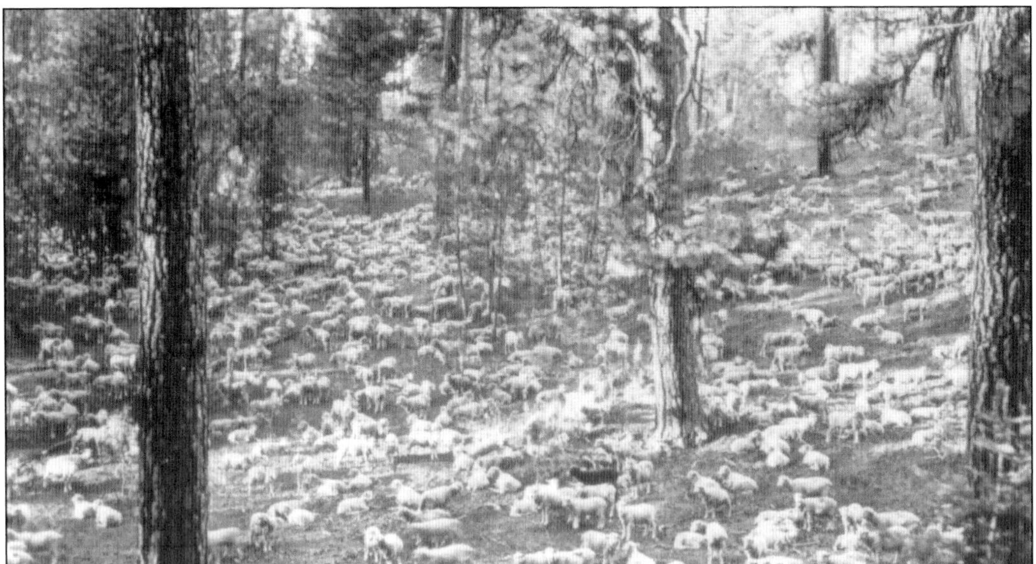

Sheep and cattle ranchers shared some of the open range for summer grazing. Lush grasses were found in the forested mountains of the Ochoco country. In 1894, the Cascade Forest Reserve was established, and grazing was withheld until administrative rules could be put into place for managed grazing. Many out-of-area sheep moved into the Ochoco Mountains, and soon friction resulted between sheep men and cattlemen. This is a large band of sheep on the Ochoco Mountains about 1900.

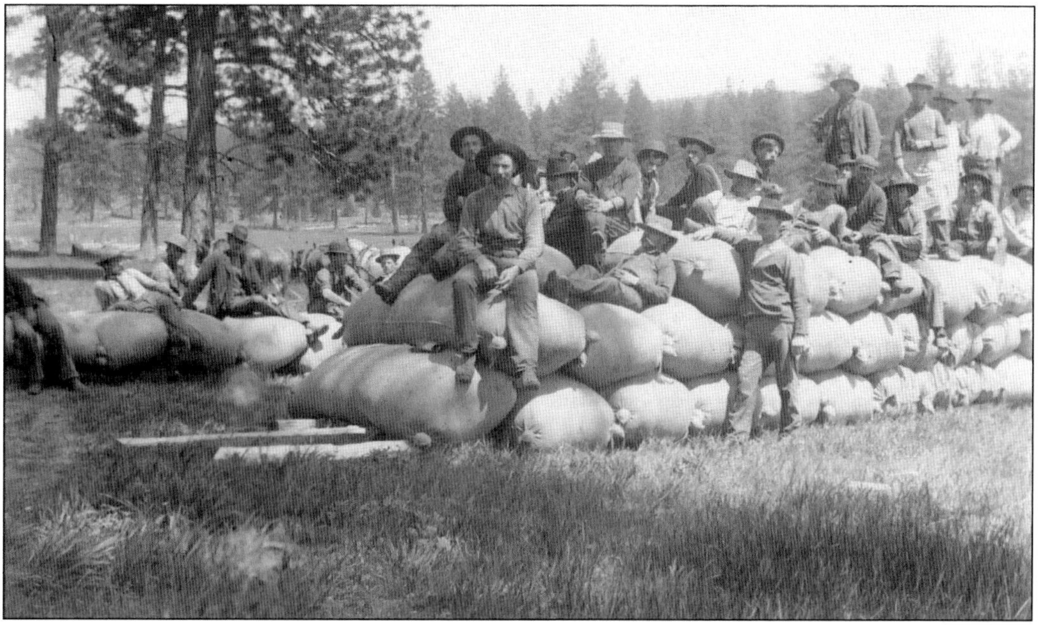

Sheep-shearing operations took place at various shearing plants in the region. This is the J.N. Williamson shearing plant, located at Dixie Meadow southeast of Prineville. After shearing, the wool was put into large canvas bags, loaded on wagons, and shipped to railheads. Prior to 1900, wool was shipped to The Dalles and, after 1900, to the railhead at Shaniko.

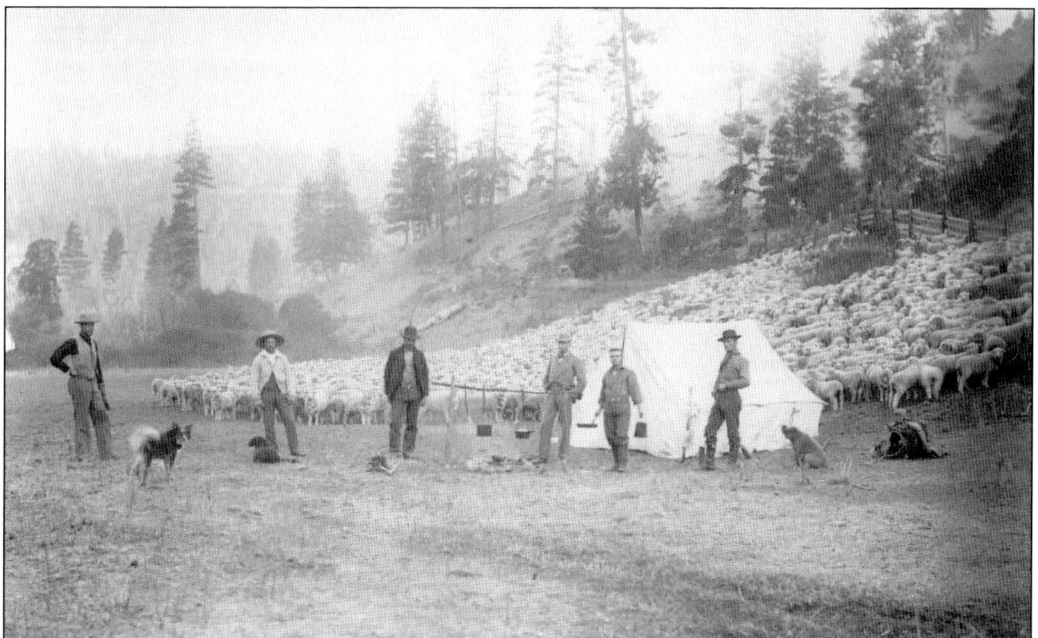

This was a typical sheep camp, located on McKay Creek north of Prineville. Sheepherders would follow bands of sheep and move them from pasture to pasture. Jesse Yancey owned this band of sheep and herded them in the forested areas north of Prineville. From left to right are Jimmy Cartwright, Al Hough, Boyd Adams, Frank Summerville, Jim Edensor, and Harry Webb about 1900.

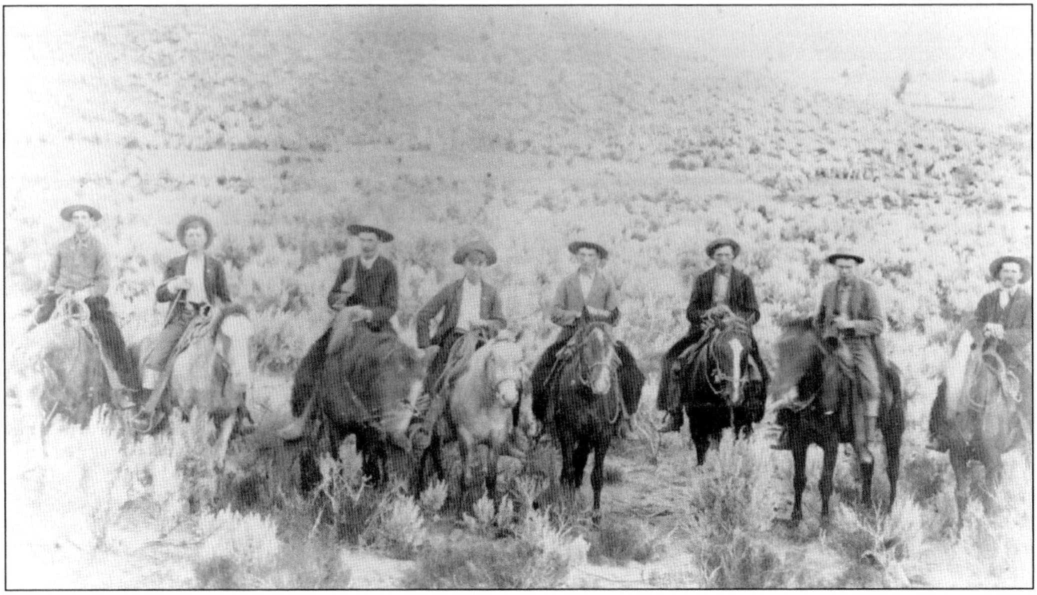

This is a group of unidentified cattlemen in the Paulina area about 1909. Some of these cowboys may have been participants in the activities of the Paulina Sheepshooter's Organization. Conflict between sheep and cattle operators led to the killing of many sheep on the open range. In some areas, sheep and cattle ranchers managed to coexist.

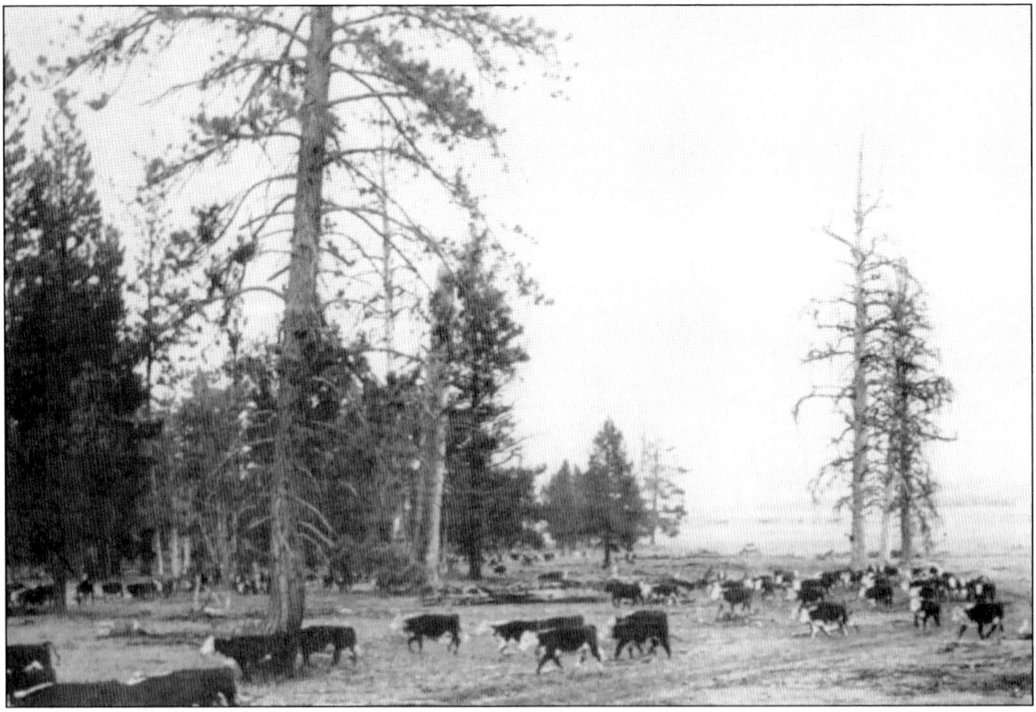

Cattle summer range was typically in the grasslands of the Ochoco Mountains, which contained some of the finest grazing in Oregon. This is a herd of cattle near Big Summit Prairie. The Sheep and Cattle War began as extensive sheep grazing infringed on open range typically utilized by cattle.

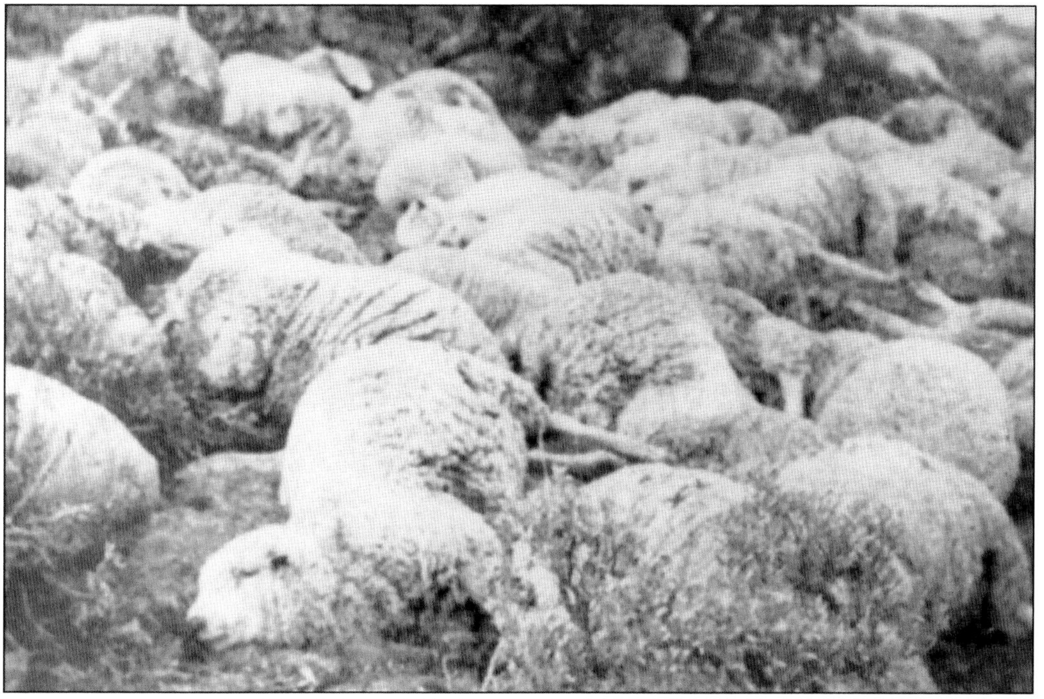

This is a photograph of dead sheep killed by masked members of the Paulina Sheepshooter's Organization. Cattlemen organized groups throughout central Oregon, including the Izee Sheepshooter's and the Silver Lake Sheepshooter's Organizations. These sheep were killed in the southern part of Crook County about 1905. The largest known sheep killing took place south of Hampton with over 1,500 sheep slaughtered.

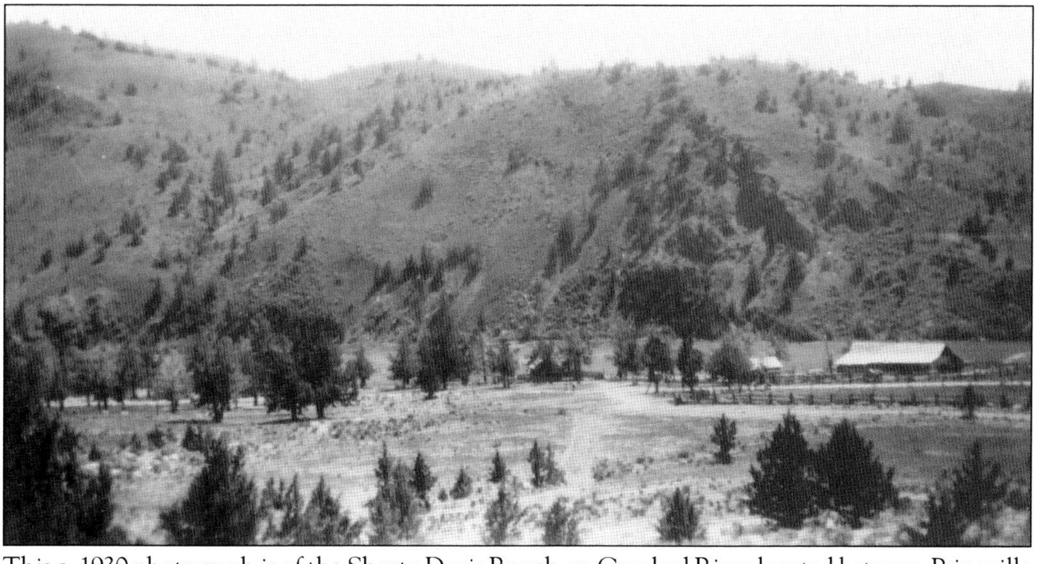

This c. 1930 photograph is of the Shorty Davis Ranch on Crooked River located between Prineville and Post. Shorty Davis was a prosperous sheep rancher. He disappeared in the summer of 1900. Rumors spread that his disappearance was a result of action by the Sheepshooter's Organization, but this was never proven. His body was never found and his disappearance is one of the long-lasting mysteries of Crook County. The ranch was later acquired by Ralph Porfily.

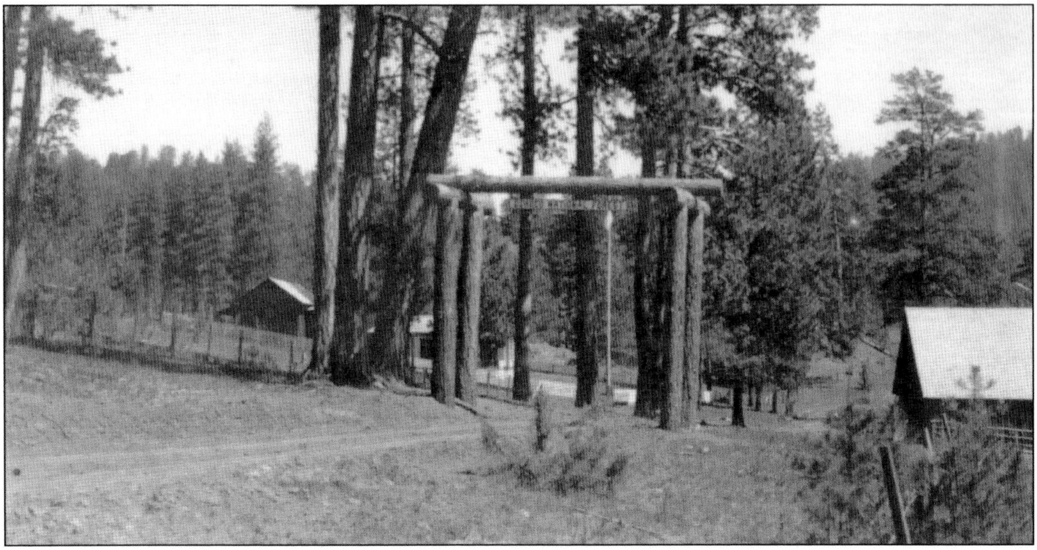

The sheep and cattle conflict was finally brought to a close when the Forest Service was established in 1905 and the Deschutes National Forest, headquartered in Prineville, began a permit system of grazing on pubic forestlands. Later, the Ochoco National Forest was created in 1911 and headquartered in Prineville. Grazing allotments were established, and permits were purchased to graze on government lands. Also the Taylor Grazing Act provided for management of public rangelands. The Taylor Grazing Act was the precursor of the Bureau of Land Management. This is a photograph of the Ochoco ranger station and the entrance into the Ochoco National Forest about 1910.

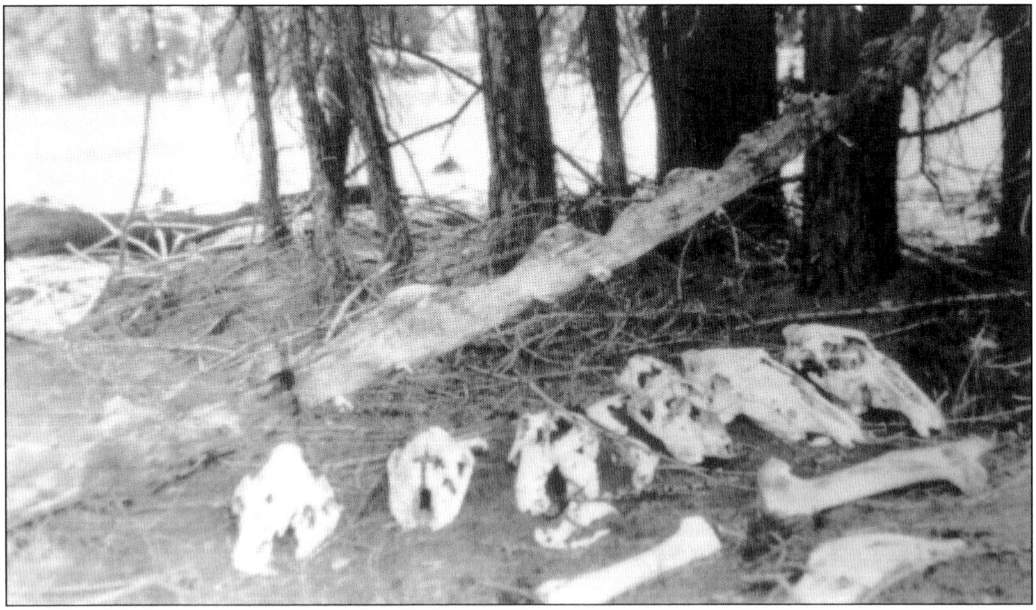

These horse skulls were found on Viewpoint, a geographic feature in the Ochoco National Forest about 30 miles east of Prineville, in 1940. The skulls are part of a legend that robbers stole gold from the mines of Canyon City in the early 1860s and made their escape east to Viewpoint where they changed horses, supposedly tying their six exhausted horses to a downed tree. The legend claims that the gold is still in the area and has inspired many treasure-seekers to visit the site.

Three

Communities and Post Offices

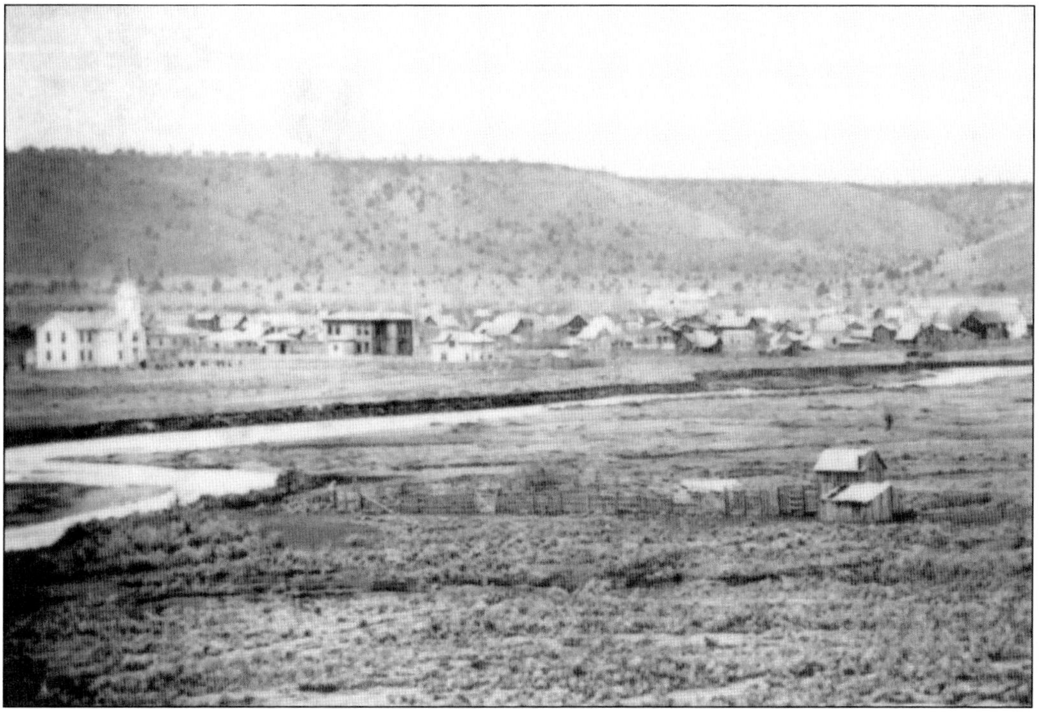

Prineville is the first community of Crook County. It is the only incorporated community in the county and has been the county seat since 1882. This photograph, taken in 1904, is looking southwest with Ochoco Creek in the foreground. The white building to the left is the Prineville School, and the flat-roofed building just to the right of it is the first Crook County Courthouse.

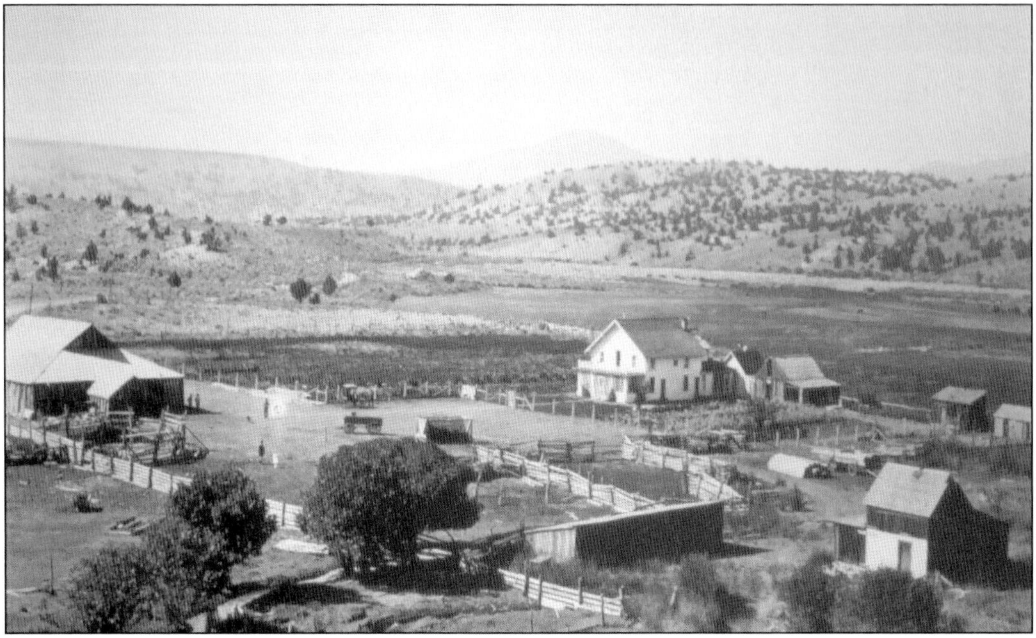

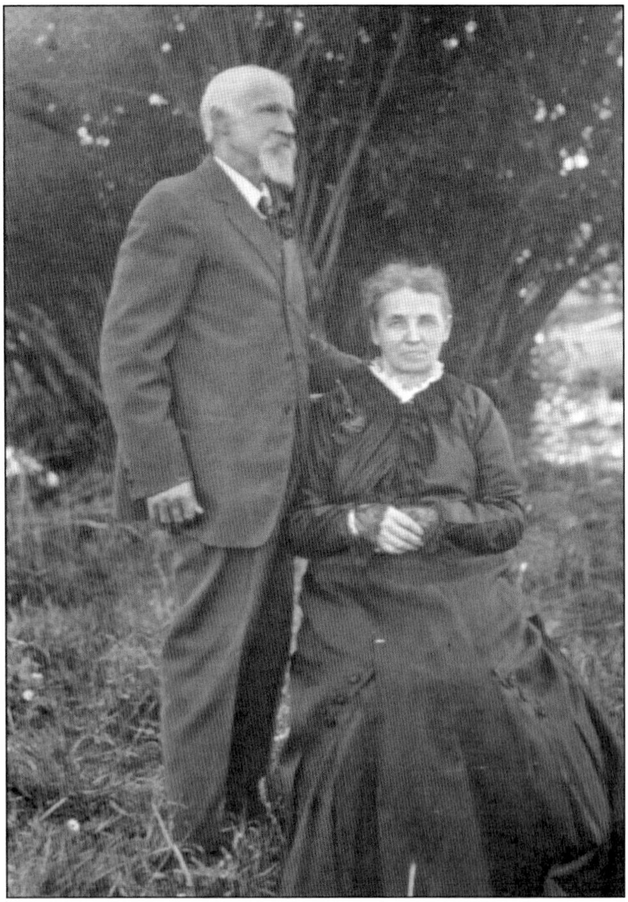

This is the Wallace Post Ranch, located on Crooked River just east of the post office of Post. The view is looking northwest and downstream on Crooked River. The building in the left background was the original location of Post.

Wallace and Lucy Post came to settle along the Crooked River southeast of Prineville in 1886. Wallace and his brother Walter settled close to each other. Walter Post became the first postmaster of Post. Wallace and Lucy operated the ranch for several years, and members of their family continued to ranch after they retired. Later, it was sold to Roscoe Knox.

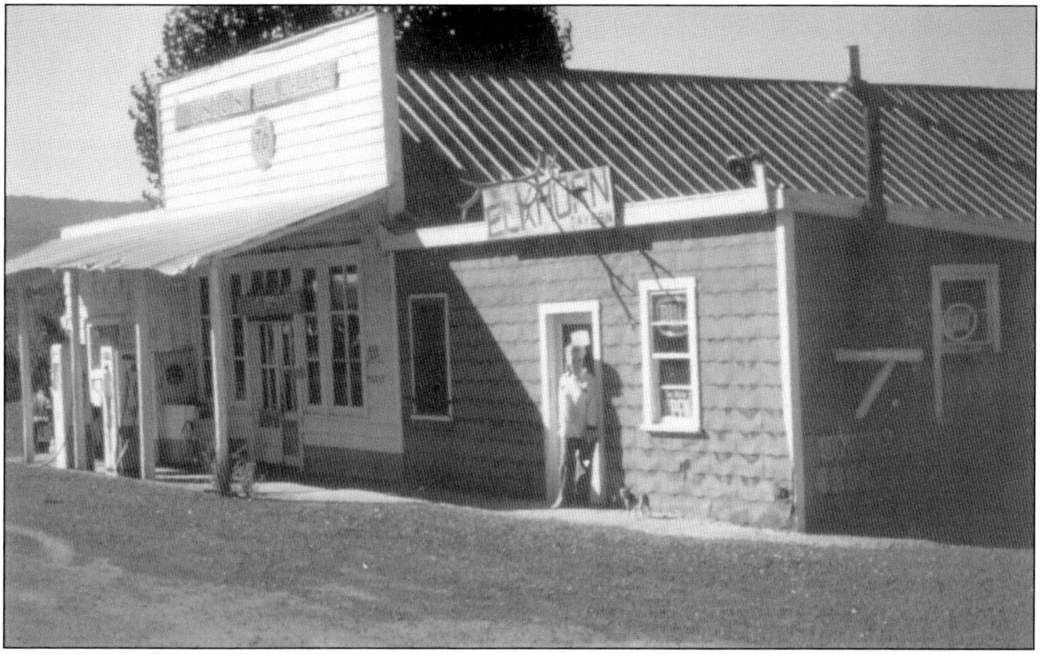

This is the post office of Post at its current location as it appeared in 1960. The site had a general store, post office, and the Elkhorn Tavern. Patricia "Pat" Wells, standing out front, operated the store for several years. The original site of Post was on the south side of the Crooked River a short distance east of the present site. Business continues to operate at the site.

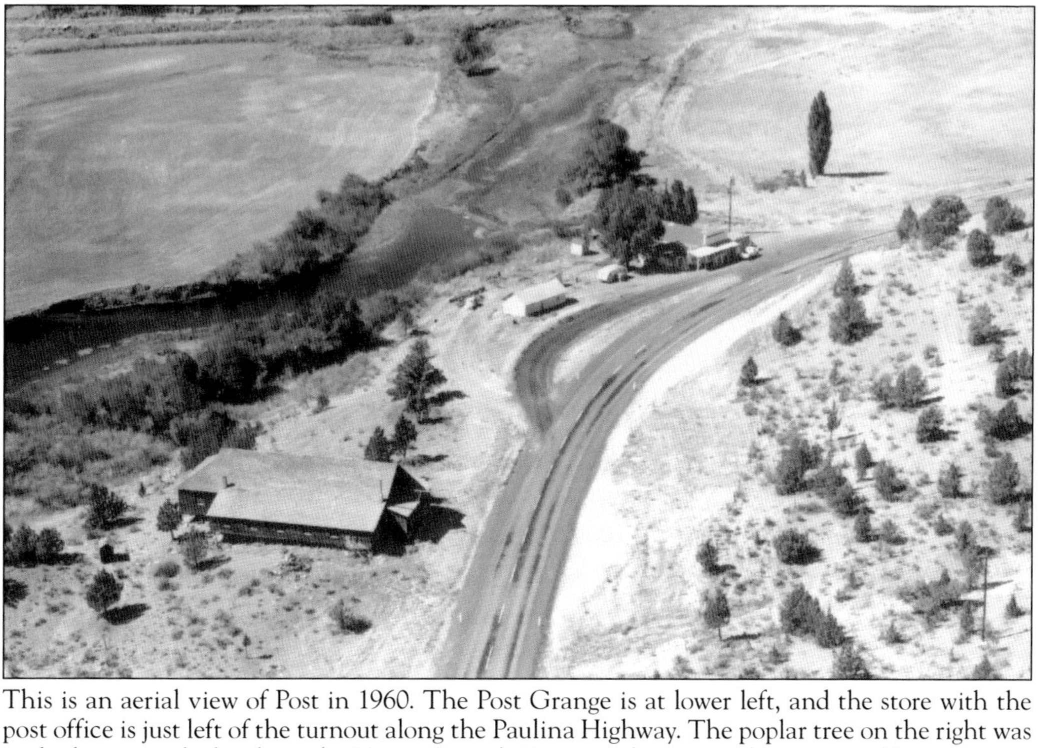

This is an aerial view of Post in 1960. The Post Grange is at lower left, and the store with the post office is just left of the turnout along the Paulina Highway. The poplar tree on the right was at the homestead of early settler Hiram Smead. Post is at the geographic center of Oregon.

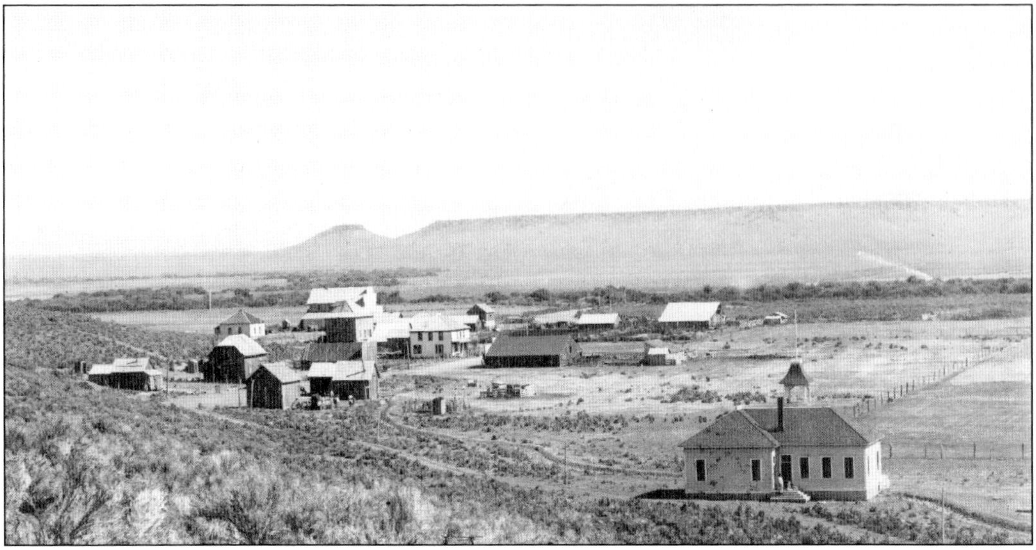

This is a view of the community of Paulina looking east in 1910. The building at lower right is the Paulina School. Hotel Paulina is located in the white building at center. The community was founded about 1870, and the first post office was established on May 23, 1882. The community was named for Indian leader Paulina, who was involved in a skirmish with Oregon volunteers that occurred to the northwest of the townsite.

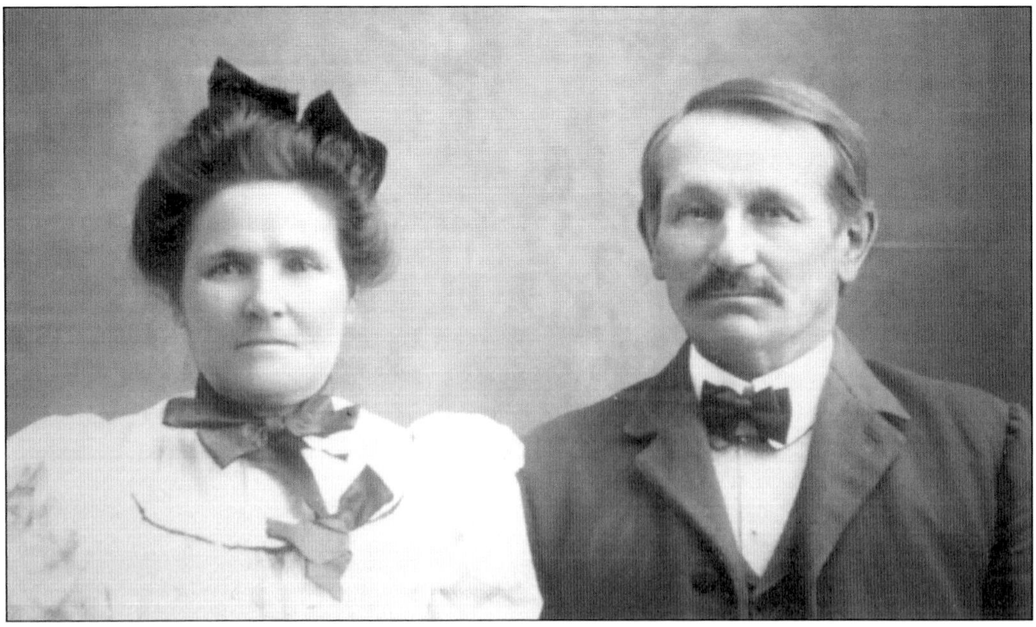

Charity and John T. Faulkner built a large house in Paulina. John served as the postmaster at Paulina for over 25 years. Charity was a practical nurse and aided many ill locals through the years.

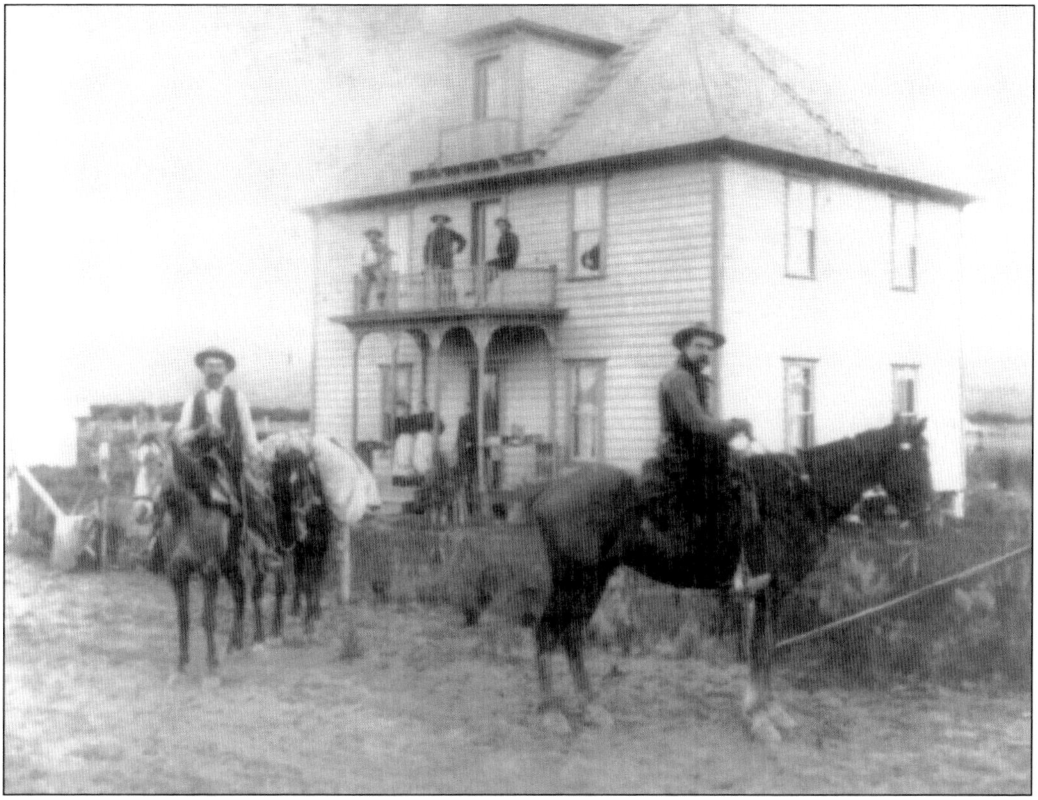

This is the John and Charity Faulkner house in Paulina. The house was built in 1885. It was the first real house to be built in the community and was three stories. It served as a hotel in Paulina for a few years. The man with the packhorse on the left is Charles Bernard, a local rancher.

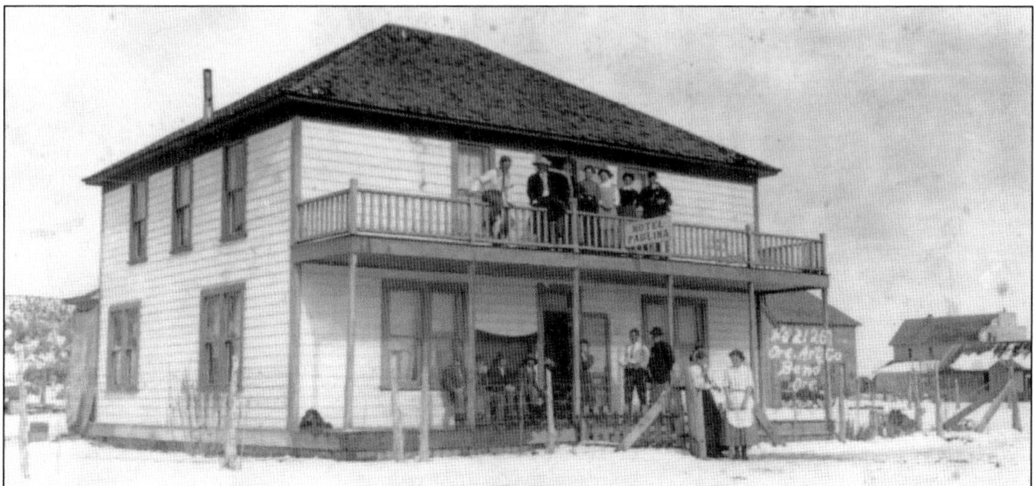

Hotel Paulina was built in 1906. It had eight bedrooms upstairs, and a kitchen, dining room, and lounge on the first floor. Elmer Clark and his wife, Frankie, operated the hotel for several years. This winter photograph shows several guests enjoying the balcony and front porch.

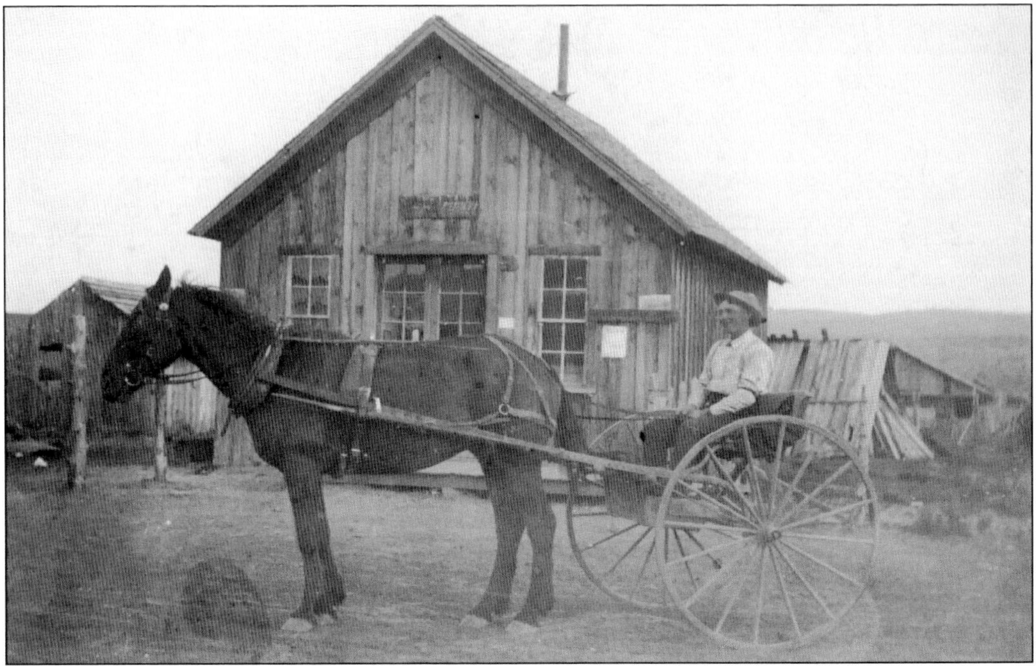

This is a small horse-drawn hack driven by George P. Lee in Paulina about 1906. He was a mail contractor and delivered mail between Paulina and Izee until 1911. Mail delivery to outlying areas sometimes was on a twice-weekly schedule.

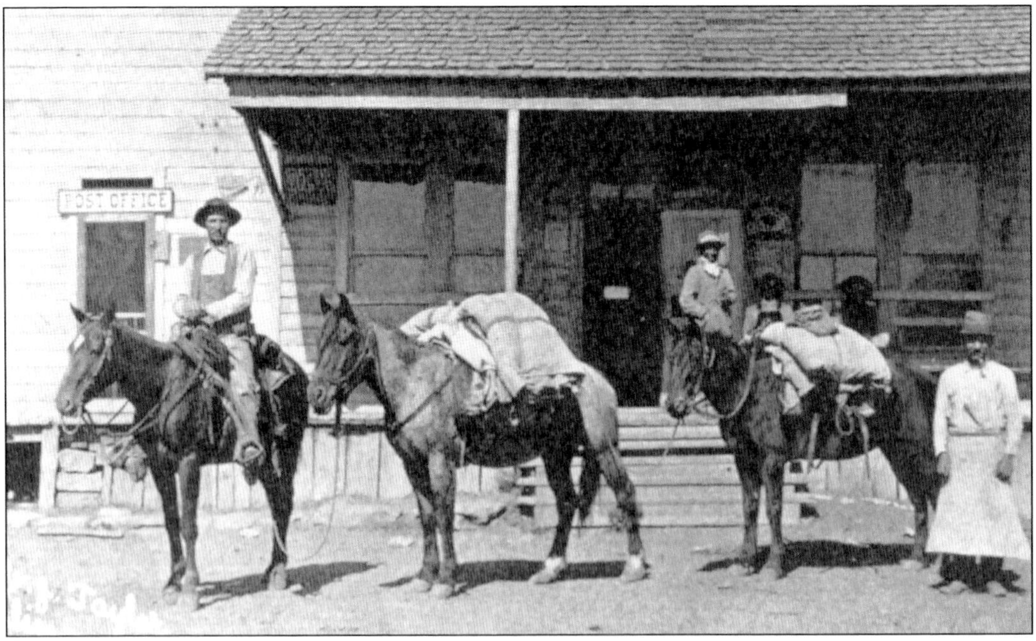

Unidentified persons are in front of the Lee Miller store in Paulina about 1906. The store was started as a general merchandise store and was located on the north side of the road through Paulina. The building contained a large dance floor and meeting hall upstairs. The post office was also located in the store. The men in front have loaded packs on horses and are heading for sheep camps.

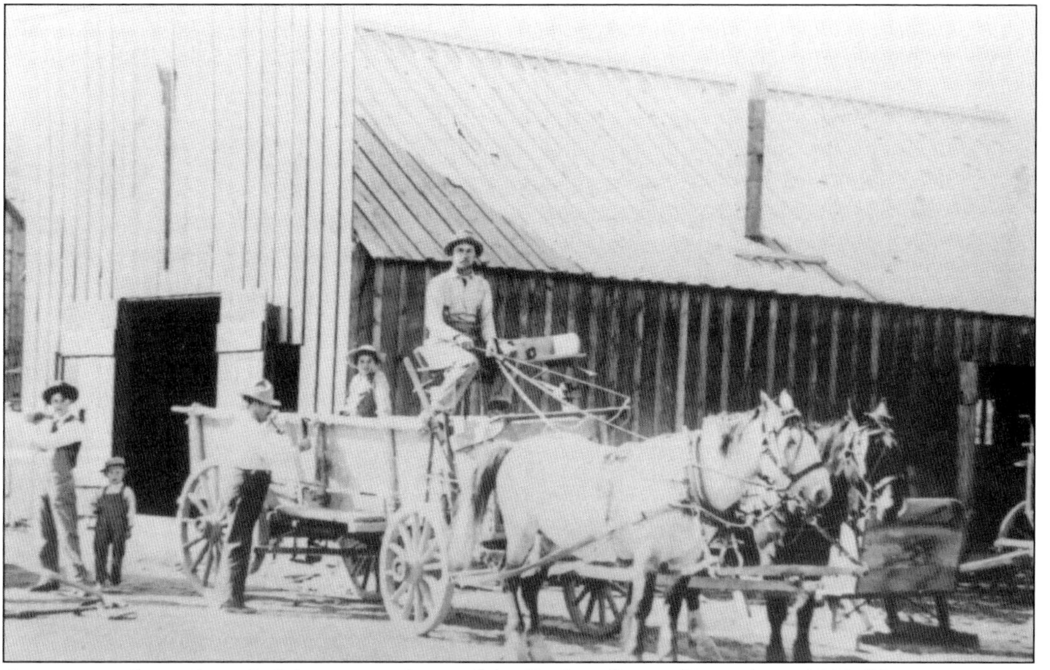

A wagon with unidentified driver is in front of the Paulina Livery Barn about 1908. The community served as a supply center for outlying ranches and camps. Travelers could rest their horses and have them fed at the livery stable.

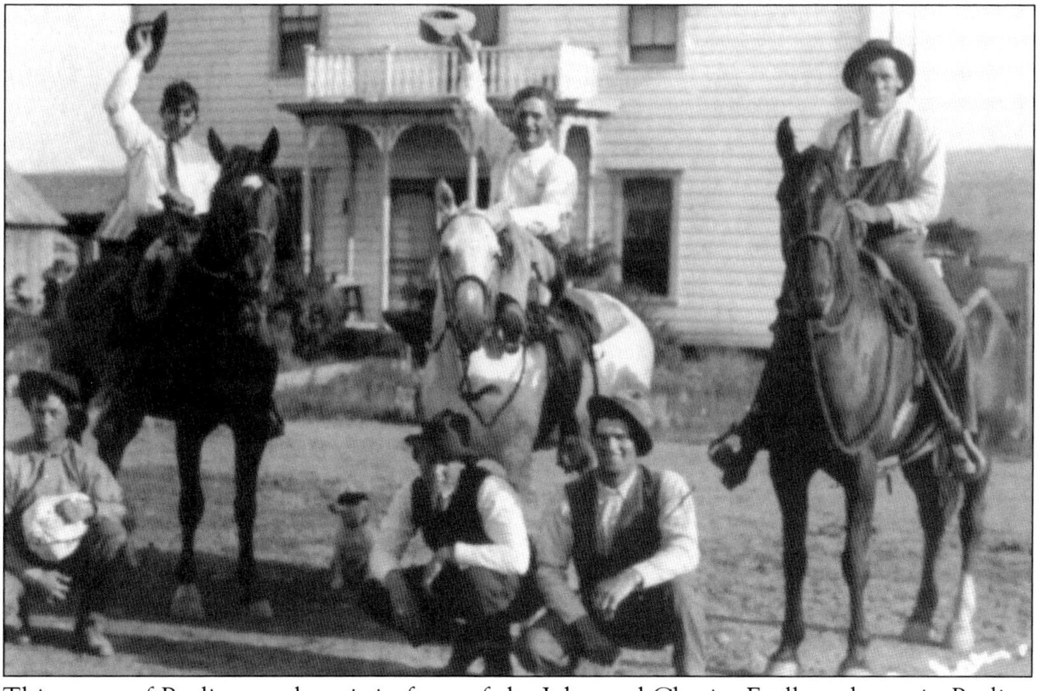

This group of Paulina cowboys is in front of the John and Charity Faulkner house in Paulina about 1909. From left to right are Joe Morskey, Henry Faulkner, Glaze Smith, Walt Nicley, Barney Bardey, and Ed Reams.

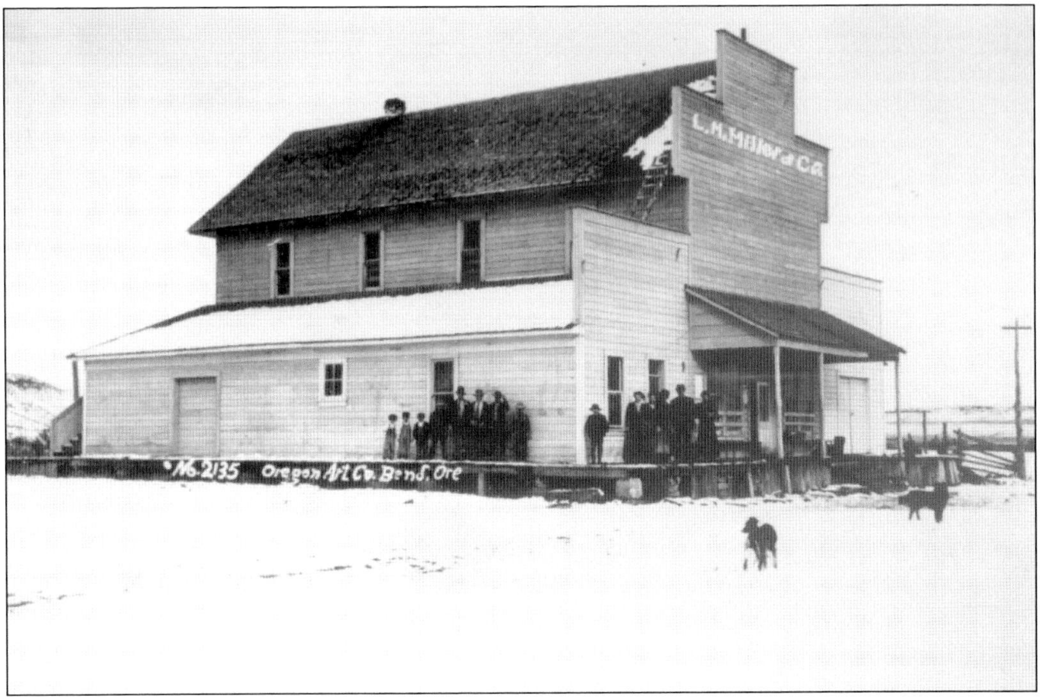

The Lee Miller store was located north of the road through Paulina and was built in 1905. George Roba was a partner with the Miller family. Later, Roba hauled merchandise from Prineville to the store in Paulina by Mack truck. The building was used as a store until 1915, when it was discontinued and a new store was built. The building burned in 1929.

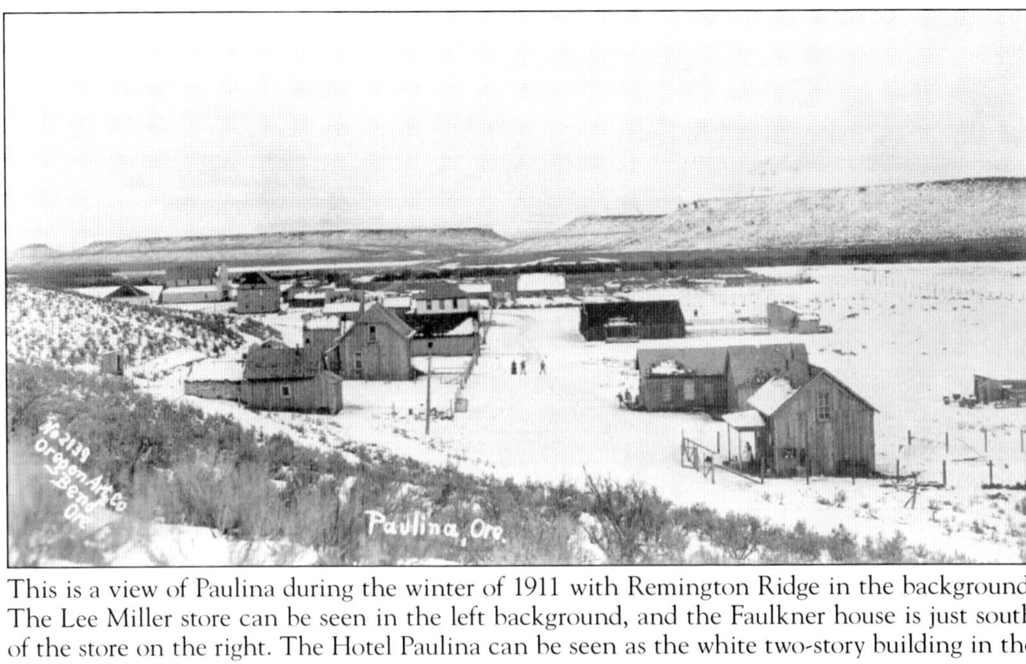

This is a view of Paulina during the winter of 1911 with Remington Ridge in the background. The Lee Miller store can be seen in the left background, and the Faulkner house is just south of the store on the right. The Hotel Paulina can be seen as the white two-story building in the middle of the photograph.

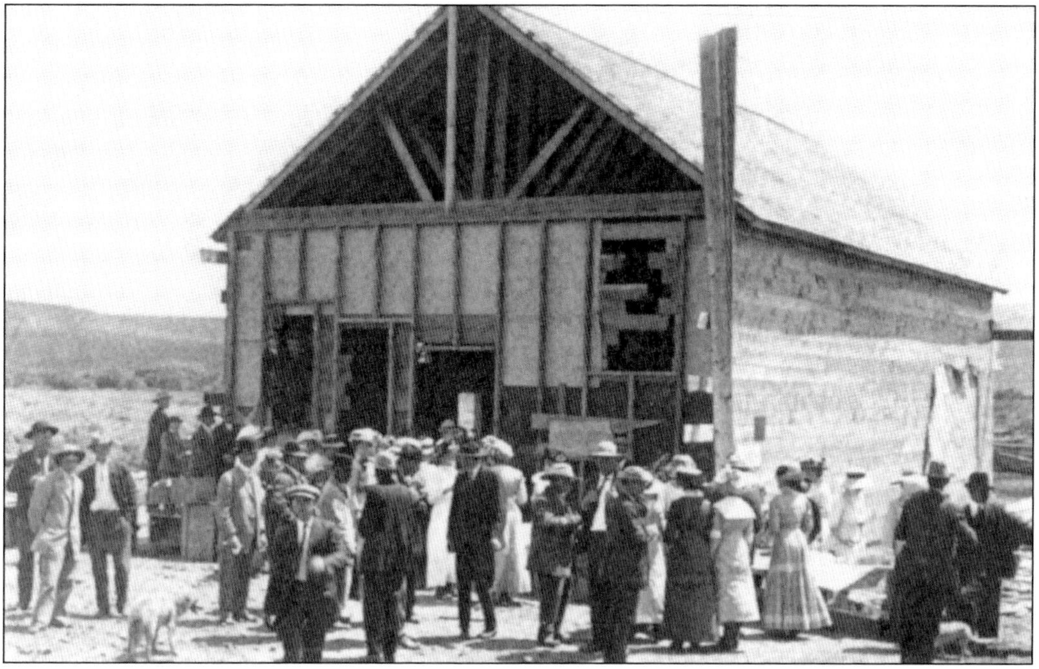

Local farmers established a creamery in Paulina in 1913. Many local ranchers had milk cows and produced butter and thought it would be profitable to have a local creamery. But poor transportation and lengthy travel times for delivery of dairy products led to the creamery only operating one year. Several locals are gathered at the creamery in this 1913 photograph.

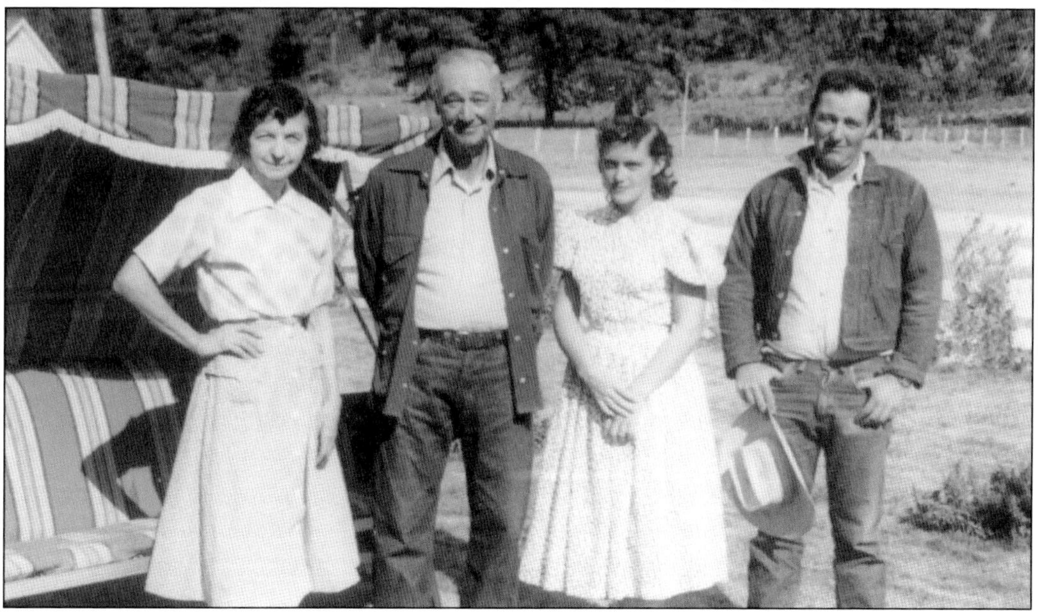

From left to right are May McCullough Miller, Lyle Miller, Naida Evans Miller, and Pat Miller. Lyle and May Miller began operating the Paulina store at its current location in 1918. May served as postmaster at Paulina for 29 years. The Millers sold the store in 1949. They had a ranch on Wolf Creek northeast of Paulina, and their son Pat Miller and wife, Naida (née Evans), and family continue to operate one of the few remaining pioneer family ranches in the region.

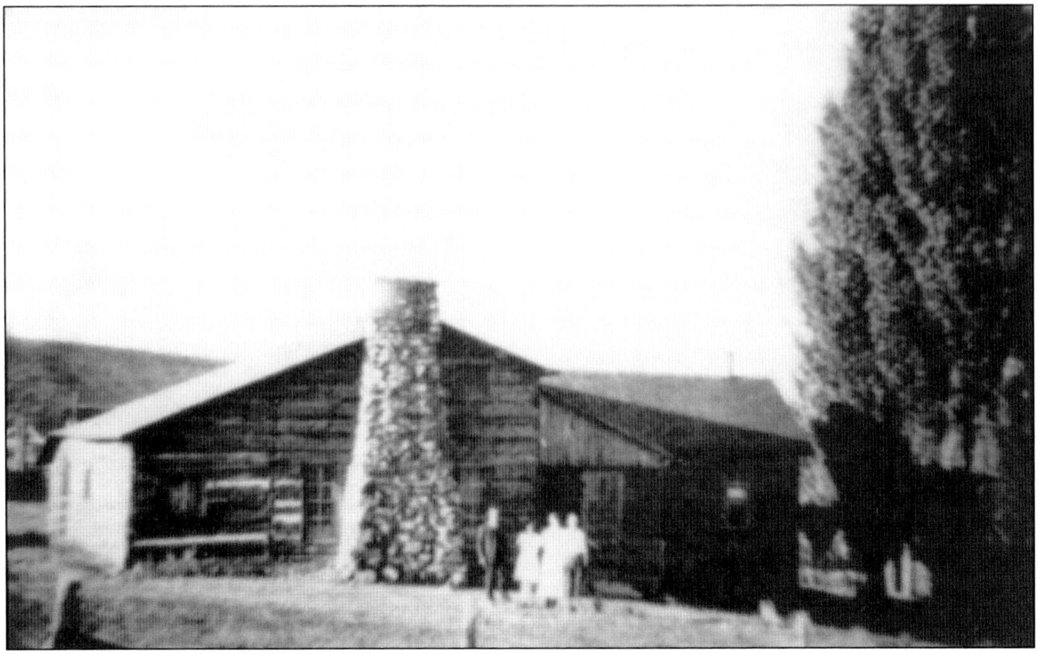

Mark and Elizabeth Carson came to settle near the confluence of Crooked River and Camp Creek in 1884. They built a log cabin and established the Mowry Post Office in their home. The name Mowry was a corruption of the last name of Col. Reuben Maury, who commanded Army volunteers in Oregon during the Civil War. The Carsons' home also became a stage station for travelers from Prineville to points east. George and Sarah Glenn later bought the cabin, and it became known as the Glenn Place. This photograph was taken around 1890. The structure is still standing. The post office was established on August 16, 1887, and was discontinued in 1899.

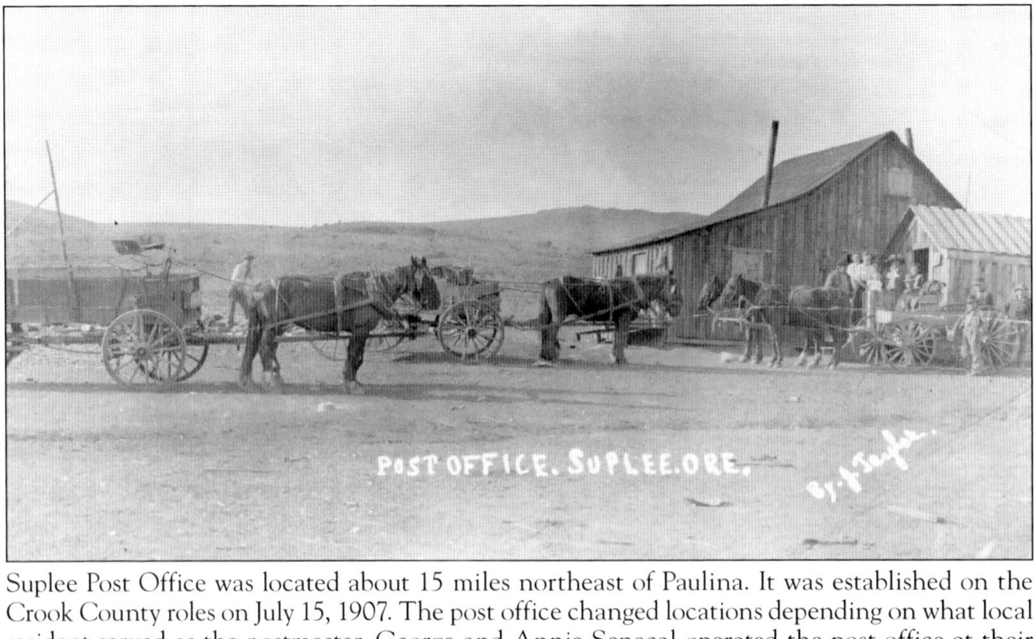

Suplee Post Office was located about 15 miles northeast of Paulina. It was established on the Crook County roles on July 15, 1907. The post office changed locations depending on what local resident served as the postmaster. George and Annie Senecal operated the post office at their home for many years. The post office was discontinued in 1941.

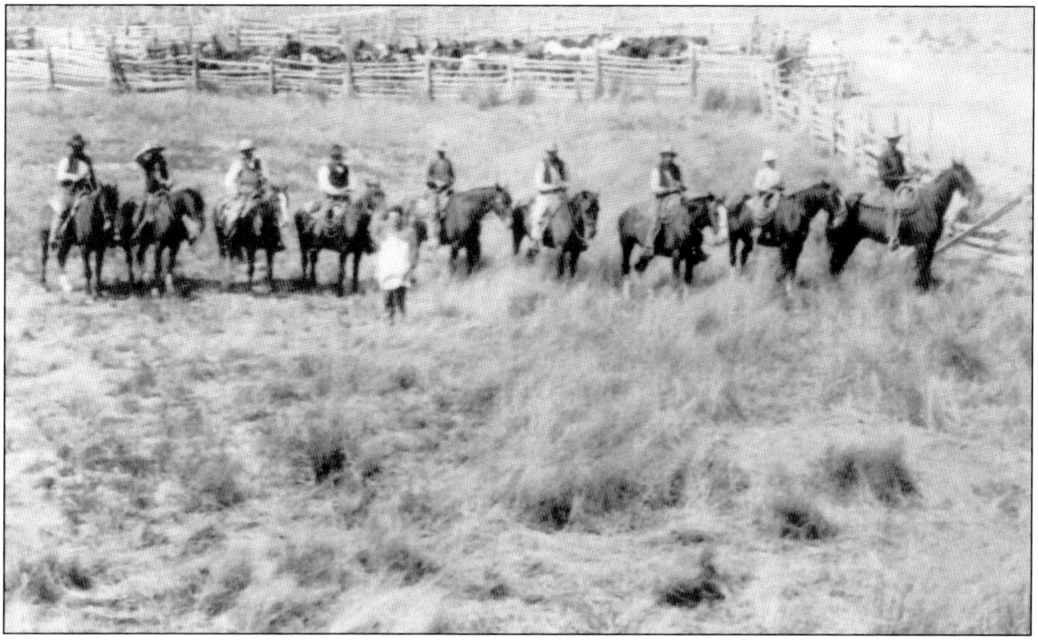

Buckaroos for legendary Bill Brown are lined up after corralling some of Brown's horses at Hardin Corrals on Twelvemile Table at the head of Grindstone Creek. A post office was established at this site with the name of Hardin on May 25, 1882. It was named for one of the partners in the Hardin and Riley Cattle Company. It was mostly a buckaroo camp.

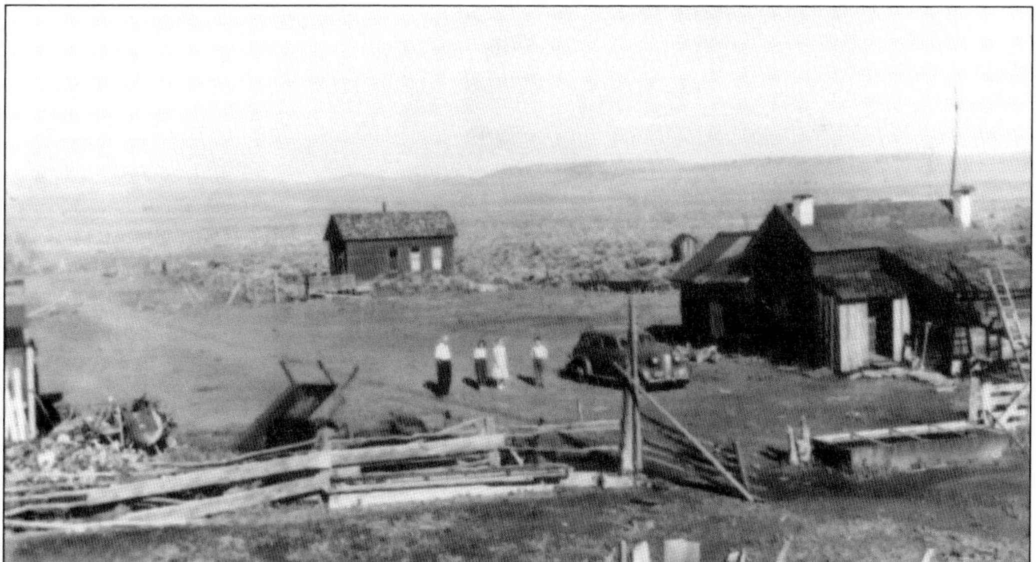

This is one of the later locations for the post office of Fife just south of the GI Ranch. The original post office was established on Buck Creek on May 17, 1890, with Bruce Balfour the first postmaster. Over the next several years, the post office moved to the home of a homesteader willing to take on the postmaster position. Stages traveled from Prineville via Roberts to Fife. The post office was discontinued in 1937.

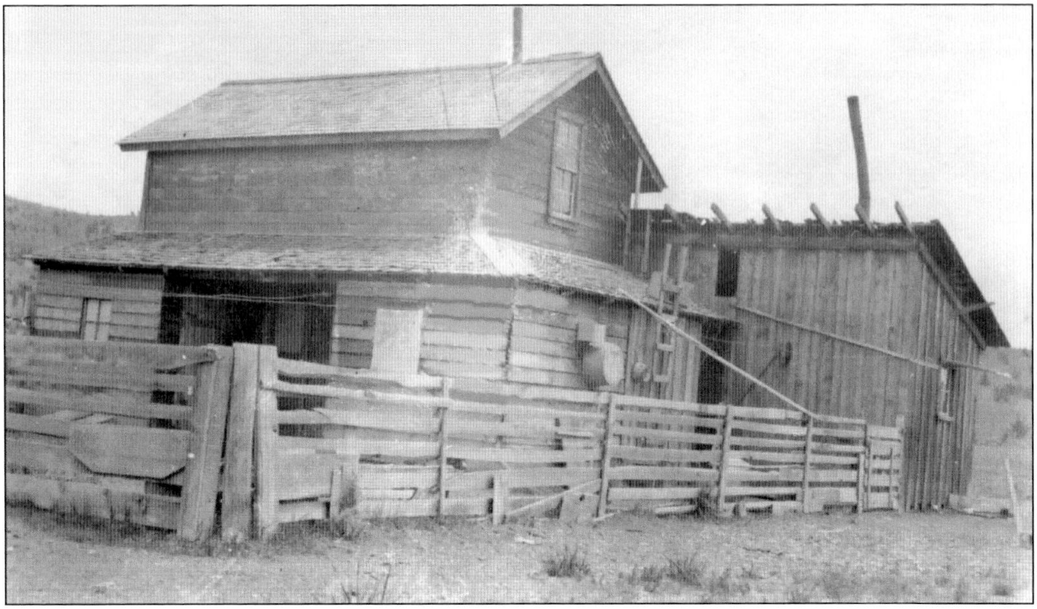

This is the Harry Barnes homestead ranch and site of Barnes Post Office on Camp Creek about 20 miles southwest of Paulina. The post office was established on May 1, 1909, and was named for Harry Barnes, the first postmaster. There was a school nearby and a small cemetery about four miles west. The post office was discontinued on July 31, 1925.

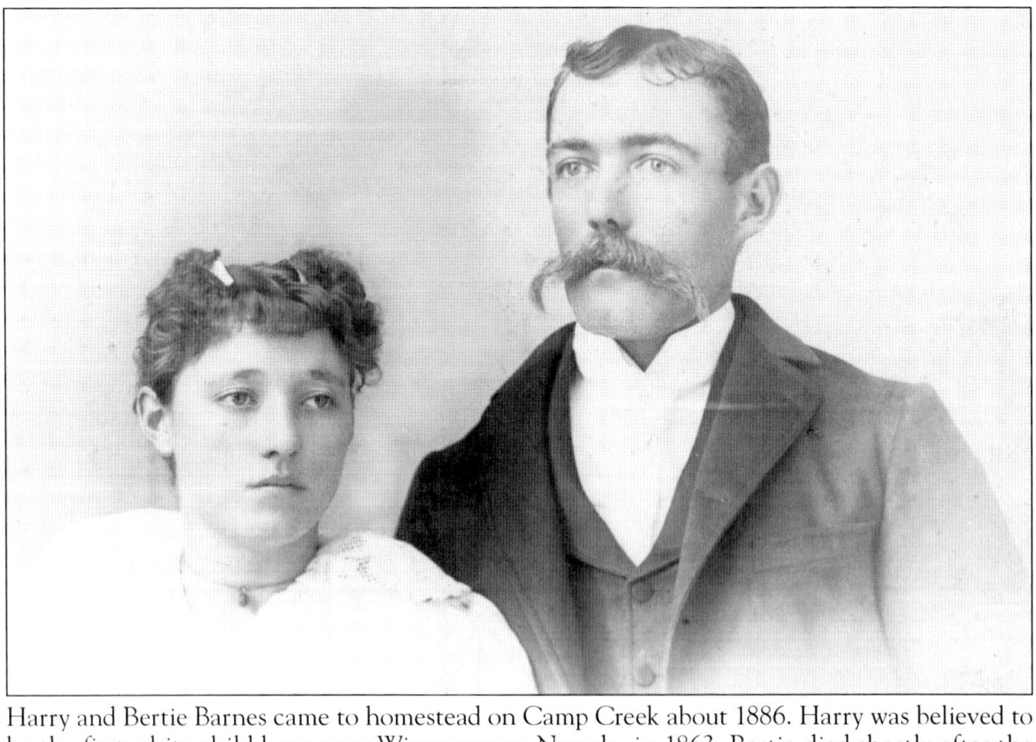

Harry and Bertie Barnes came to homestead on Camp Creek about 1886. Harry was believed to be the first white child born near Winnemucca, Nevada, in 1863. Bertie died shortly after the birth of their son Charles. Harry's mother moved to the ranch to help take care of his son. He lived at the ranch site for over 75 years.

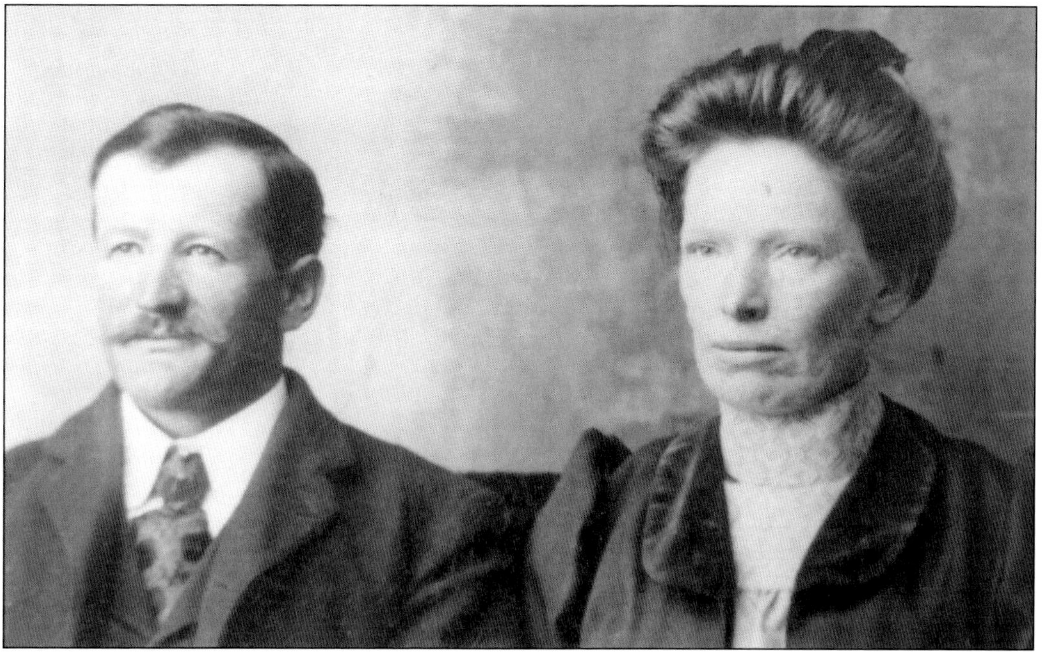

Paul and Eva Ammons Held settled at a site between Camp Creek and Bear Creek off of the main wagon road. A post office was established in the Held home on May 1, 1909, with the post office named for Paul Held, the first postmaster. A school was established nearby. The Helds established a cattle ranch and lived in the area for several years. The post office was discontinued on May 15, 1919.

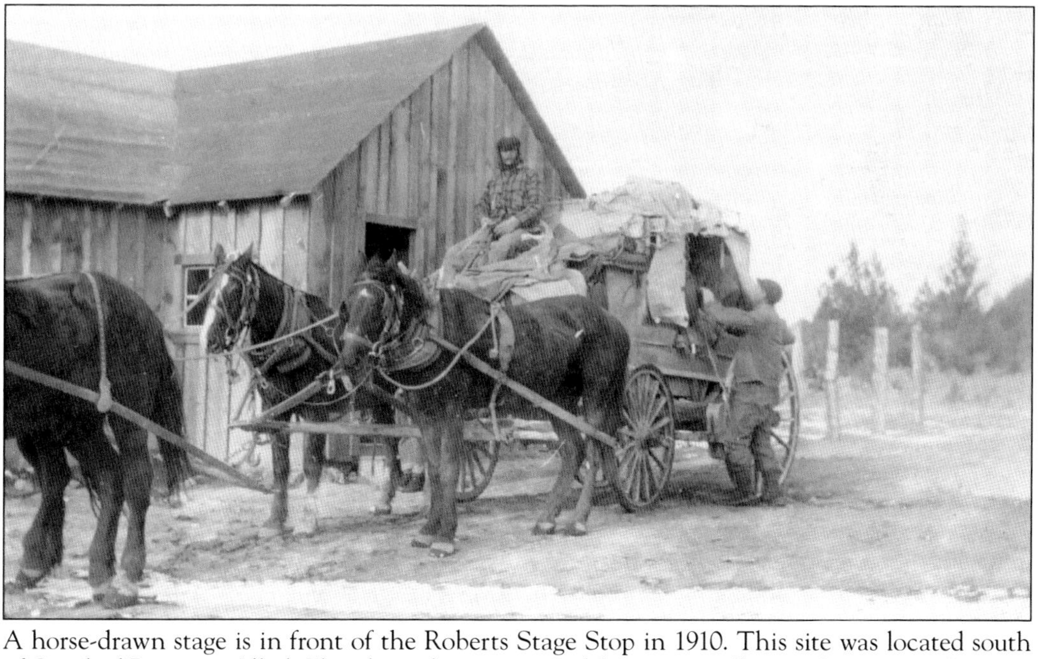

A horse-drawn stage is in front of the Roberts Stage Stop in 1910. This site was located south of Crooked River on Alkali Flat along the wagon road from Prineville to Fife. A post office was established at the site on May 6, 1910, and named for a nearby rancher Joseph Roberts. The stage driver is unidentified.

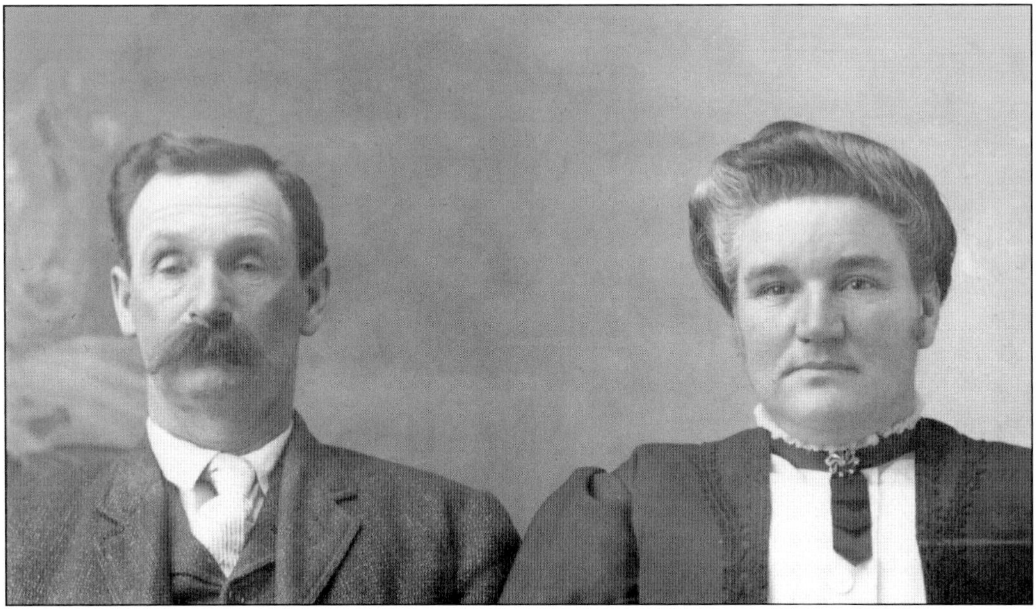

Joseph E. "Gede" and Sophronia Rice Roberts settled along Newsome Creek in 1887 and bought the Arthur Johnson Ranch on Alkali Flat in 1894. The homestead era after the turn of the 20th century created a short-lived boom in the area. Gede and Sophronia donated land for a school and a cemetery. They sold their ranch in 1930; they are buried in the Roberts Cemetery.

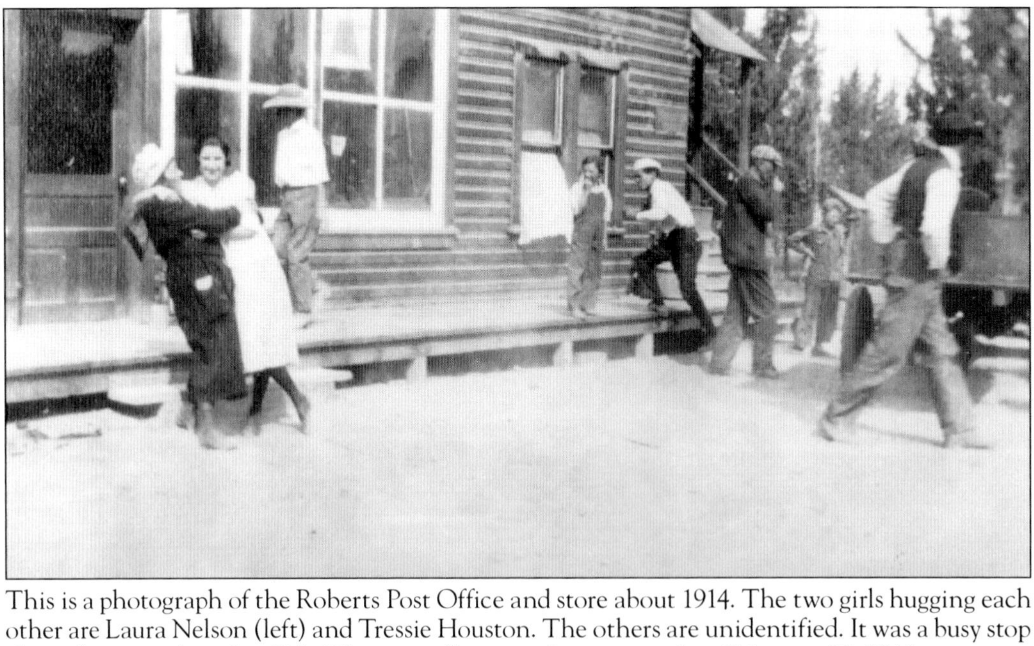

This is a photograph of the Roberts Post Office and store about 1914. The two girls hugging each other are Laura Nelson (left) and Tressie Houston. The others are unidentified. It was a busy stop along the rugged road to Fife. The post office was discontinued on February 29, 1940.

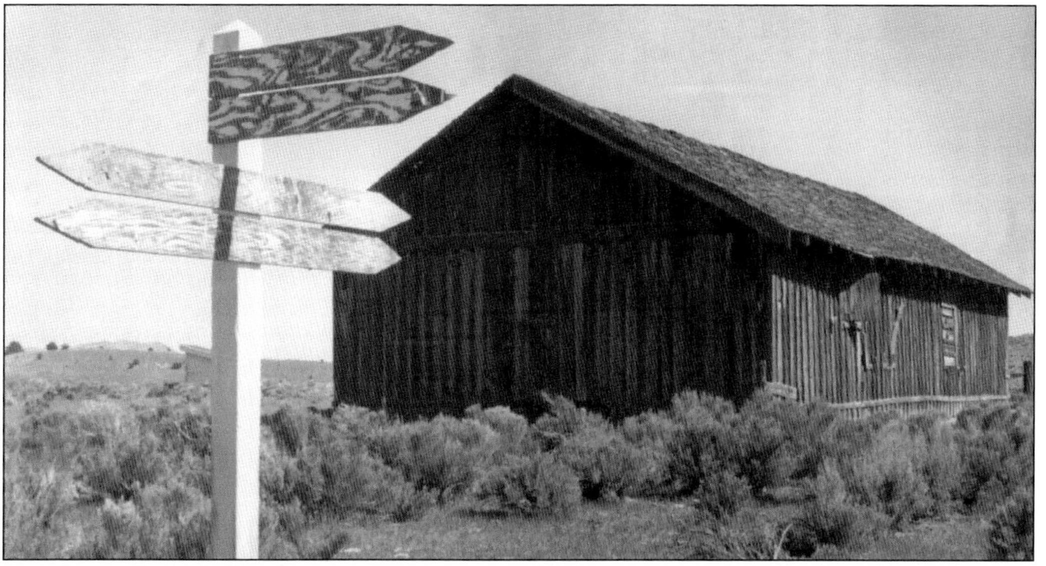

Pringle Flat dance hall and community center was located on Pringle Flat about five miles north of Brothers near the Crook-Deschutes County line. Numerous homesteaders settled the surrounding region, and this hall was built for community gatherings about 1910. A Fourth of July event at the hall in 1915 attracted over 250 people. The once-thriving area is now the home of isolated ranches, and the building has collapsed.

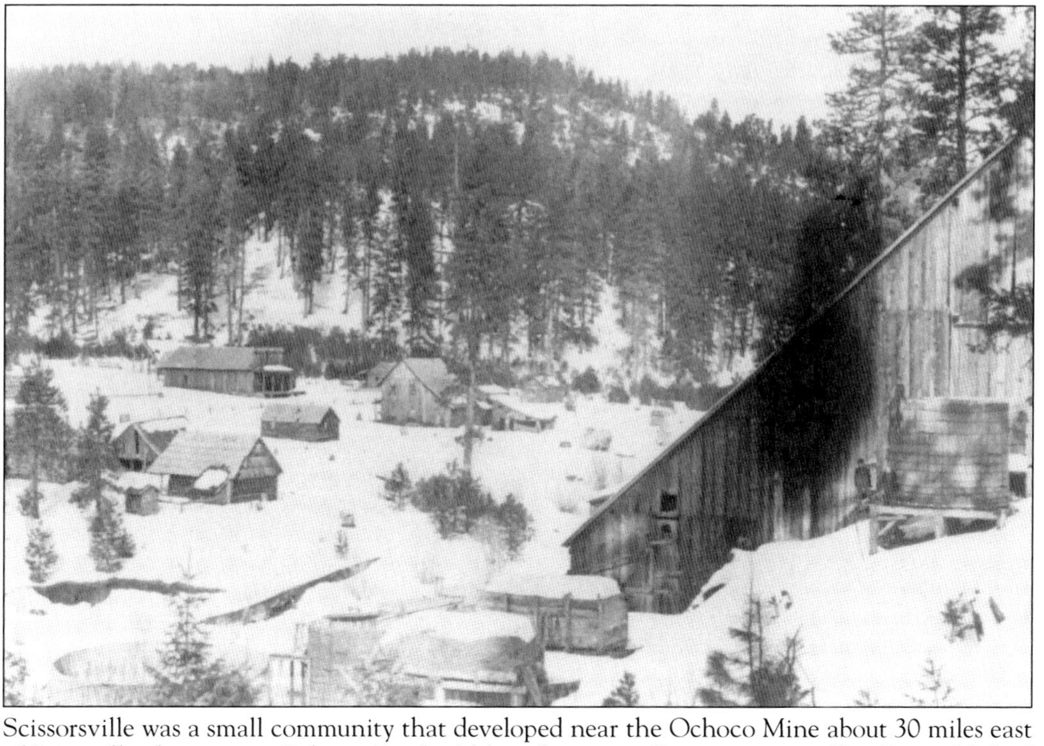

Scissorsville was a small community that developed near the Ochoco Mine about 30 miles east of Prineville along upper Ochoco Creek. Although a post office was never officially established by that name, the mining community was identified on maps as early as 1875. This 1890 view is looking north from the mine with Ochoco Creek in the background near the hill.

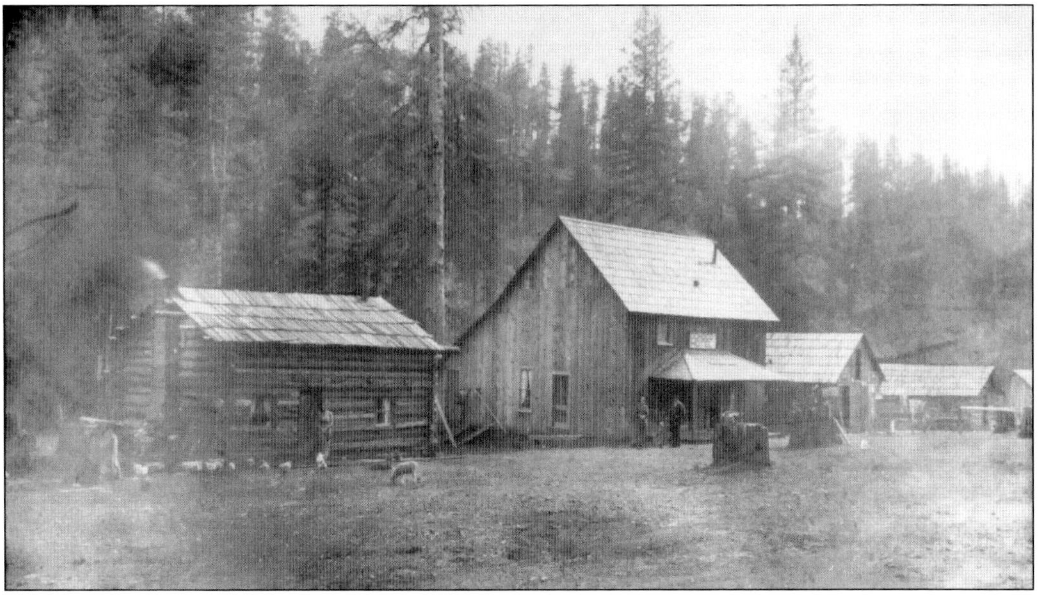

Scissorsville became known as Howard when a post office was officially established on May 10, 1877. The post office was named for James Howard, one of the first discoverers of gold in the area. The Ochoco Hotel is the larger building at center. This photograph was taken about 1900.

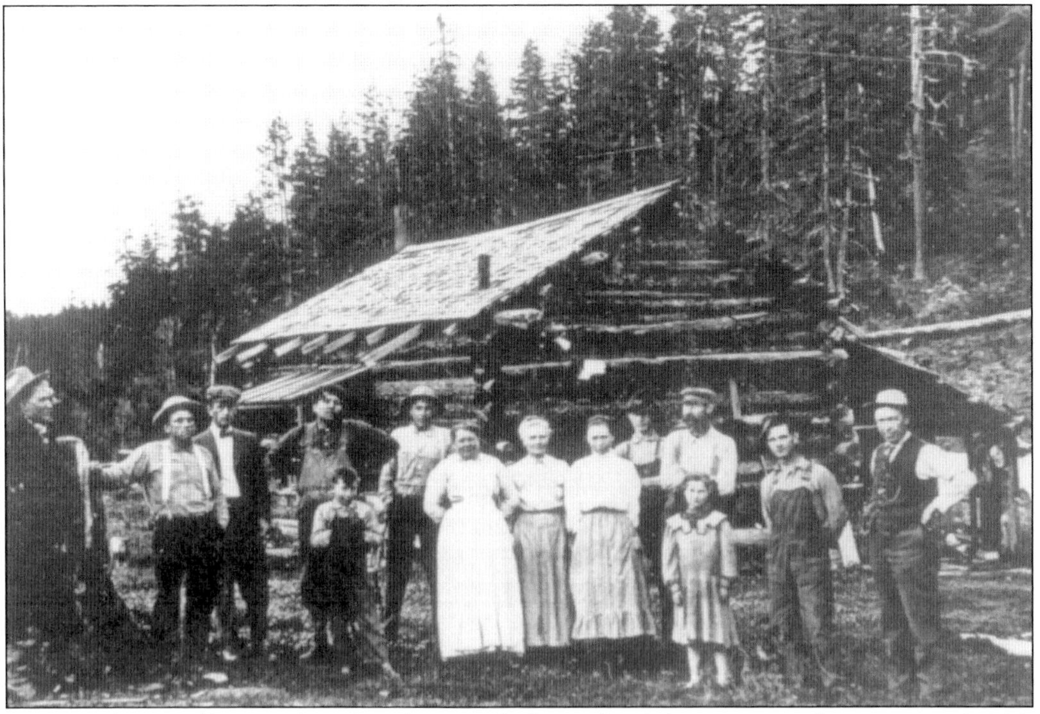

Taken at the McAllister Cabin, this photograph shows the Ochoco mining district around 1900. A few people attempted to keep the mining activities at Ochoco Mine a viable enterprise, and this group was among the last to live and work there. Mining at the site ceased about 1920. Most signs of the mining district are now vanished.

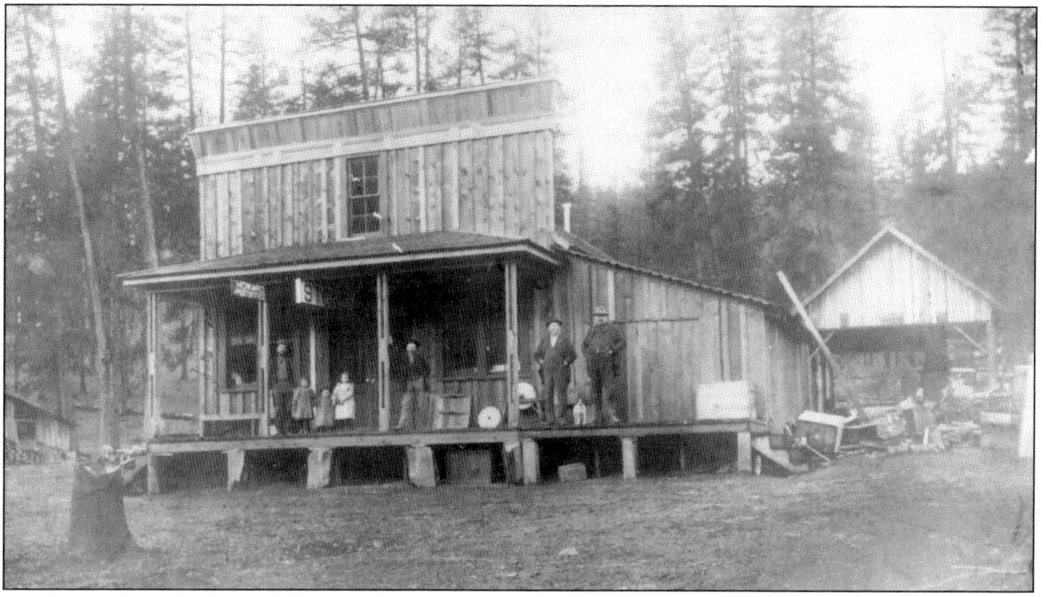

This is a merchandise store at Howard. The population of Howard probably never exceeded 50 people. As mining activity decreased, the post office was moved to various locations along Ochoco Creek depending on who was willing to be the postmaster. The Howard Post Office was discontinued on May 15, 1918.

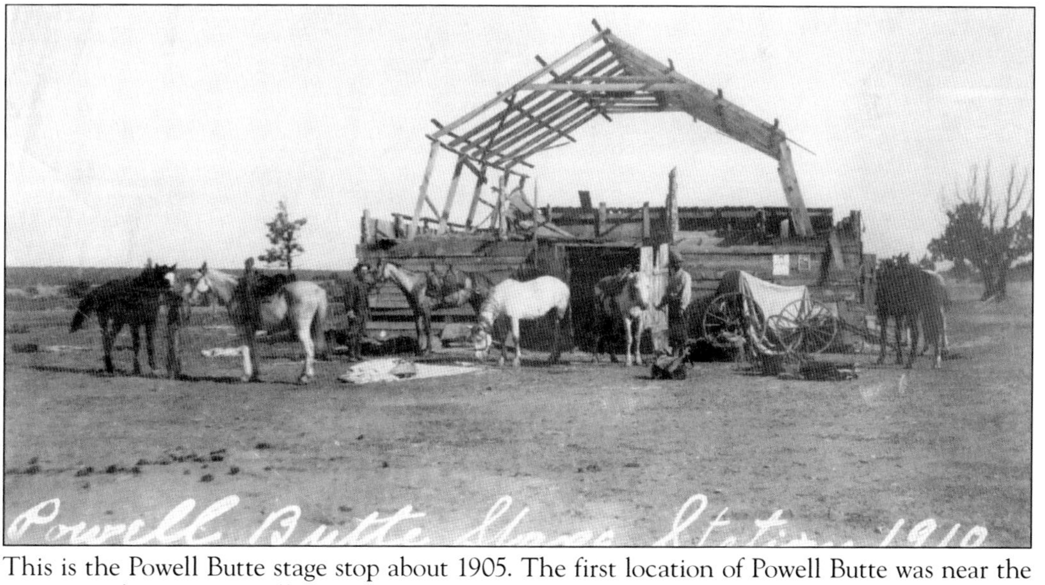

This is the Powell Butte stage stop about 1905. The first location of Powell Butte was near the junction of present Powell Butte Highway and Shumway Road. The stage stop was along the old wagon road from Prineville to Bend. The vicinity became a dryland-farming center until irrigation arrived about 1908.

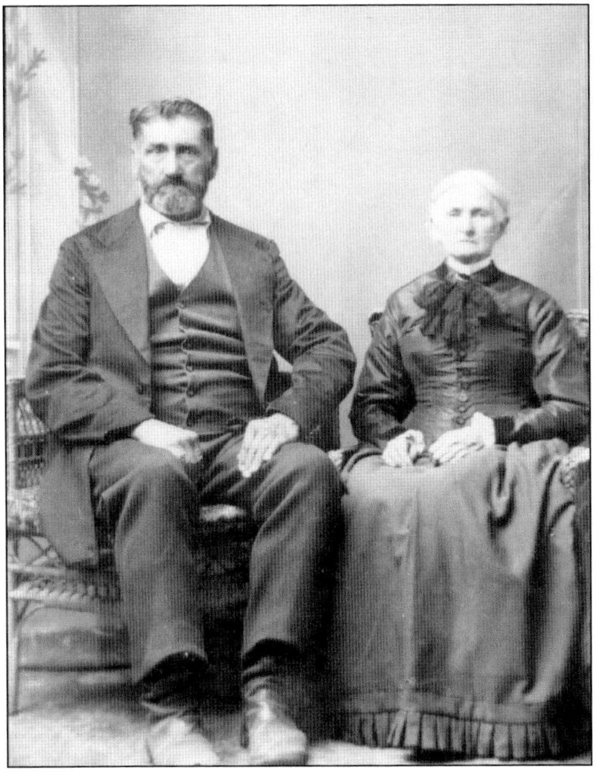

John and Emily Powell settled in central Oregon in 1870 near Crooked River to the north of a series of buttes named for them. John was the son of noted early circuit-rider preacher Joab Powell. Later, the post office of Powell Butte was named for the nearby buttes.

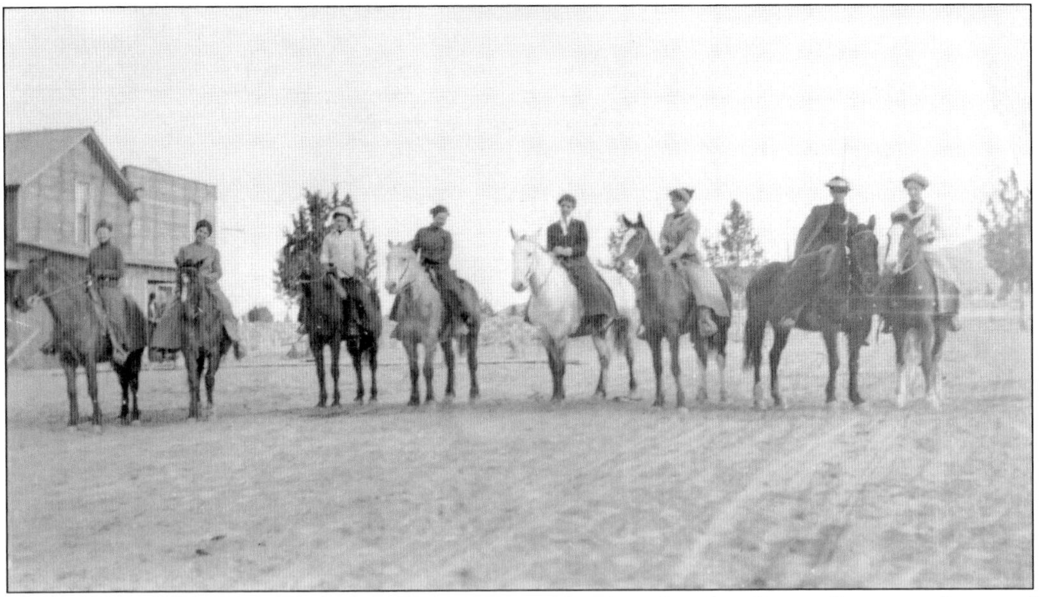

This is a group of unidentified young women traveling from Bend to Prineville to watch one of the first football games in central Oregon in 1911. They are stopped at Powell Butte. The buildings in the background house the post office, a hotel, and a store. The location was near the junction of present Shumway Road and Powell Butte Highway. A post office was established at this site on March 12, 1909. The post office was later moved to its present location at the junction of Highway 126 and Powell Butte Highway.

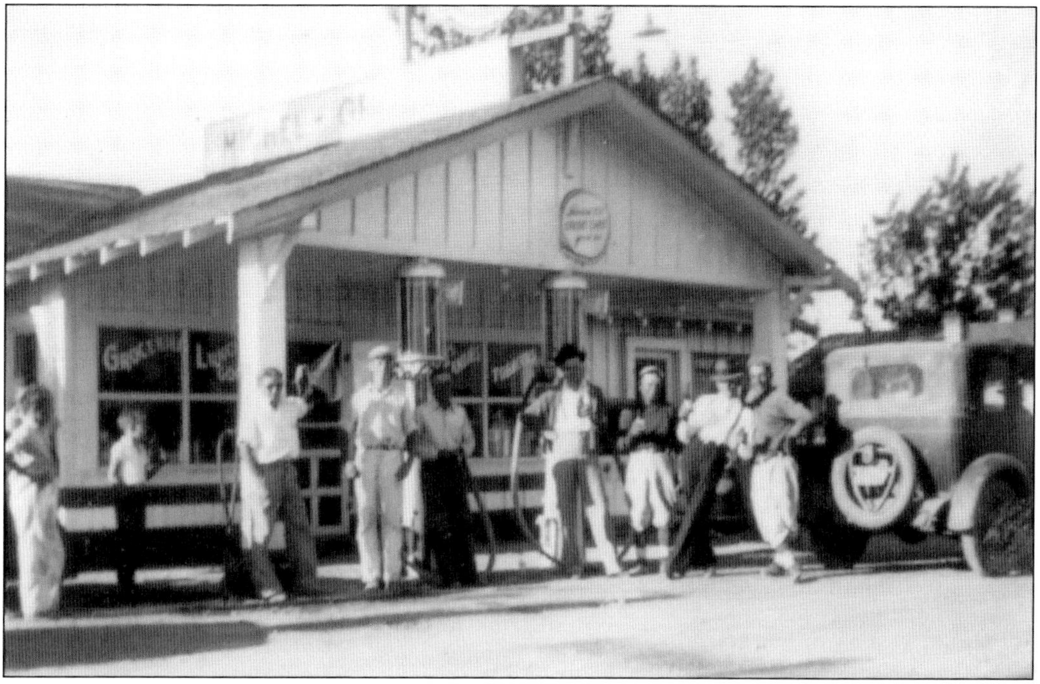

A new store was built at the present site of Powell Butte around 1938 across the road from the new Powell Butte School. Here, a group of men is pictured at the gas pump of Ayers store at Powell Butte.

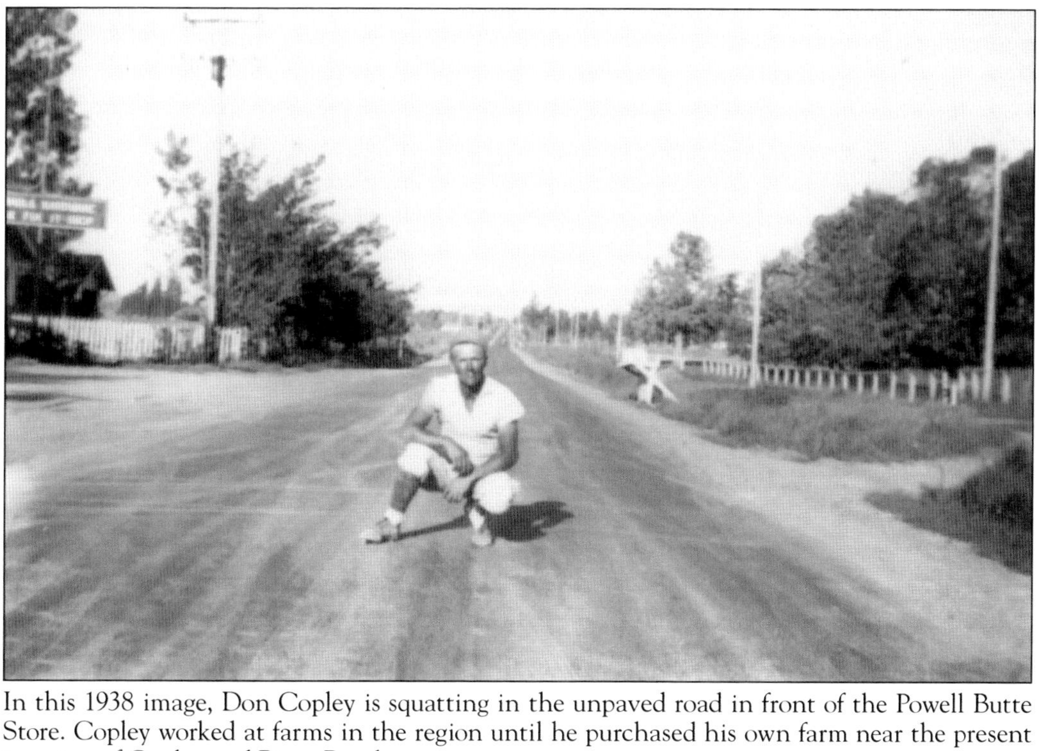

In this 1938 image, Don Copley is squatting in the unpaved road in front of the Powell Butte Store. Copley worked at farms in the region until he purchased his own farm near the present junction of Copley and Riggs Roads.

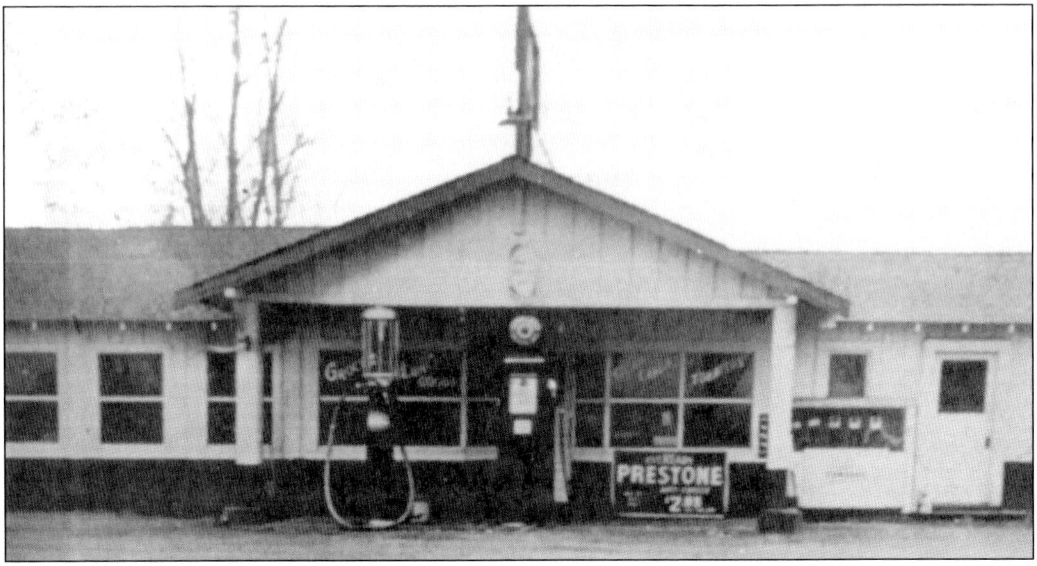

This is the Powell Butte Store at its present location around 1950. The present store at Powell Butte is now a modern structure.

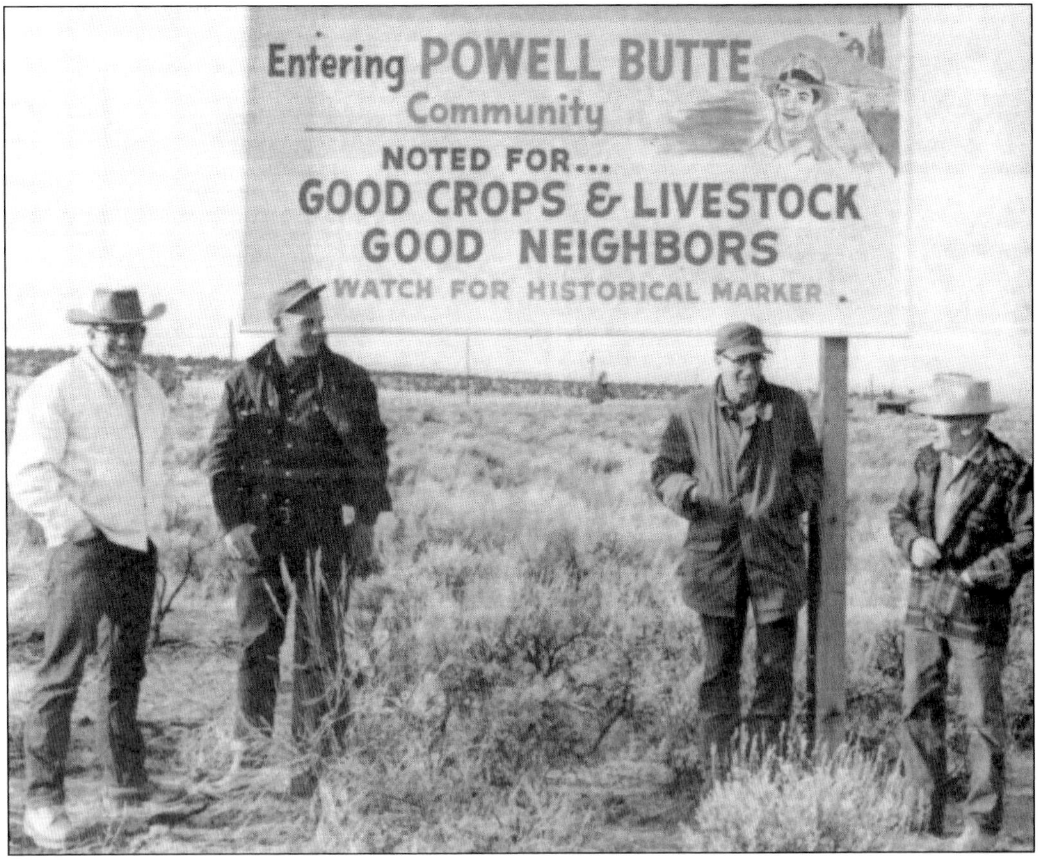

Powell Butte farmers are standing in front of a welcome sign to the community of Powell Butte. From left to right are Darrell Dickson, Gene Hargis, Ernie Hall, and R. Shepard.

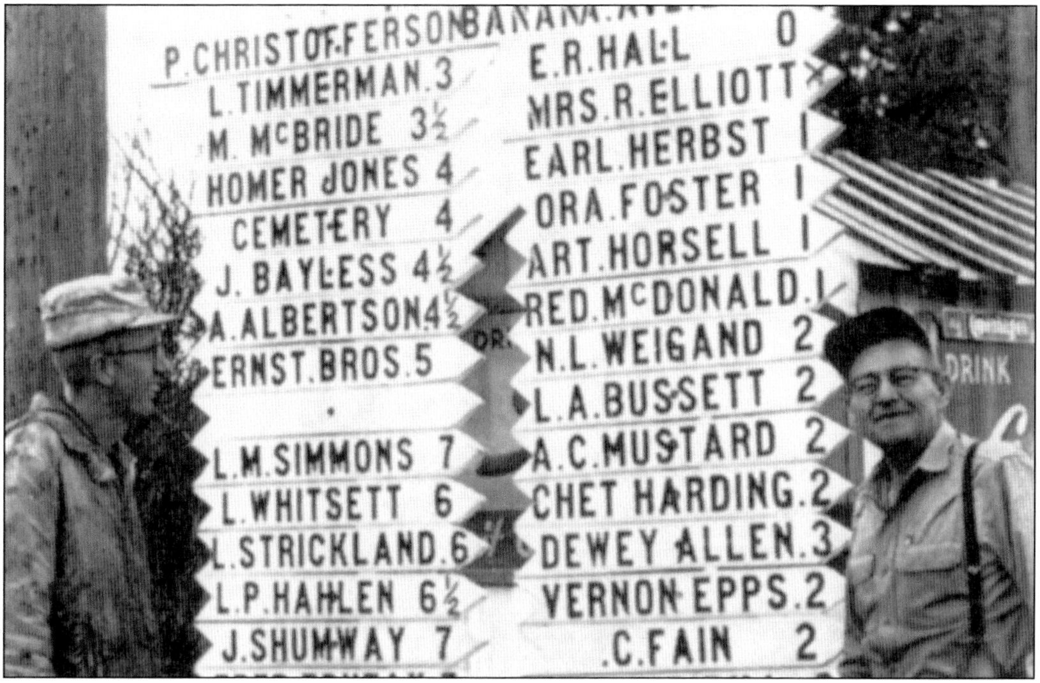

Many farmers became established in the Powell Butte vicinity. This sign was located at the junction of Powell Butte Highway and Highway 126 at the site of the new post office and the Marshall store. Family names were identified for travelers to locate the different farms in the region. On the left is Ken Werth, and on the right is Edgar Peterson.

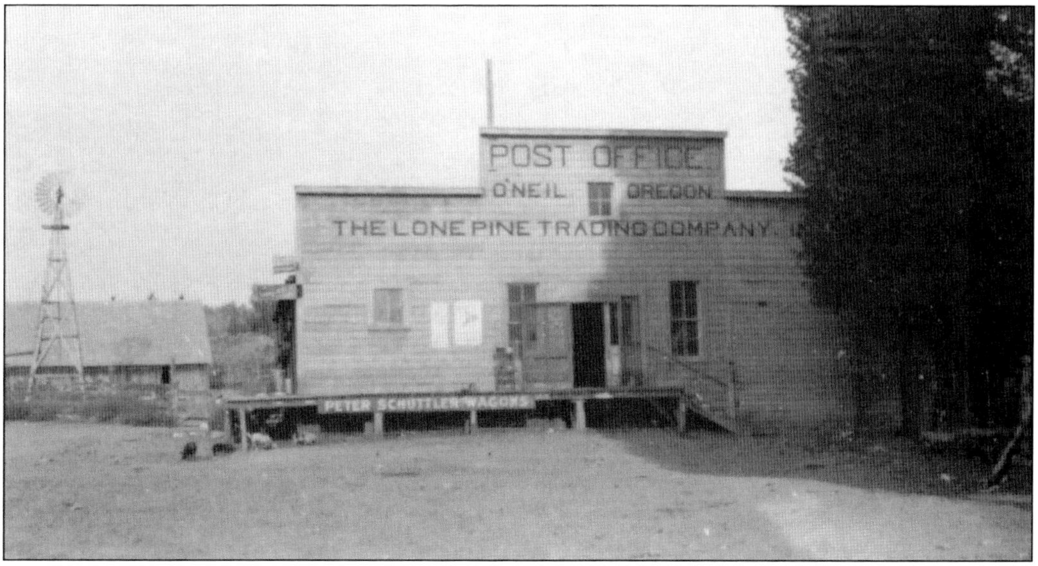

The Lower Crooked River Valley had rich farmland and was the site of early transportation routes on the Crooked River. The flat region became known as Lone Pine for the solitary ponderosa pine that grows in the upper portion of the valley. It was first known as Carmichael's Crossing, then Forest Crossing, and finally as O'Neil. This is the Lone Pine Trading Company, operated by the O'Neil brothers, at what became the post office of O'Neil. The post office was established on February 16, 1906.

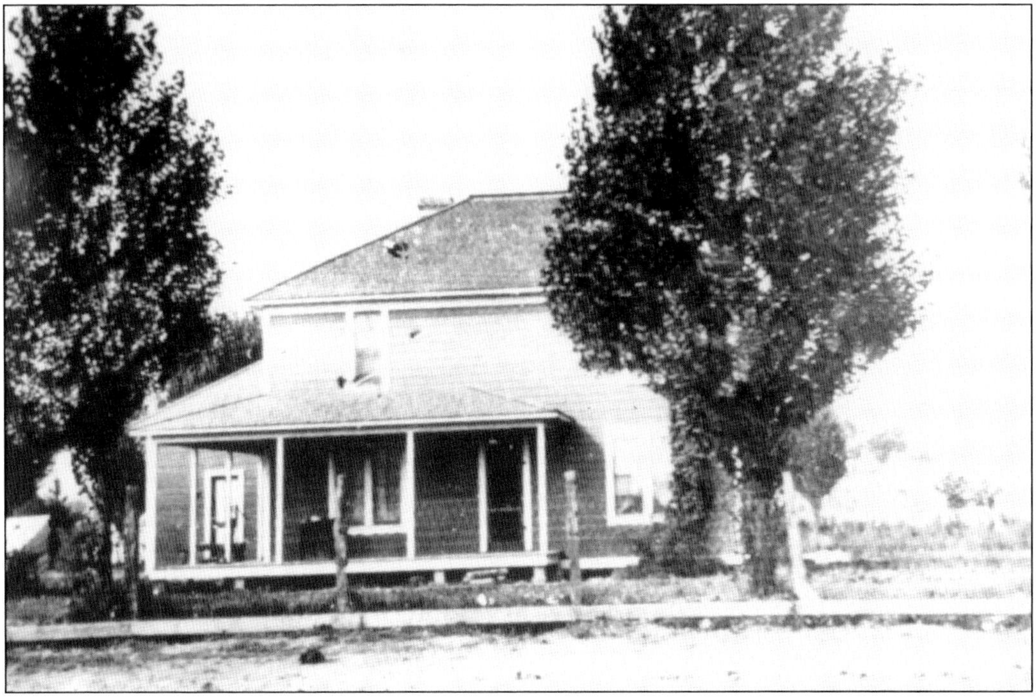

Frank Forest established a hotel at his home just north of present-day O'Neil. Forest operated a stage stop at his home, which was near the Crooked River Crossing. It later became known as the O'Neil Hotel when the O'Neil brothers purchased Forest's holdings. This is a view of the O'Neil Hotel.

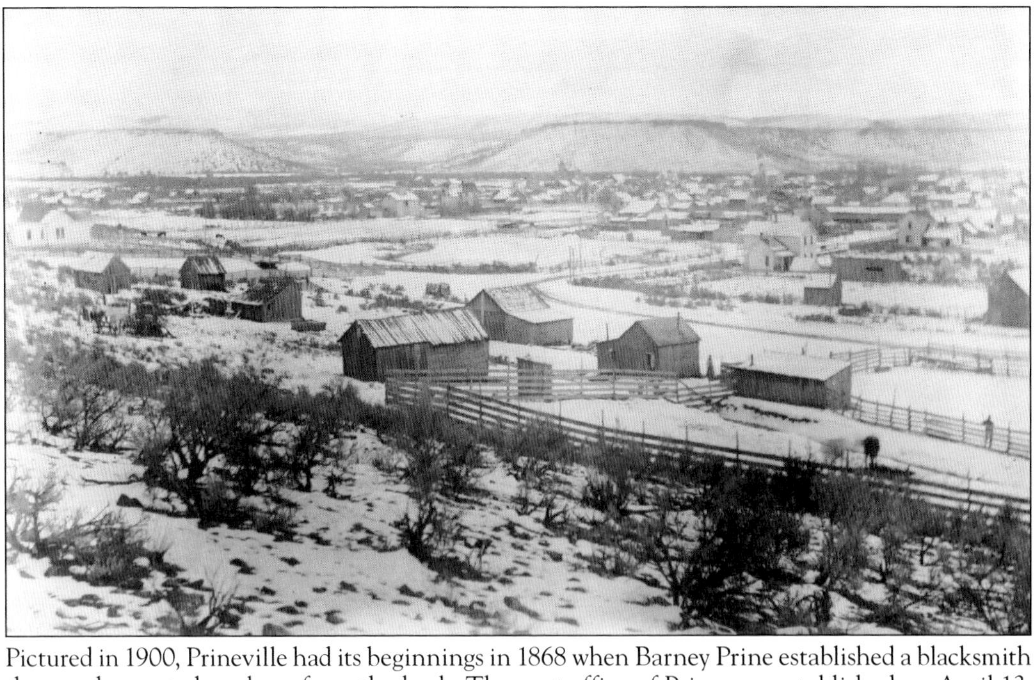

Pictured in 1900, Prineville had its beginnings in 1868 when Barney Prine established a blacksmith shop and operated a saloon from the back. The post office of Prine was established on April 13, 1871, and was named for Barney Prine. The community was officially incorporated in 1880.

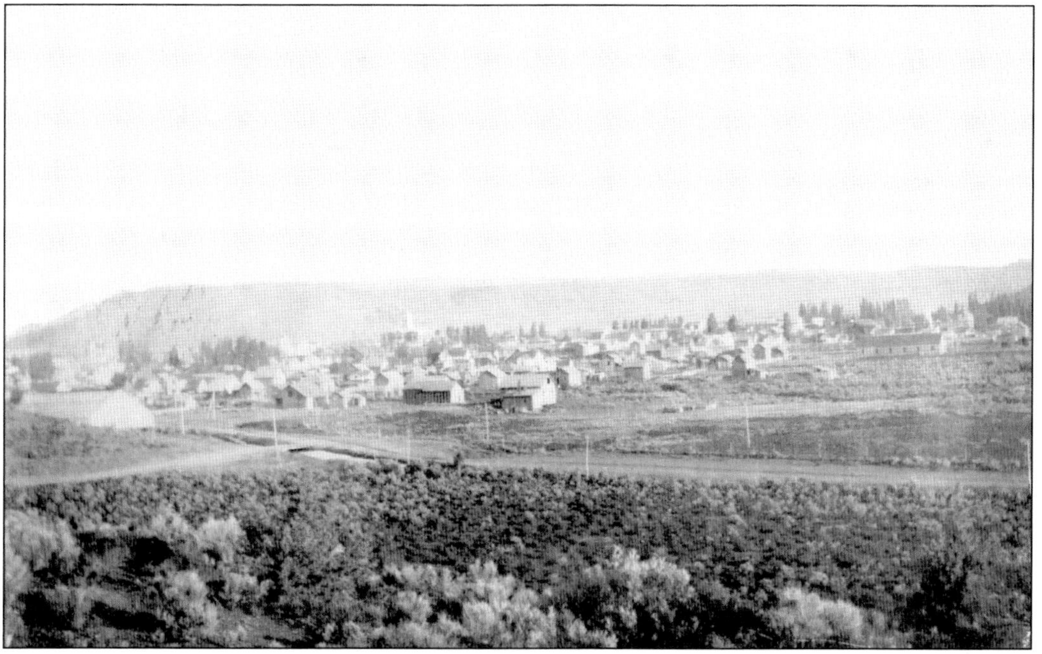

This is a view of Prineville looking southeast in 1911. The large building in the middle background is the Crook County Courthouse, built in 1909. Vacant sagebrush flats are at the immediate border of the town.

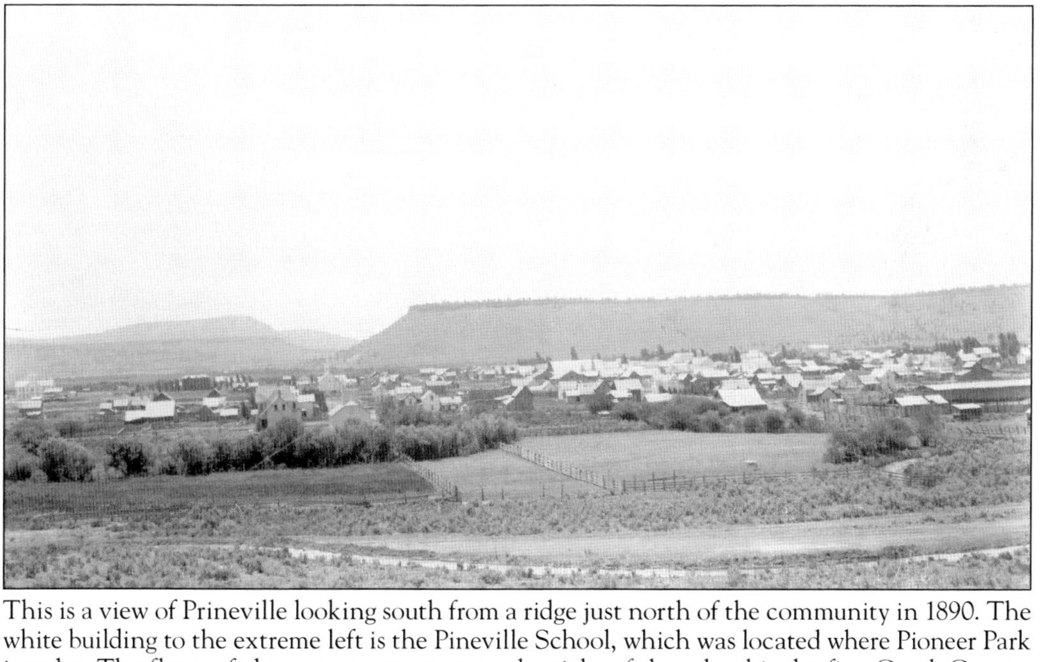

This is a view of Prineville looking south from a ridge just north of the community in 1890. The white building to the extreme left is the Pineville School, which was located where Pioneer Park is today. The flat-roofed two-story structure to the right of the school is the first Crook County Courthouse, built in 1885. Willow-lined Ochoco Creek is in the foreground.

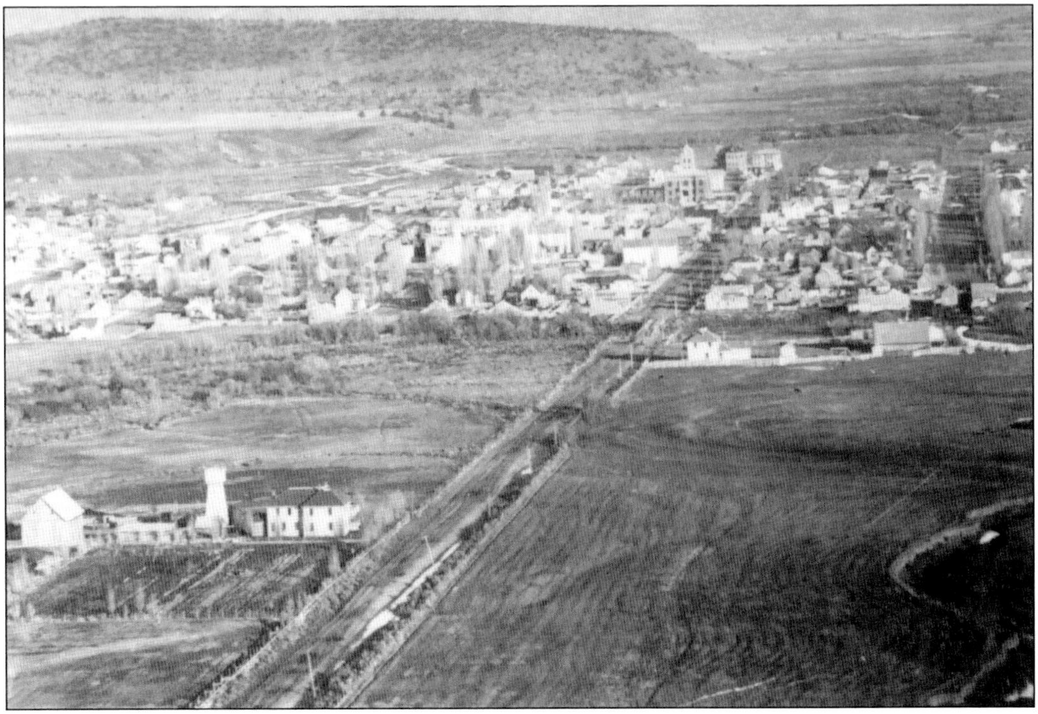

This view is looking east from a rimrock west of Prineville in 1909. The lined street entering town from the lower left is Second Street, which was the main entrance into the community. The Poindexter Home Hospital at lower left. The newly constructed Crook County Courthouse is at upper right. The Crooked River is flowing on the edge of the community.

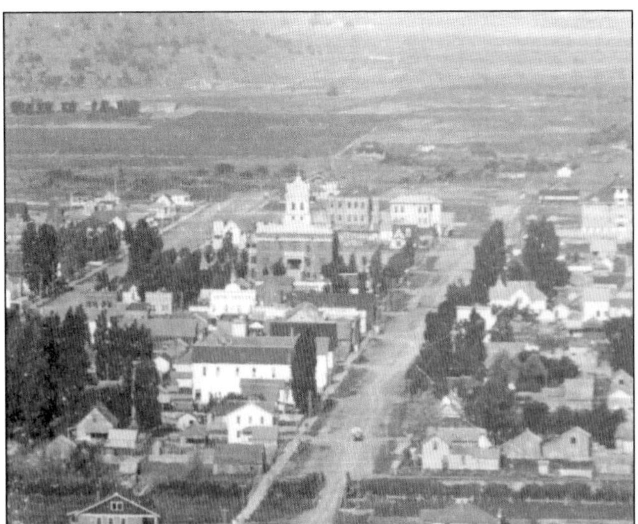

This is another view looking east from a rimrock west of Prineville in 1911. The large white building at lower left is the Odd Fellows Hall. The Crook County Courthouse is in the middle, and just beyond the courthouse is Crook County High School in the brick building. Next to the high school is the old courthouse; it had been moved near the school for use as an annex. To the right of Second Street is Prineville Elementary School. Crooked River Elementary School now occupies the location of the old schools.

Four

Taming the Wide-Open Spaces

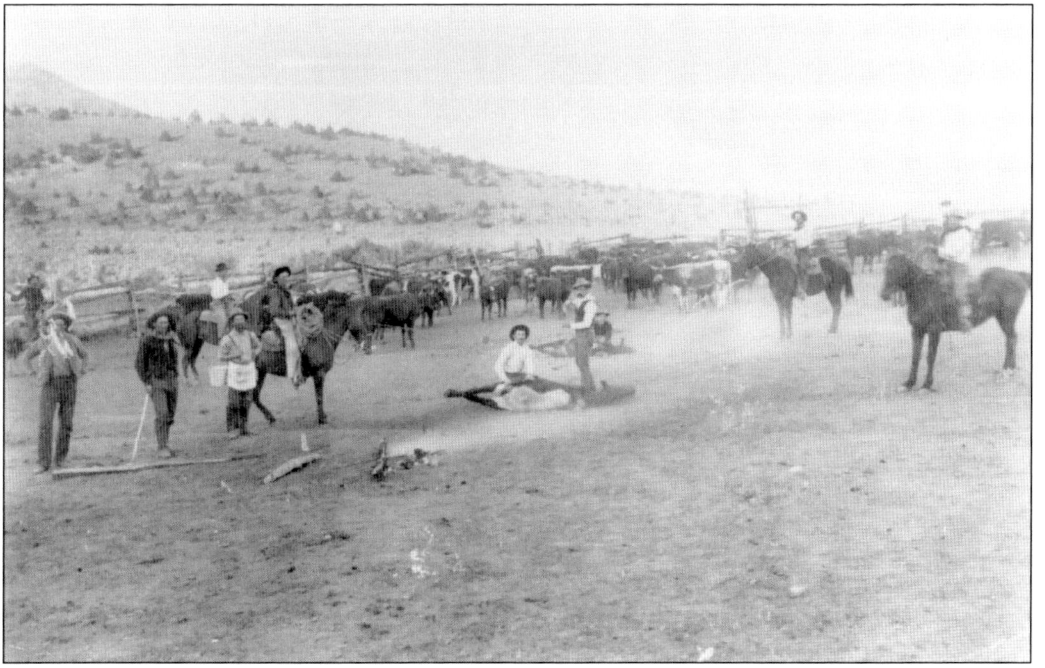

The lush grasslands of the region attracted many of the early settlers to raise cattle and sheep. Stock raising was the first major business enterprise. This c. 1885 photograph is of cattle branding at the Q Ranch on Camp Creek several miles southeast of Prineville. In addition, farming, lumber production, and homesteading helped settle central Oregon. From left to right are Lew Carson, Kit Carson, Johnny Schmeer, Johnny Huffman, Poley Moses (heeling), Leighton Morgan (branding), Frank Hackleman (branding), Billy Edwards, and Charlie Parrish (heading).

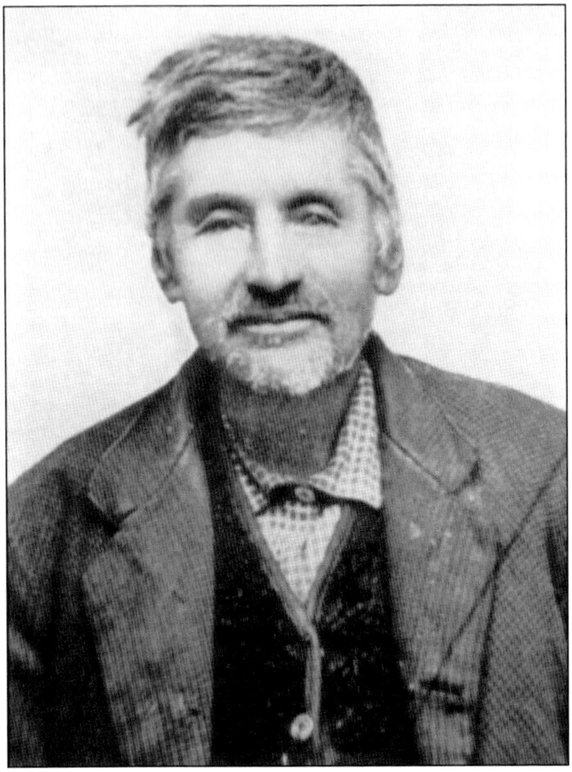

Peter DeLore was among the earliest to begin ranching in the Upper Country in the Suplee vicinity. He had served as a scout in early Indian campaigns in the Oregon country and as a packer for several years. In 1882, he moved to what would soon become Crook County and established a ranch.

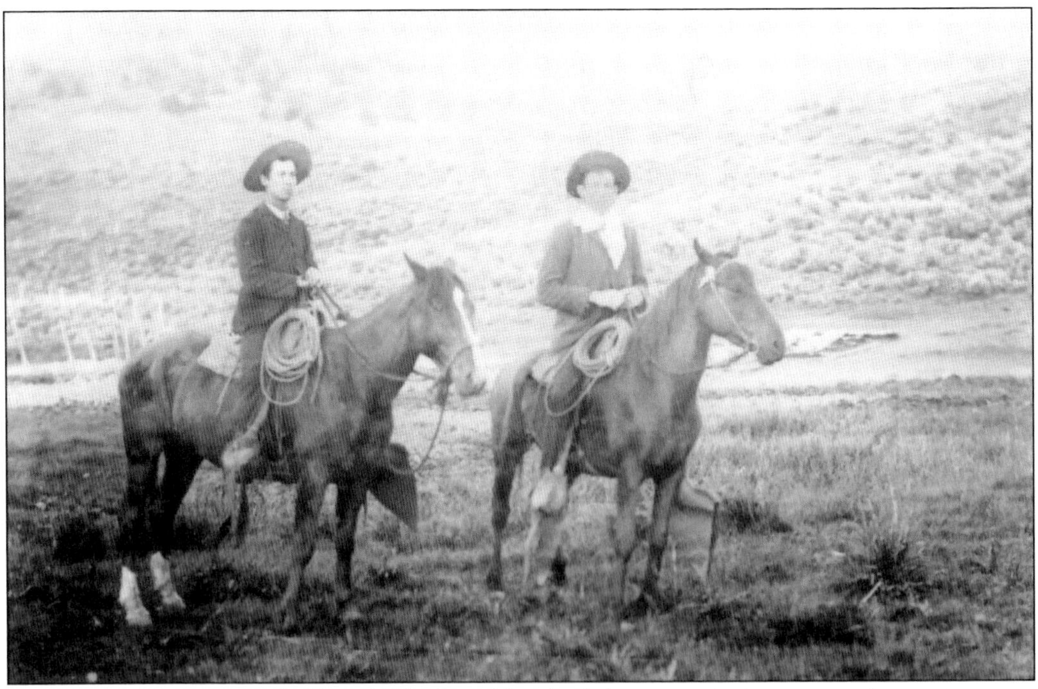

Augustus "Gus" DeLore (left) and Ellis Laughlin (right) are astride horses at a hot spring near Suplee about 1908. Stockmen ranged cattle and sheep on the Upper Country range on the far eastern boundary of Crook County.

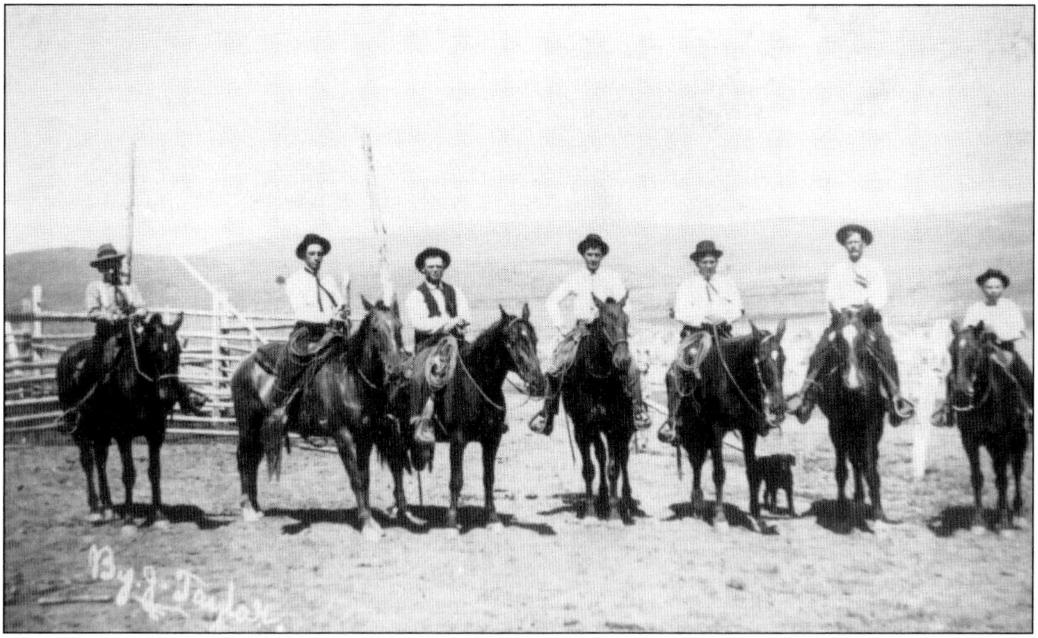

This is a group of Suplee ranchers ready to round up some cattle on the range. Local ranchers often helped each other on roundups and at branding time. From left to right are Walter Colpitts, Henry Bernard, Ed Laughlin, Andrew Bernard, Goodie Senecal, Walt Dunkel, and young Floyd Senecal.

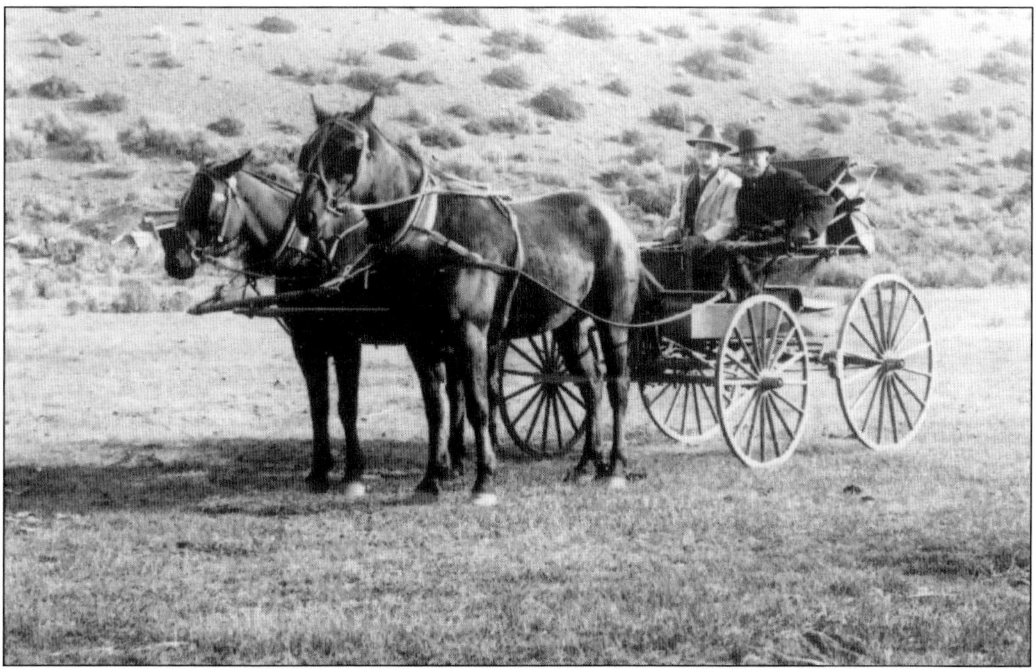

Melvin Weberg and his father, John Peter Weberg, are riding in a buggy near their ranch just southeast of Suplee about 1905. John and his wife, Mina Washburn Weberg, purchased the ranch in 1900 from Joe and Mary Abbot. Melvin and his wife, Mary, operated the ranch after his father's death in 1910. Melvin served as a Crook County commissioner for several years.

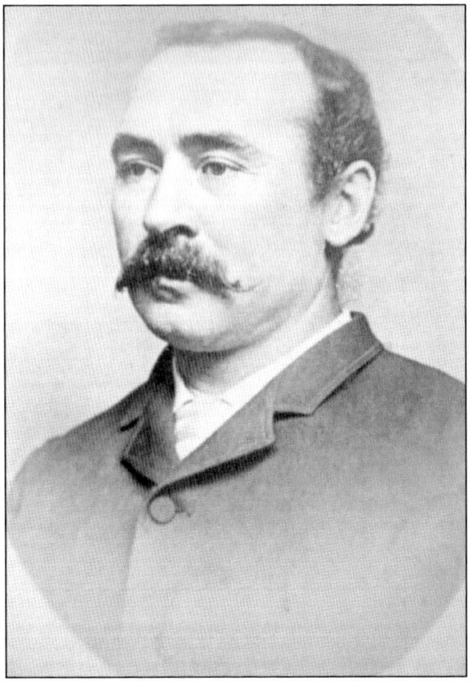

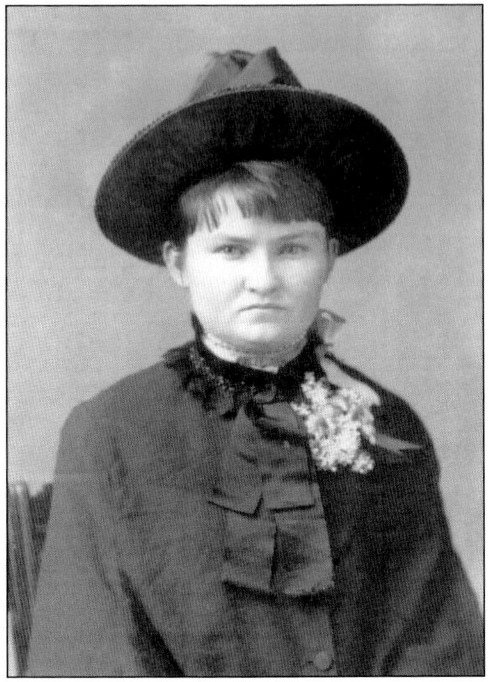

Thomas Brennan (left) and his wife, Polly Hinkle Brennan (right), operated a ranch on Grindstone Creek between Paulina and Suplee. Thomas came to central Oregon in 1880 and homesteaded at Suplee in 1888. Polly Hinkle's family lived in the Suplee area, and after she married Thomas, they purchased a ranch on Grindstone Creek. Their ranch holdings included almost 33,000 acres. They later separated, but both lived most of their lives in the Upper Country.

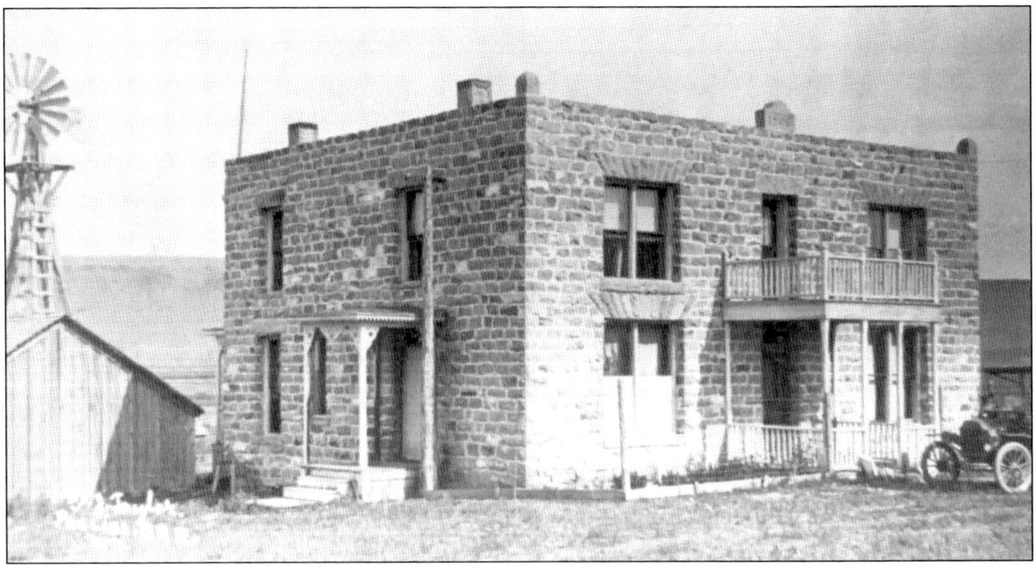

Thomas Brennan built a house made of native stone at his ranch on Grindstone Creek in 1908. Each corner of the house had a fireplace; two of the chimneys are visible in this photograph. A stone above the balcony is engraved with the date the house was built. The stone is now in the Bowman Museum in Prineville. The house was once a center of early-day activities and hospitality. It long stood as a historical landmark until it was demolished.

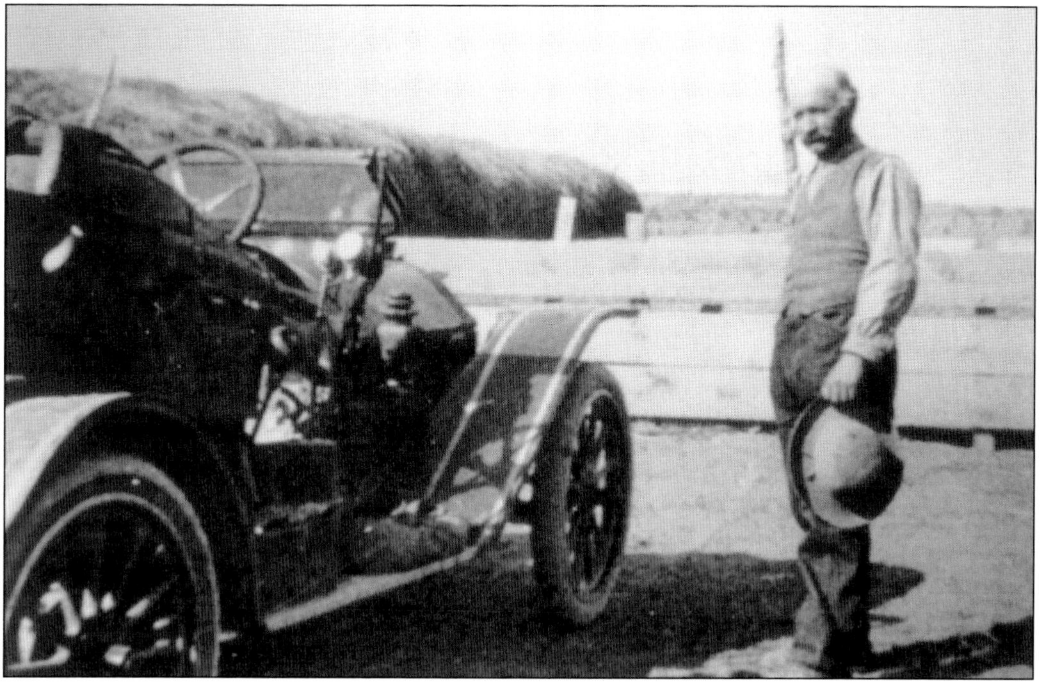

William Walter "Bill" Brown became a legend of the High Desert. He came to central Oregon in 1882 with his brothers Ellis, George, and Bob. They raised sheep near Wagontire Mountain south of Hampton. A devastating snowstorm in 1885 decimated their herd, and his brothers sold out to Bill. He began investing in herds of horses as well as sheep. He became one of the largest stockmen in the region and established his headquarters on Buck Creek on the eastern boundary of Crook County. He was widely known for his eccentric actions.

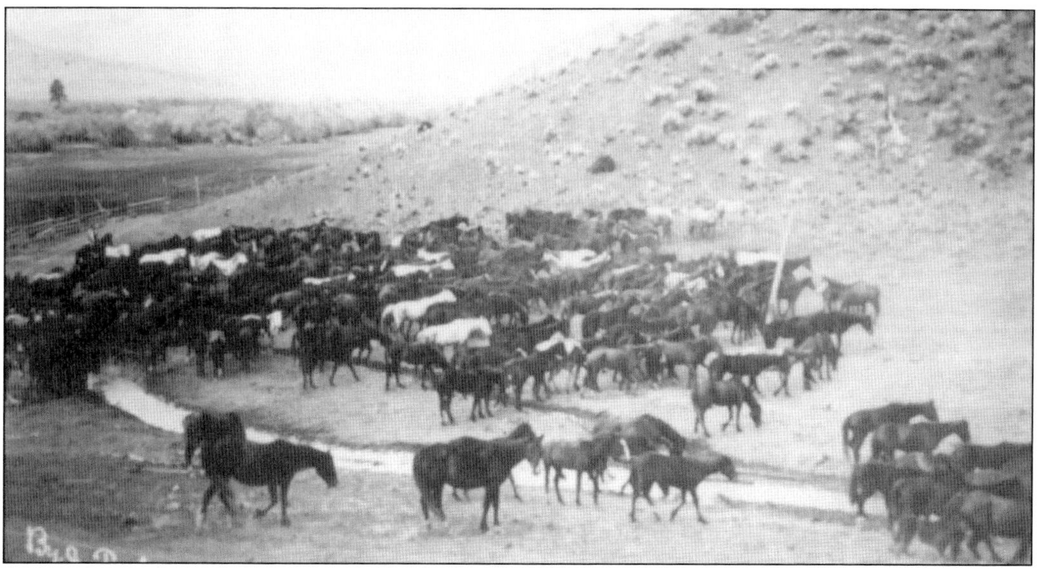

This is a herd of Bill Brown's horses near Wade Butte in the Grindstone country south of Paulina. It is estimated that Brown herded over 5,000 horses on the desert and, along with his sheep operations, accumulated a fortune. Many local ranchers and hired hands worked as buckaroos for Brown, and he had several camps located at water holes he had deeded on the desert.

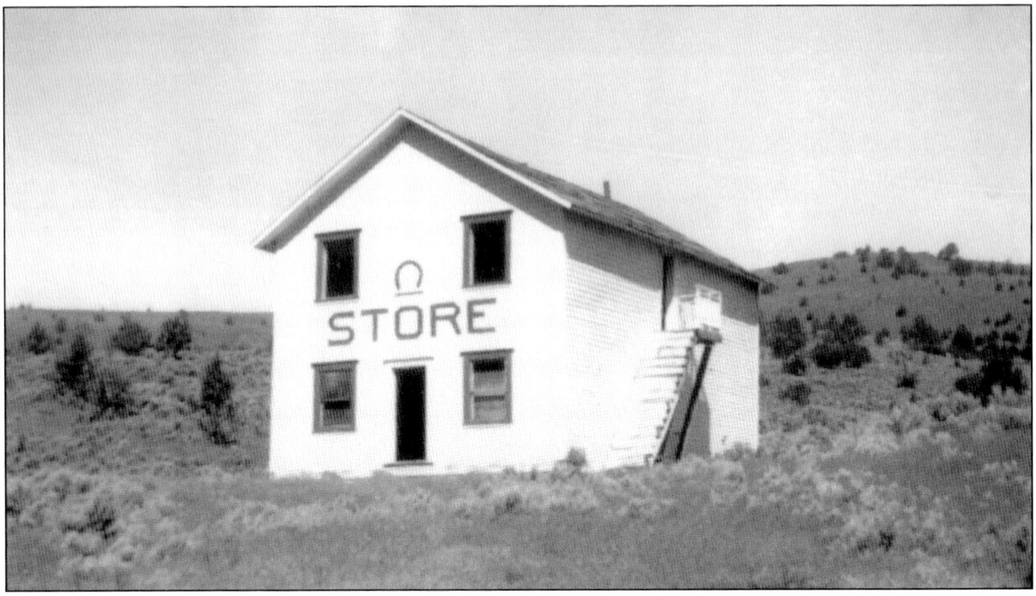

Bill Brown established a mercantile store at his ranch headquarters on Buck Creek, known as the Horseshoe Bar Store. His horseshoe bar brand was one of the most widely recognized brands in the northwest. He freighted supplies to the store from The Dalles and later Shaniko. Merchandise was bought on the honor system, as there was no proprietor. A ledger book in the store was provided for purchasers to note what they had purchased. Payment sometimes was delayed or bartered.

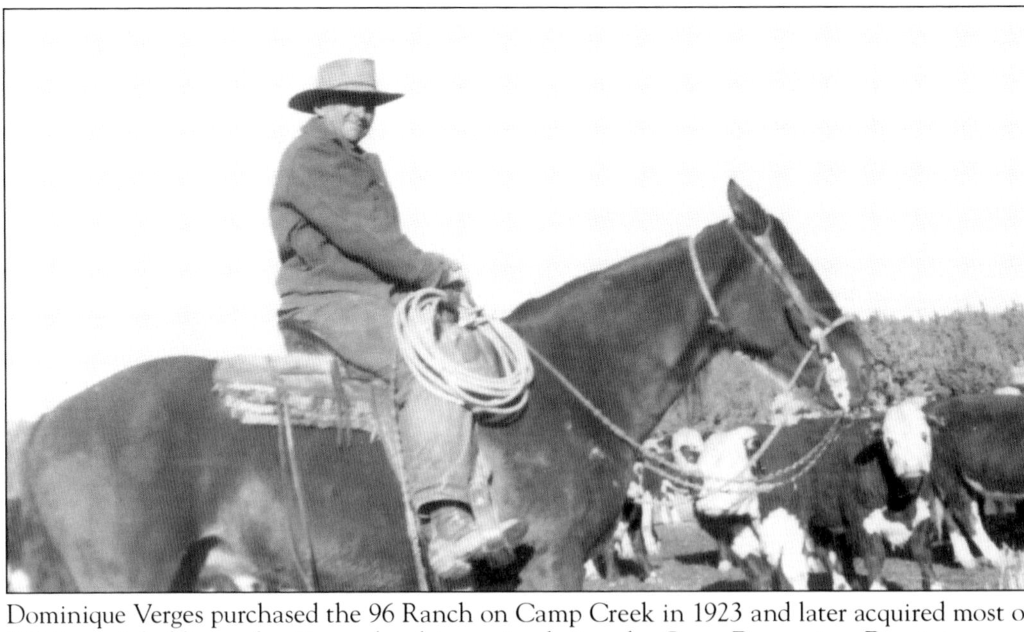
Dominique Verges purchased the 96 Ranch on Camp Creek in 1923 and later acquired most of Bill Brown's holdings after Brown lost his empire during the Great Depression. Dominique was born in southern France and came to the United States in 1908. After purchasing the 96 Ranch, he raised sheep and cattle and expanded his operations.

Charles and Effie Short Sherman and their young son Calvin moved to Crook County in 1909 and bought the Sheppard Place on the South Fork of Crooked River. They operated the ranch for several years, and Calvin managed the ranch after his parents retired. The ranch grew to include over 50,000 acres of deeded and permit lands. The ranch was primarily a cattle ranch. From left to right are Charles, Calvin, and Effie Sherman.

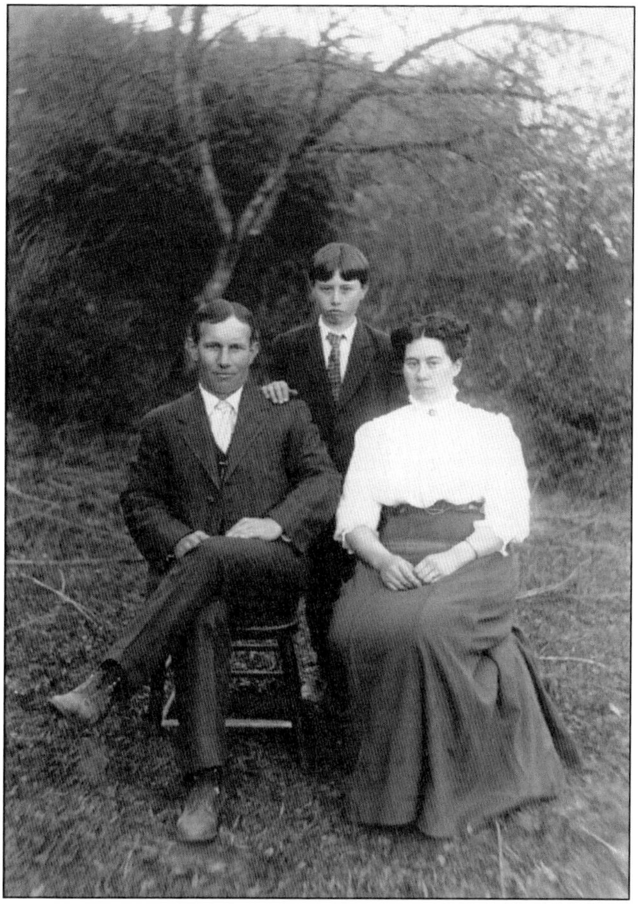

Calvin Sherman is roping a horse in a log corral at his ranch on the South Fork of Crooked River. Calvin was widely known for his large girth. He married Martha Houston, and they lived with his parents until taking over the ranch operations. Calvin and Martha operated the ranch until selling it in 1958.

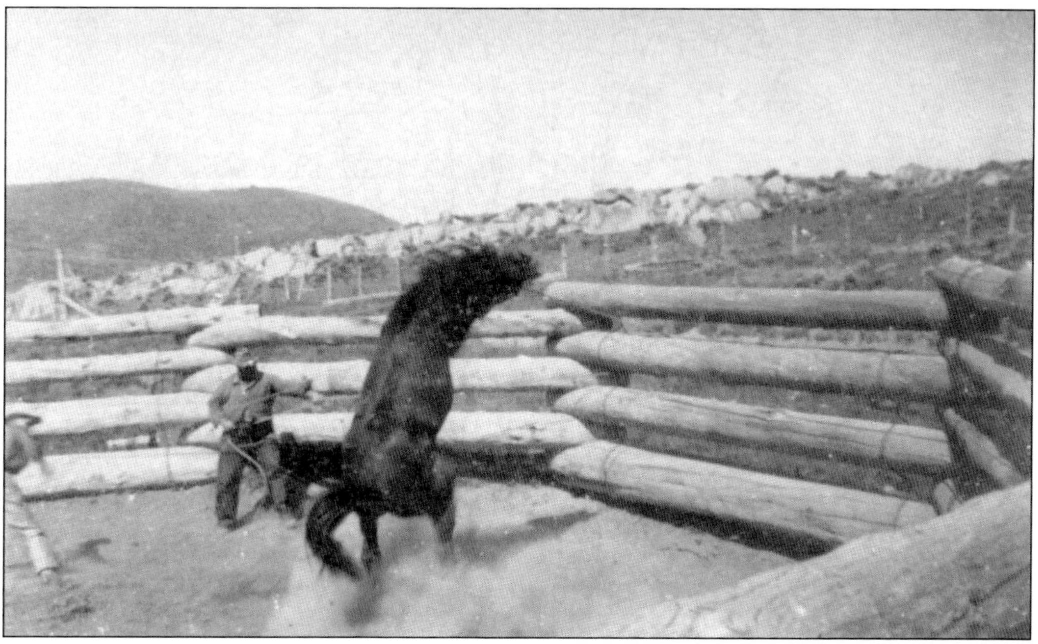

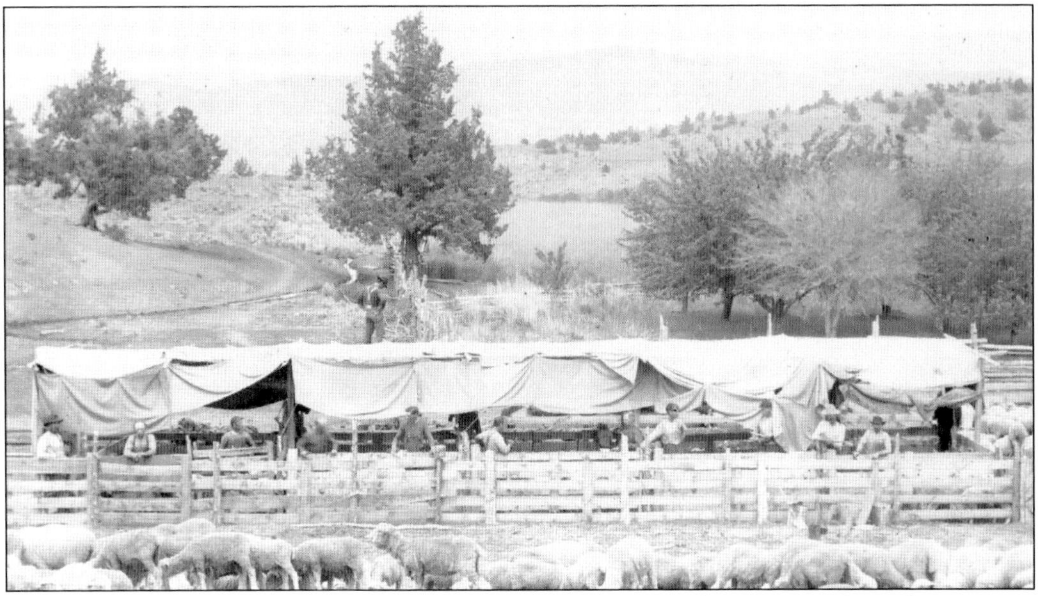

This is a view of the Knox sheep shearing plant on Newsome Creek near Post. Sheep shearing was done in late spring or early summer when wool was at its most luxuriant growth. Trained sheep shearers traveled to various plants to conduct shearing of the wool. An experienced shearer could shear a sheep in a few moments using razor sharp hand-held shears. The photographer caught a gentleman behind the shearing pens in a moment of relief. The sheep in the foreground have already been sheared. The photograph was taken about 1895.

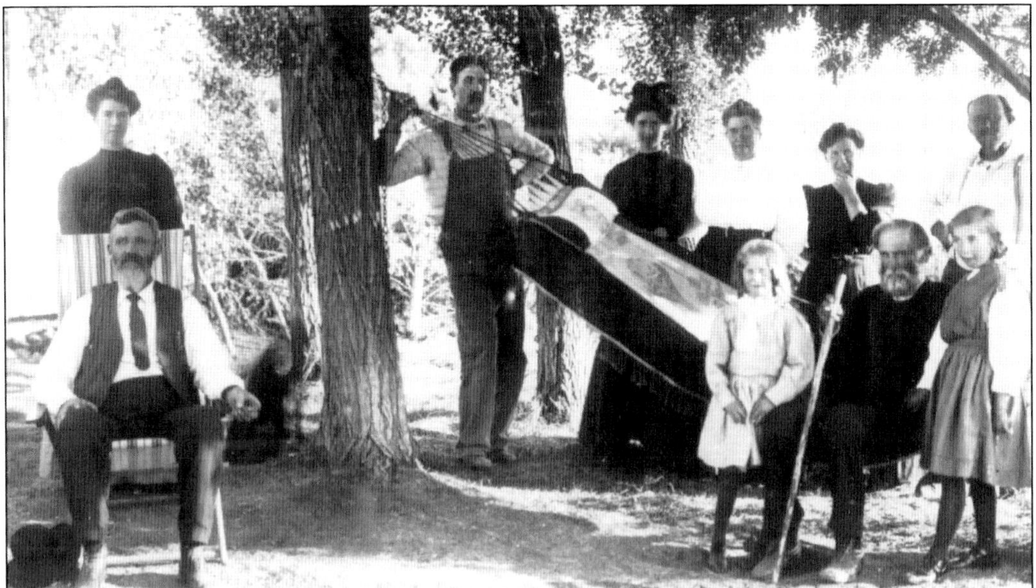

Roscoe Knox purchased the Wallace Post Ranch just east of Post about 1888. Roscoe and his wife, Matilda Buoy Knox, had 13 children. The Knoxs raised sheep and later cattle. Pictured around 1906 are, from left to right, (sitting) Roscoe Knox, Cassie, Roscoe's brother Jerome Knox, and Velma; (standing) Lillian Knox, Edward Baker "Bake," Ina Lavicy, John Knox's wife Grace Caldwell Knox, Margaret, and John Knox.

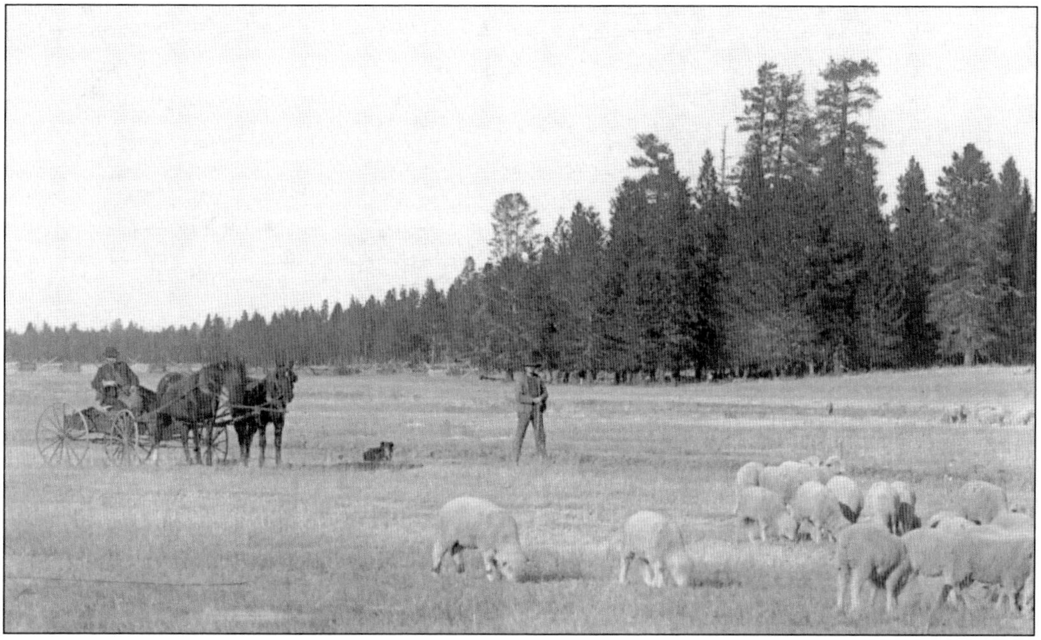

The Knox family, as well as many other ranchers, raised sheep and summer grazed on the open range of the forested mountains of the region. John Knox, the son of Roscoe Knox, is in the wagon, and Grover Caldwell is the herder with his trusted dog to his right. The sheep are grazing in a meadow in the Ochoco Mountains.

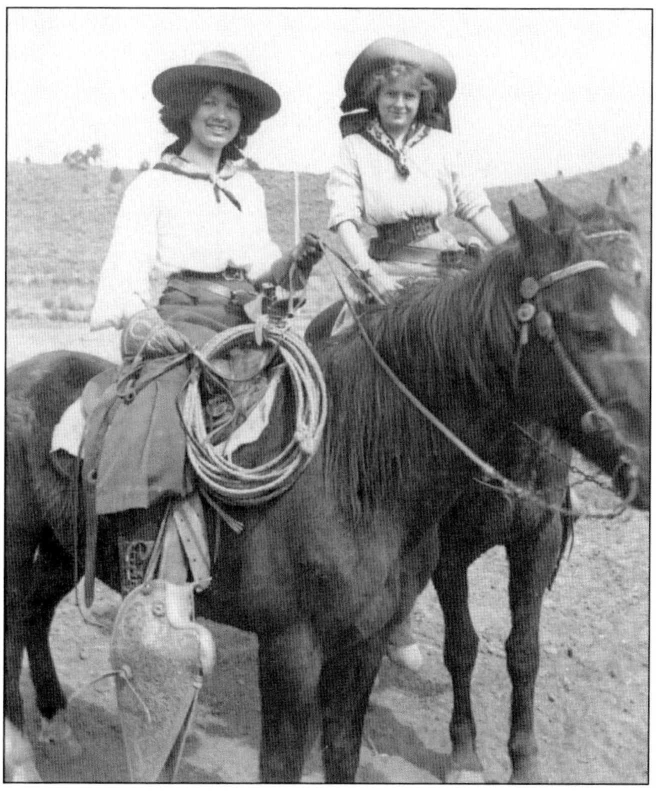

Ruth Brennan (left) and Lillian Reed (right) are outfitted and ready to take to the range in this c. 1909 photograph. Note the extreme narrow waists on the young women. Lillian is wearing a gun belt, as guns were used to kill rattlesnakes or predators. Both women appear to be enjoying their activity.

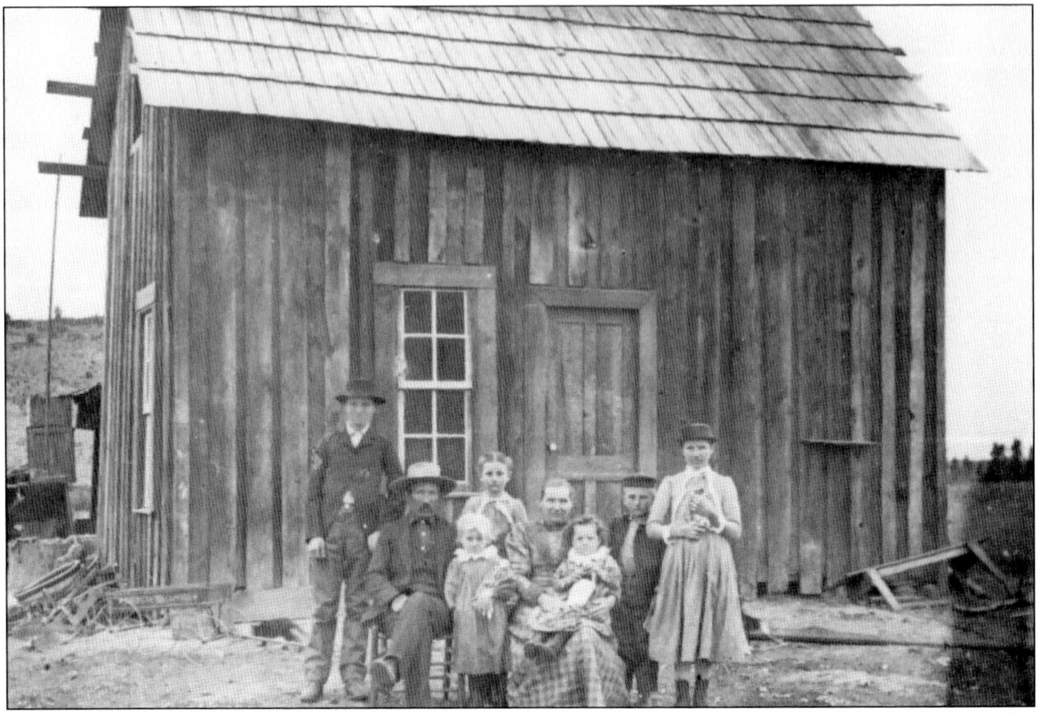

The George Roba family is posing at their ranch in Paulina Valley. George and Mary Soijka Roba came to the Paulina vicinity in 1889. They originally engaged in the sheep business, but because of the grazing disputes between sheep men and cattlemen, he sold his sheep. From left to right are Joe, George Sr., Eula, young Mary, Mary holding Ruby, George Jr., and Anna.

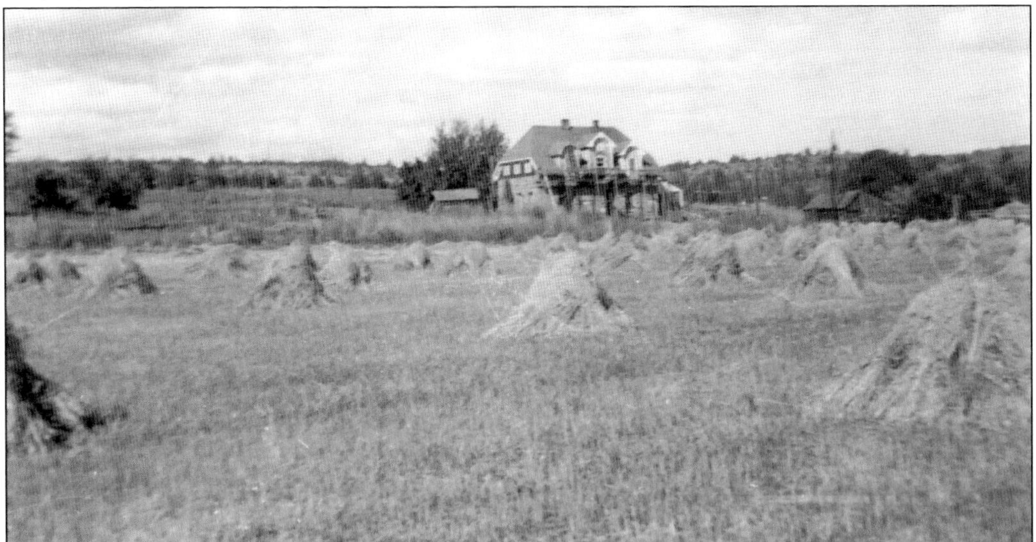

George Roba built a two-story, six-bedroom stone house at the upper end of Paulina Valley in 1910. This became the headquarters for ranch operations including raising hay for forage, as seen here in the field in front of the house. Paulina Valley had fertile soil and water from Paulina Creek, allowing favorable crop growth. The Roba house was listed in the National Register of Historic Places in 2007.

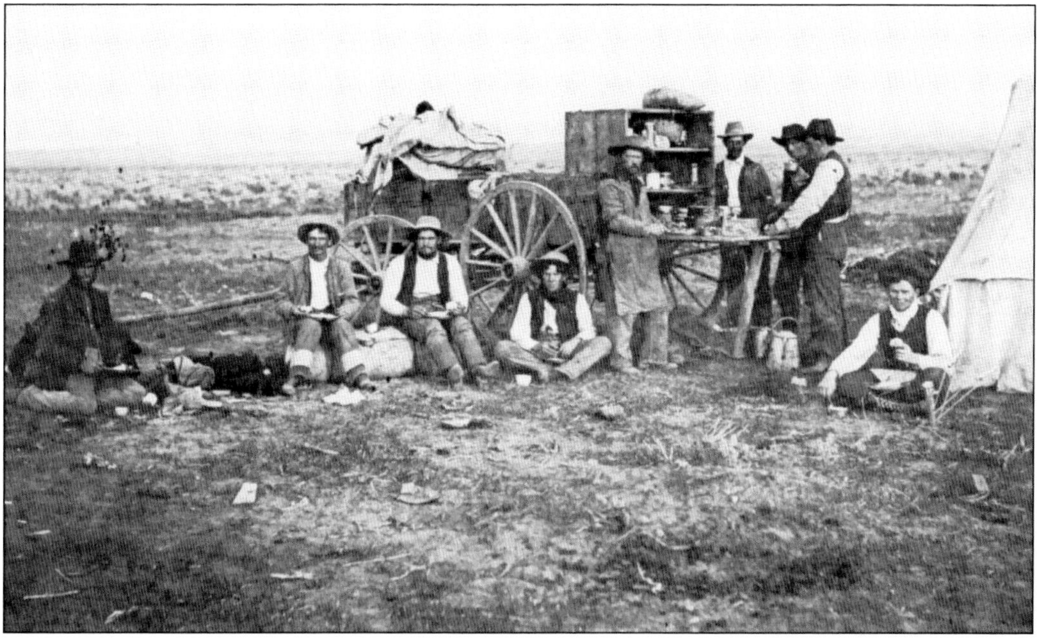

Here, cowboys enjoy dinner on a cattle drive from Paulina to Klamath Marsh in 1906. Local ranchers often teamed up to drive cattle to shipping points or summer pasture, which entailed long and arduous journeys. From left to right are Arch Gibson, Henry Faulkner, Ed Reams, Martin Brummer, Bud Hinton, Frank Smead, Johnny Heisler, Ed Rannels, and Les Duncan.

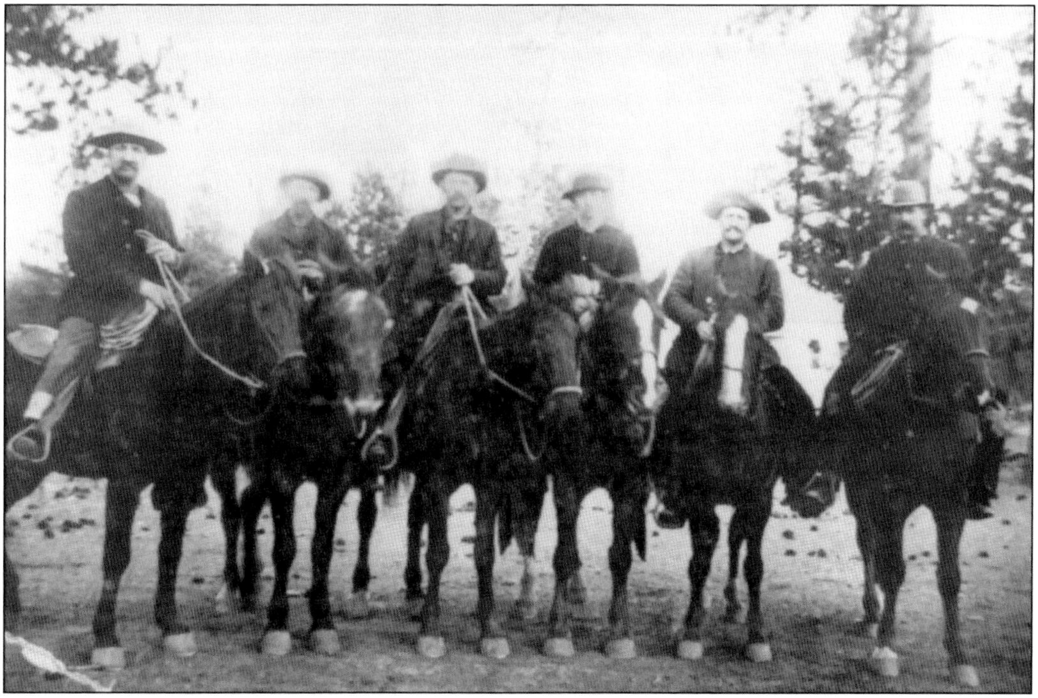

This is a c. 1900 group of Paulina cattlemen after returning from a cattle drive from Paulina to the railheads at Ontario, Oregon. From left to right are Jeff Heisler, Vince Circle, Andrew Noble, Elmer Clark, Alec Heisler, and Luther Claypool.

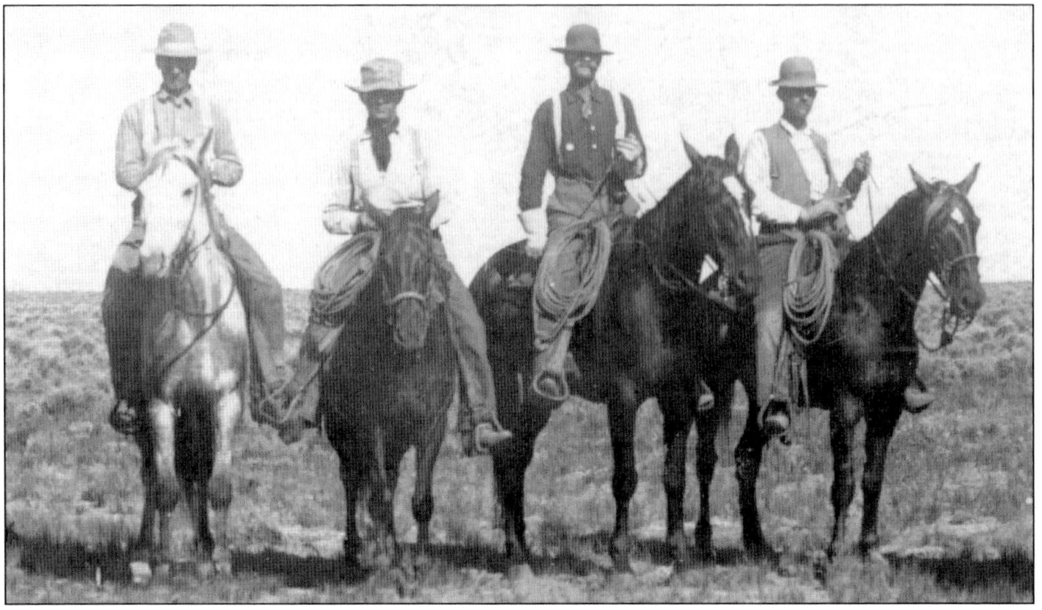

These Held area ranchers prepare to round up cattle for branding in 1906. From left to right are Fisher Logan, Paul Held, Sid Rogers, and Alex Rickman. These ranchers herded cattle along Camp Creek and into the High Desert. Paul and Eva Held established a post office at their ranch, which was a popular stopping place for travelers.

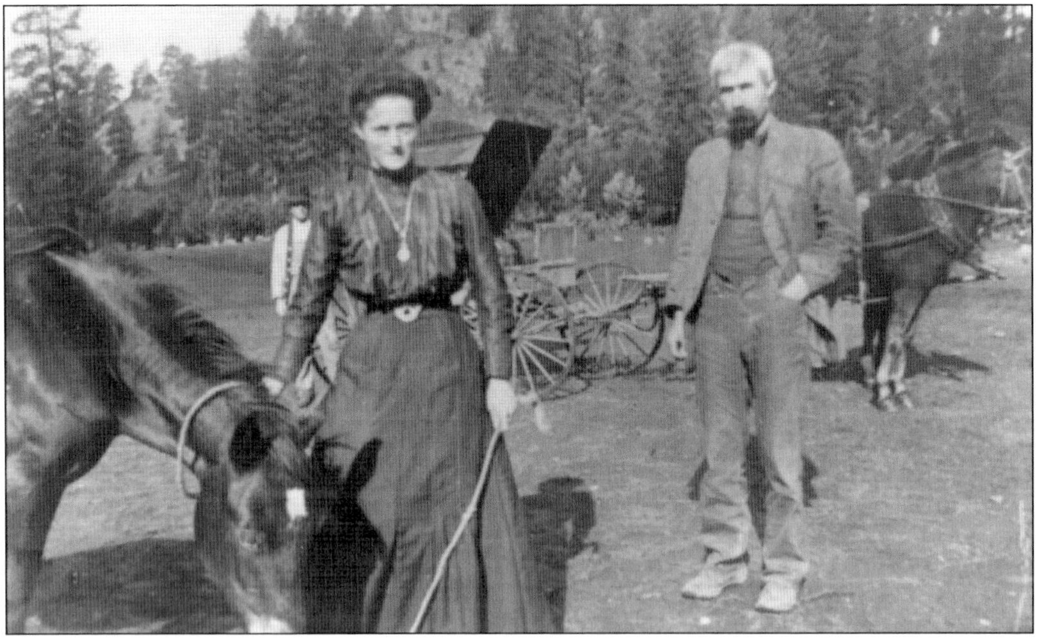

This photograph was taken on Ochoco Creek, about 25 miles east of Prineville. Dana Wright (left) and Farquhar McRae (right) are having a neighborly visit at the Wright cabin. The Jasper Wright family was among the early settlers on upper Ochoco Creek. Farquhar McRae was a colorful sheep man who had a reputation for vulgarity. McRae had a ranch on Muddy Creek near the John Day River and summer grazed his sheep in the Ochoco Mountains. He had a house near the present Ochoco National Forest boundary on Ochoco Creek.

Manford Nye purchased the Silas Hodges ranch on Little Bear Creek in 1895. Manford is riding his horse near his ranch with Sheep Rock in the background. Manford married Adell Yancey in 1892, but she later left with a hired hand. He bought up adjoining property from homesteaders and built up a large ranch. He operated the ranch for over 50 years, and his second wife, Margaret Wiltsie Nye, and hired hands George and Johnny Pearce later operated it.

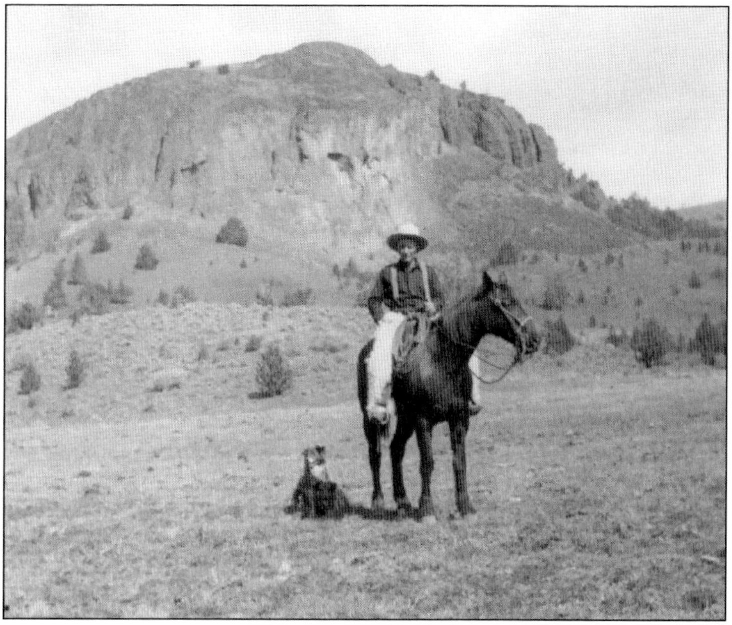

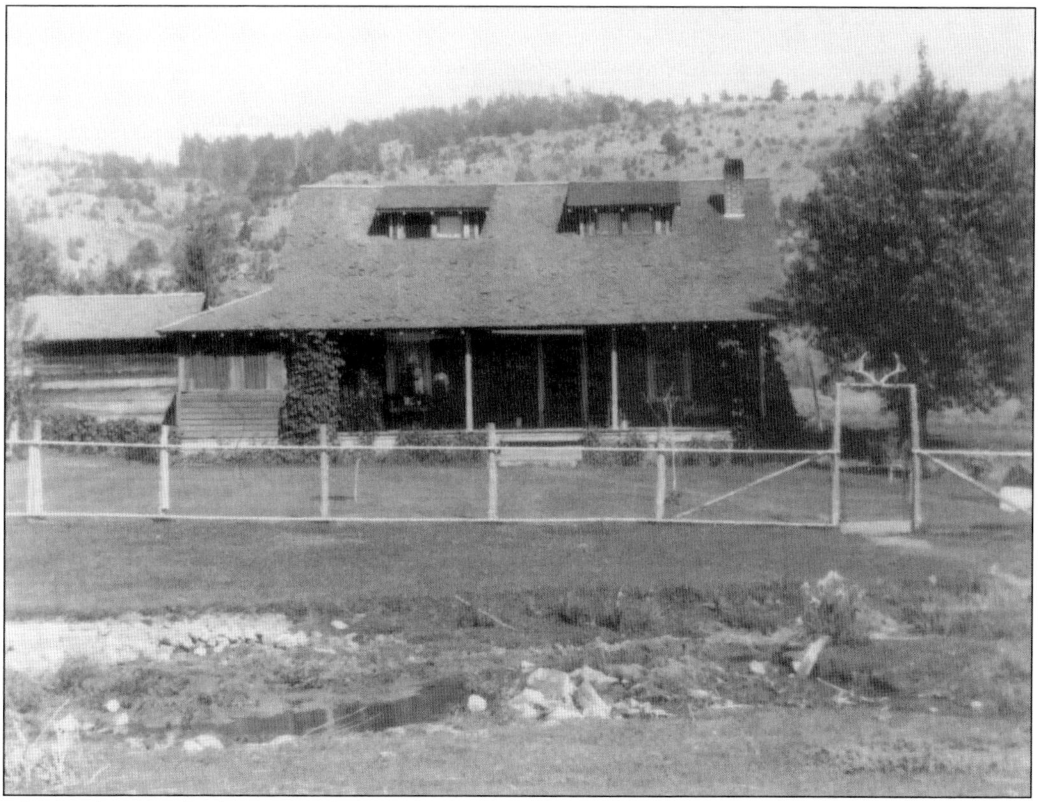

This is the Manford Nye ranch house on Little Bear Creek. The stream is running in front of the house. There was plenty of natural meadowland along Little Bear Creek that provided hay crops for feeding cattle during the winter. This house burned down in the early 1960s. A barn that was located just south of the house is still standing.

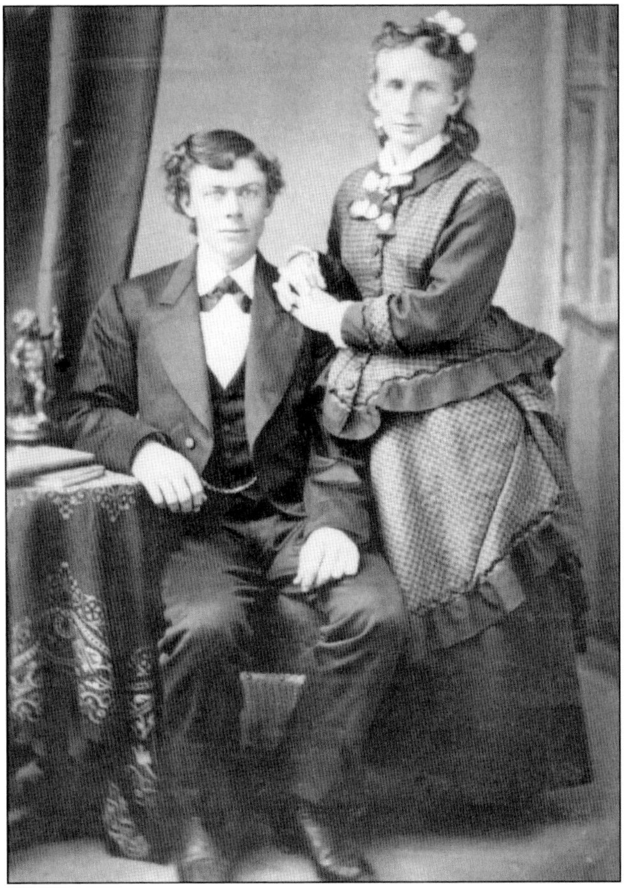

John Henry and Rebecca Hunsaker Gray came to central Oregon in 1876 and settled on Combs Flat about 10 miles southeast of Prineville. They purchased a ranch on Crooked River just west of Post in 1899. The ranch became known as Bonnie View Ranch. They operated it for several years. John served as Crook County assessor, sheriff, and treasurer at various times.

Looking southwest, this is a c. 1905 view of the Bonnie View Ranch. The Crooked River is at rear center near the base of the ridge. Later, the name Bonnie View became the Bonnieview Ranch, one word. The ranch was a popular location for local social events, such as picnics and dances. The house was removed in the early 1970s, but the barn is still standing and being utilized. The current Post-Paulina Highway is located near the road in the foreground.

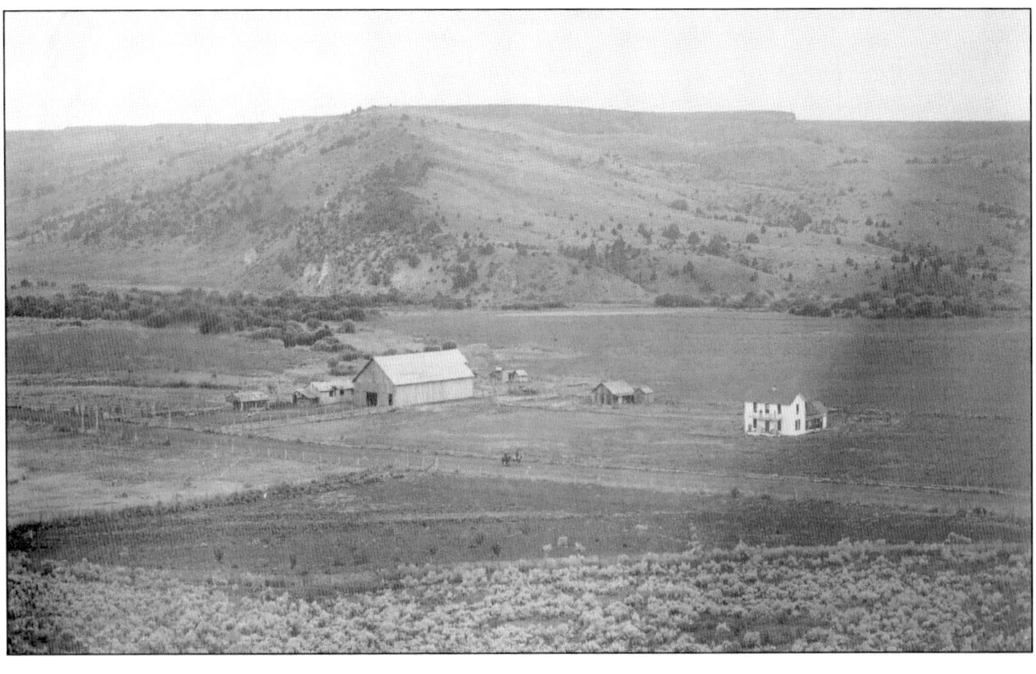

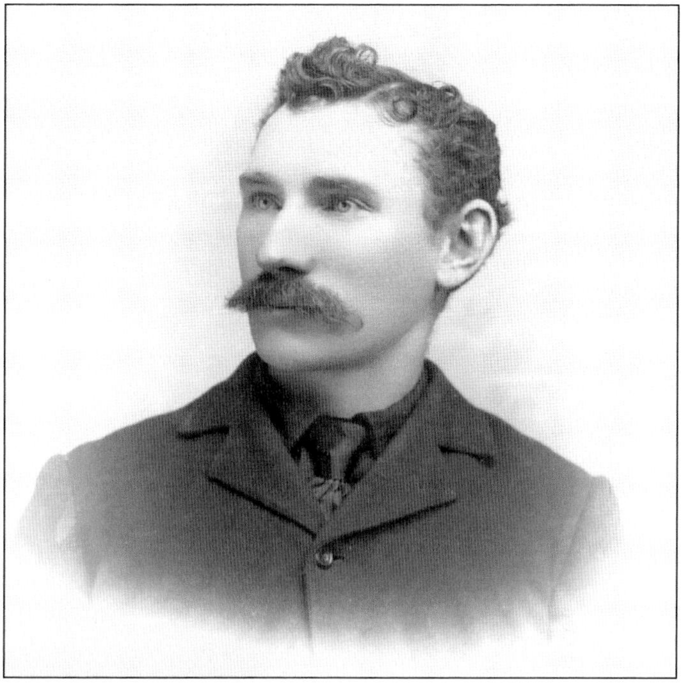

Isaac "Ike" Mills came to central Oregon in the mid-1880s and worked as a cowboy at different ranches in the Paulina area. He homesteaded near Suplee and married a local rancher's daughter, Ann Laughlin. Ann died in 1895. Ike expanded his operations into a large cattle business known as the Mills Land and Livestock Company. His headquarters was near the confluence of Wolf Creek and Beaver Creek east of Paulina. The ranch operation was among the largest in the Upper Country. Ike married Effie Hale in 1900. After his death in 1941, his heirs sold the ranch to Darrel Mills, who operated it for several years before selling out.

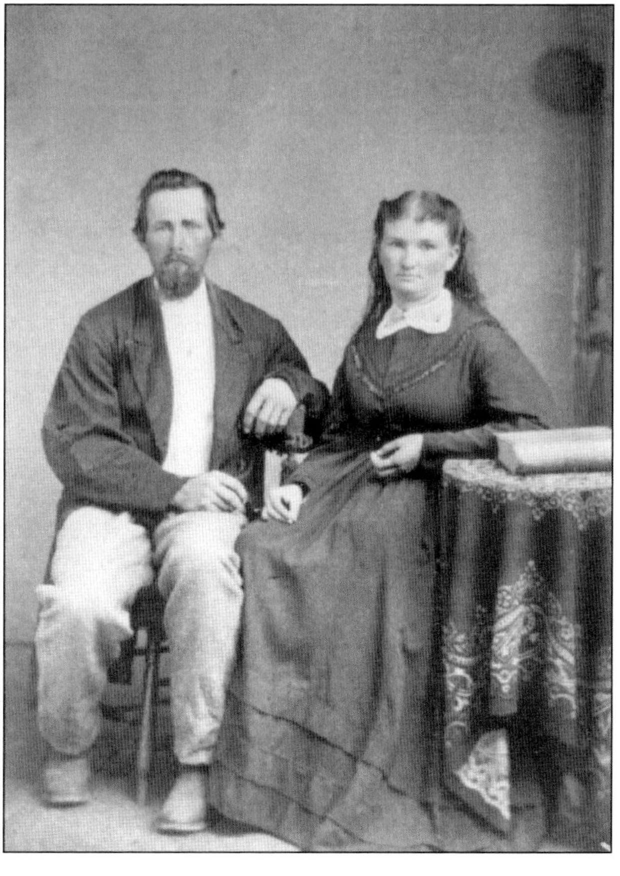

Thomas and Amanda Smith Powell were among the earliest settlers on upper Beaver Creek east of Paulina. They came to central Oregon with his parents to settle near Prineville in 1872. They soon established a ranch on Beaver Creek and handled horses, cattle, and sheep. The ranch became a large cattle operation. Powell Creek and Powell Mountain were named for the Powells. Their sons Richard and Fred later managed the Beaver Creek holdings, and Thomas and Amanda moved to a small ranch on McKay Creek north of Prineville.

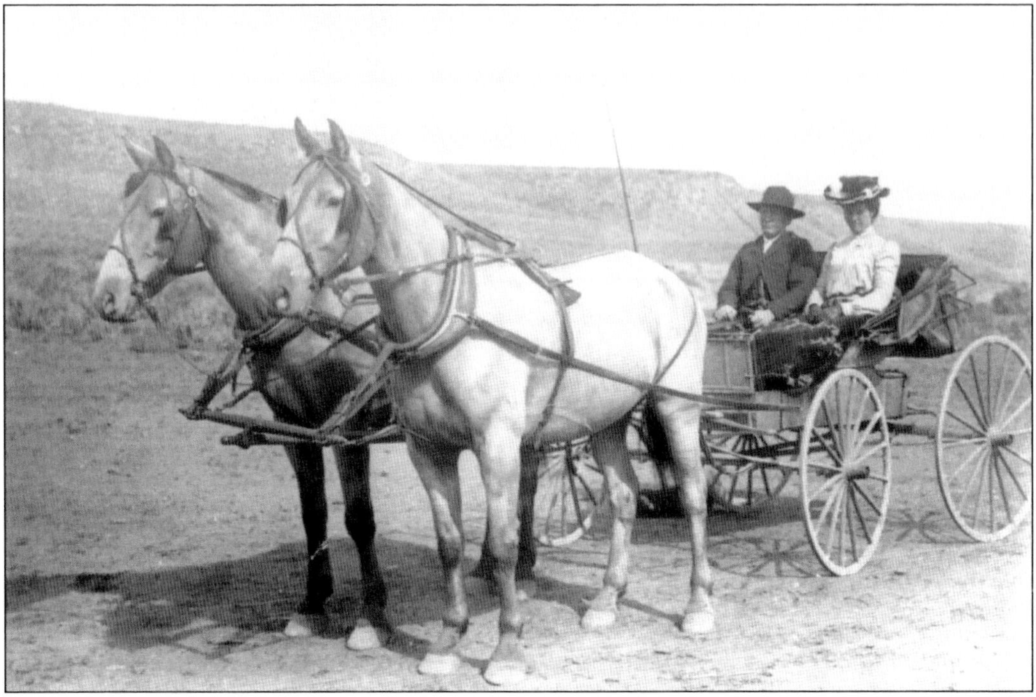

Fred and Eva Brown Powell are seen here in a buggy near their ranch on Wolf Creek. Fred was the son of Thomas and Amanda Powell and helped manage his parents' ranch on Beaver Creek until he started his own ranch on Wolf Creek. He married Eva Brown in 1899. They developed their ranch into a large stock operation.

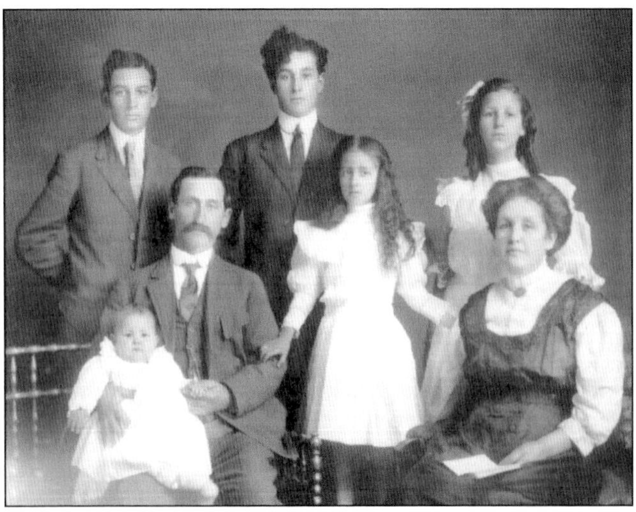

This is the family of Charles and Rosa DeLore Bernard. Charles and Rosa settled north of Suplee in the mid-1880s. Charles was born in France and came to the United States in 1883 and began herding sheep. He married Rosa DeLore in 1891. They had five children. Charles moved to The Dalles in 1902 and began farming, but his son Andrew continued to operate the Suplee Ranch. From left to right are (sitting) Charles holding Harvey, and Rosa; (standing) Henry, Andrew, Noemi, and Iva.

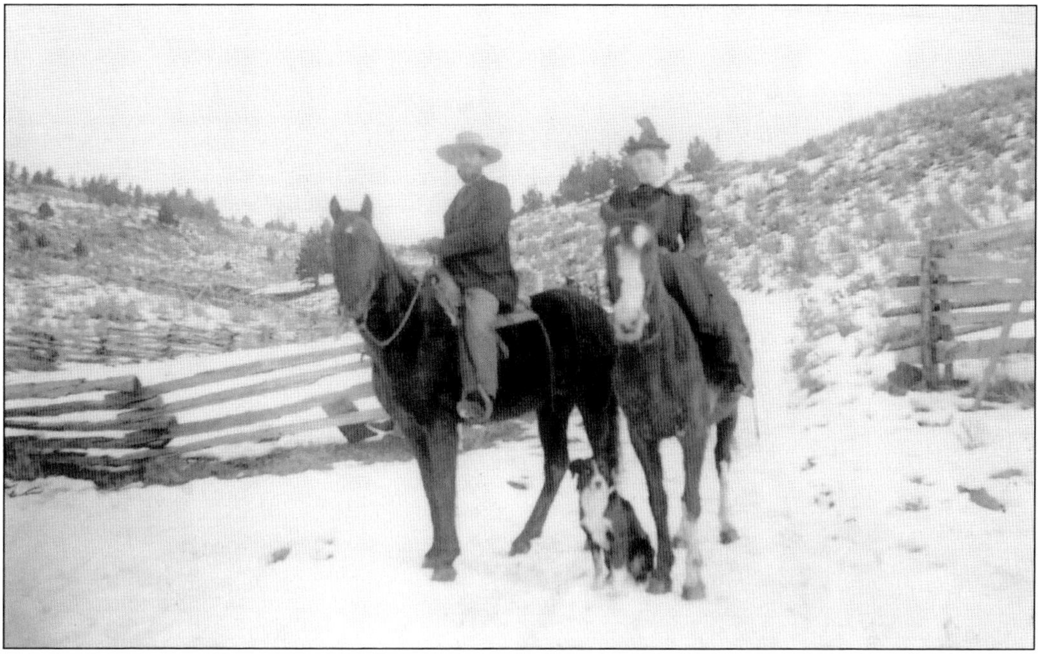

Floyd and Alva Houston are riding horseback at their ranch near Bear Creek. Floyd came to the Bear Creek vicinity from North Carolina in 1896 and homesteaded. He married Alva Allen in 1897. They increased their ranch to 10,000 deeded acres and 35,000 acres of leased and permit lands. Several of Floyd's brothers followed him from North Carolina to central Oregon.

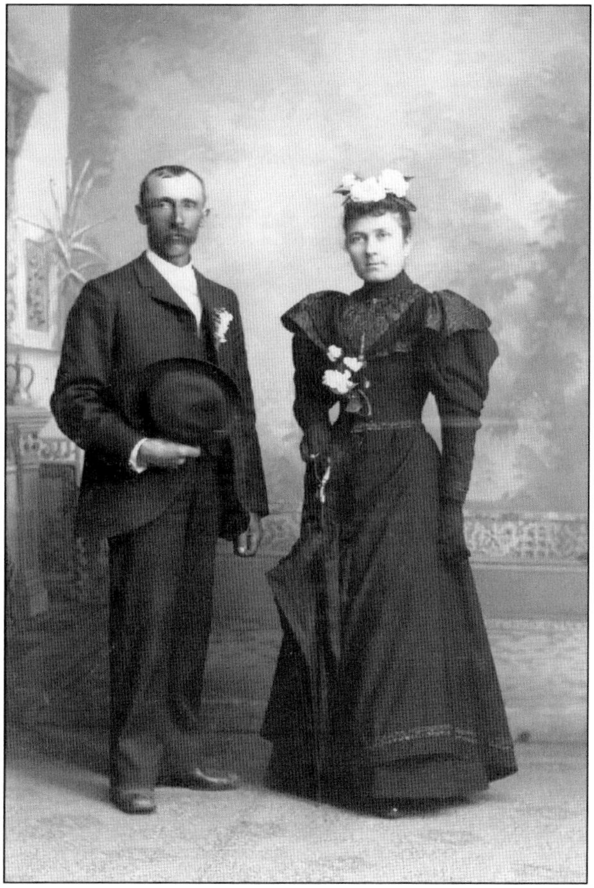

Isadore and Phillipinia Berz Meyer were prominent ranchers near Paulina. Isadore came to central Oregon in 1882 and worked for wages in the Hay Creek area. He formed a partnership with Michael Brown and raised sheep. He and Brown moved their headquarters to the present Twin Buttes Ranch east of Post in 1884. Isadore married Phillipinia Berz in 1894. Meyer and Brown operated for several years.

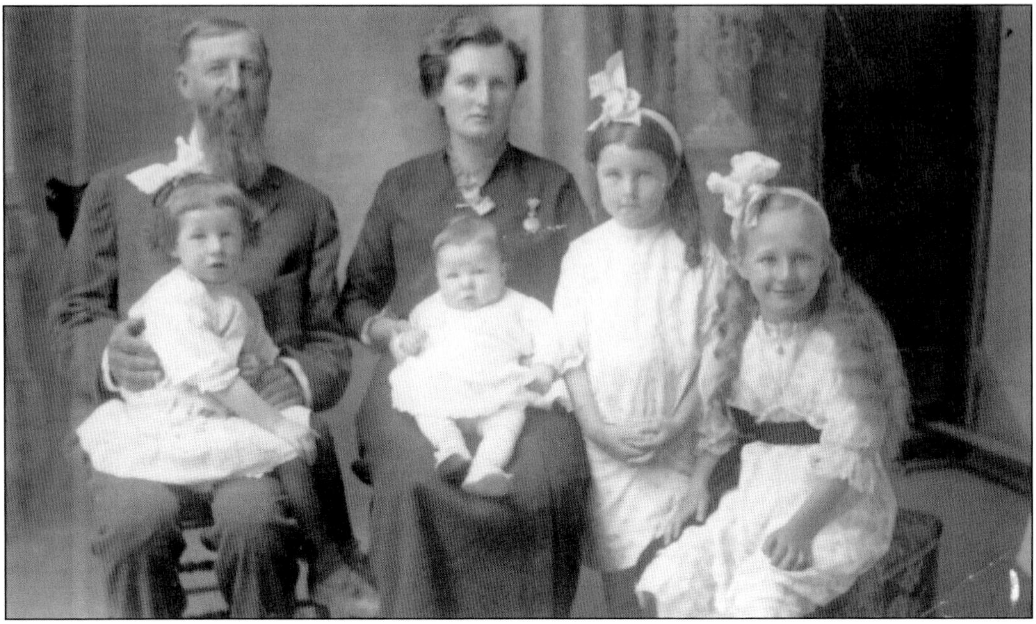

Michael Brown partnered with Isadore Meyer to operate a sheep enterprise near Hay Creek. They later moved operations to Crooked River near Twin Buttes. Michael married Jennie McCullough, and they had four children. Pictured are, from left to right, Michael holding Catherine, Jennie holding Aaron, Lena, and Mary. Michael Brown passed away in Mount Vernon, Oregon, and Jennie later married George Meyer, the brother of Isadore Meyer. Jennie and George had two daughters, Georgia and Joan.

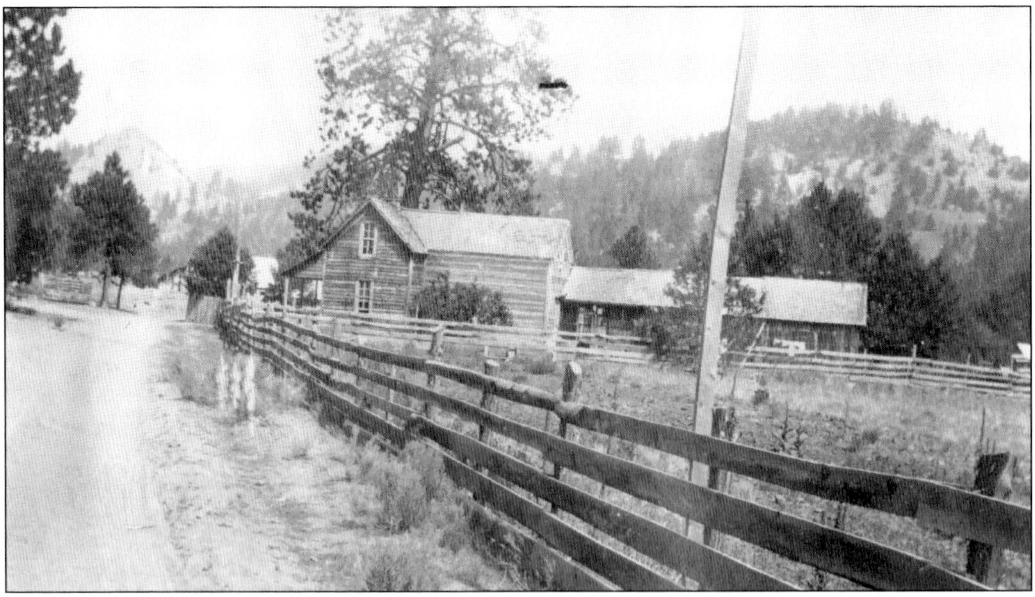

This is the Demaris Ranch on upper McKay Creek north of Prineville. Members of the Demaris family were early settlers on Mill Creek and McKay Creek. John Walter "Walt" Demaris, the son of John Demaris, established a ranch at this site and also operated small sawmills in the vicinity. The house was near the Ochoco National Forest boundary. The house stood for many years but has been destroyed by a fire.

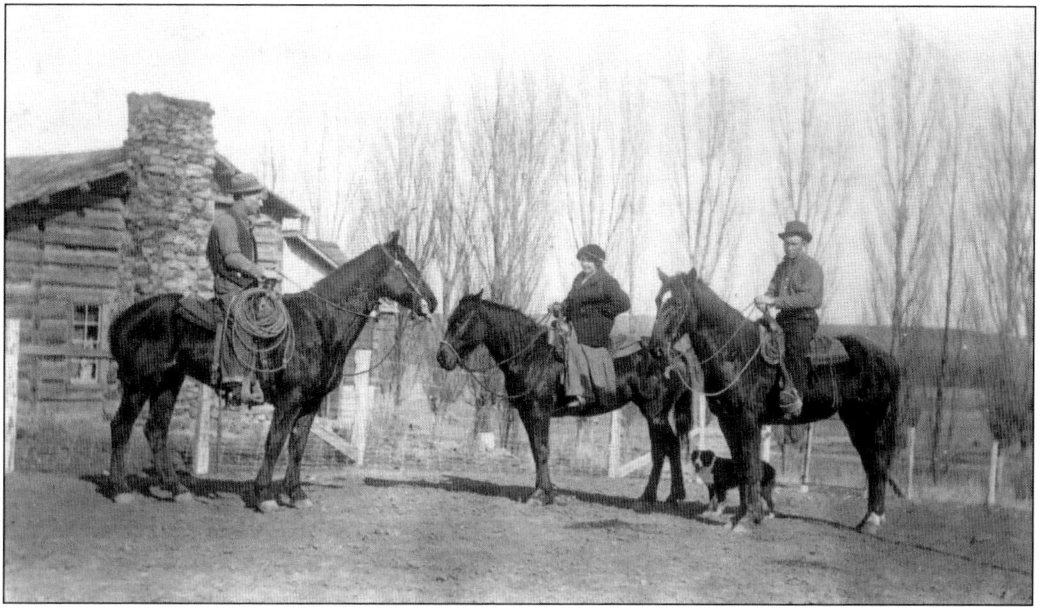

From left to right, Bob McCullough, Eva Hennard, and Harry Severance are at the Glenn Place near the confluence of Camp Creek and Crooked River about 1913. Harry Severance came to central Oregon about 1911. He worked on many ranches in the Paulina area. He met Eva Hennard, a teacher at the Maury School, and they were married in 1914. They first lived at the old Jake Place on the South Fork of Crooked River, and eventually expanded their operations. The ranch became known as Twin Buttes Ranch.

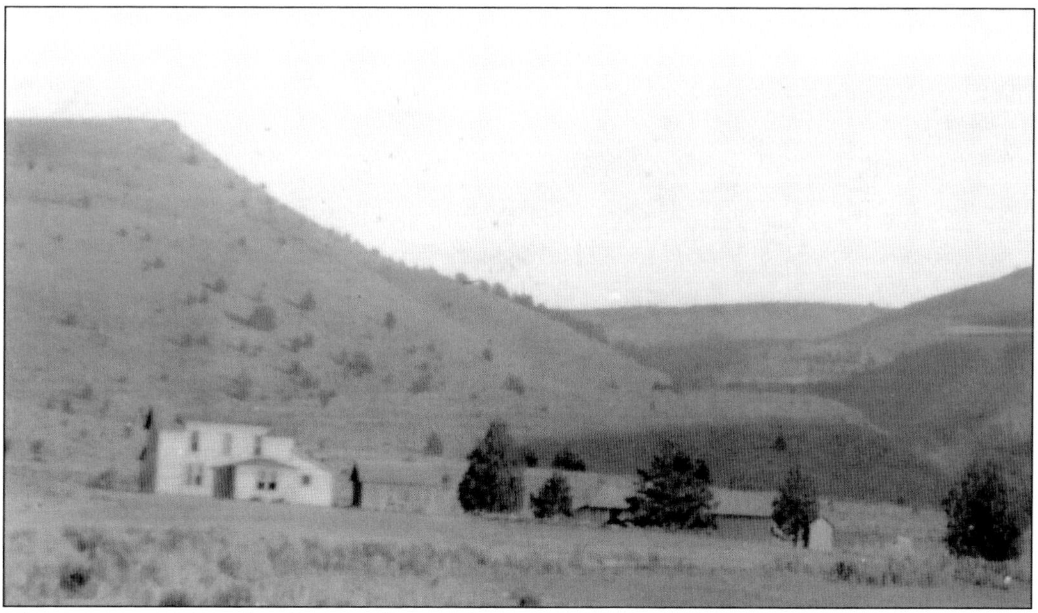

This is a view of the Jake Place on the South Fork of Crooked River about 1909. William Jacobs, who freighted supplies for Bill Brown on Buck Creek, originally settled the ranch. It became known as the Jake Place as an abbreviation of Jacobs's last name. Harry and Eva Hennard Severance later purchased the ranch and expanded operations. There is little left of the original buildings at the Jake Place. (Photograph courtesy of Barbara Severance.)

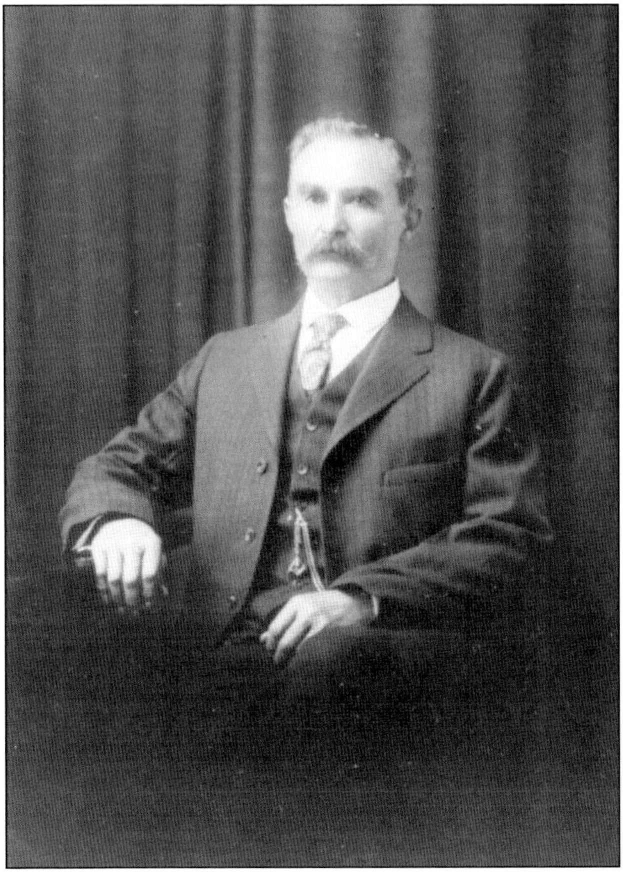

William J. Schmidt came to central Oregon in 1885 and homesteaded on Big Summit Prairie 30 miles east of Prineville. He became dissatisfied and wandered the West working for wages. He came back to his homestead in 1892 and became involved in the cattle and horse business. He increased his holding and had a sizable ranch on the prairie. He married Sarah Lowery Swift in 1900. They lived on the ranch for several years.

William J. Schmidt and his wife, Sarah, built a large two-story house on their ranch at Big Summit Prairie in 1902. The house had six bedrooms, a kitchen, a dining room, and a sitting room. Mr. Schmidt also had a special men-only room upstairs in the house, which was reserved for smoking and card playing. The house is still standing but in a dilapidated state. The man with the fur coat is Dr. Charles Edwards, and to his left is W.J. Schmidt.

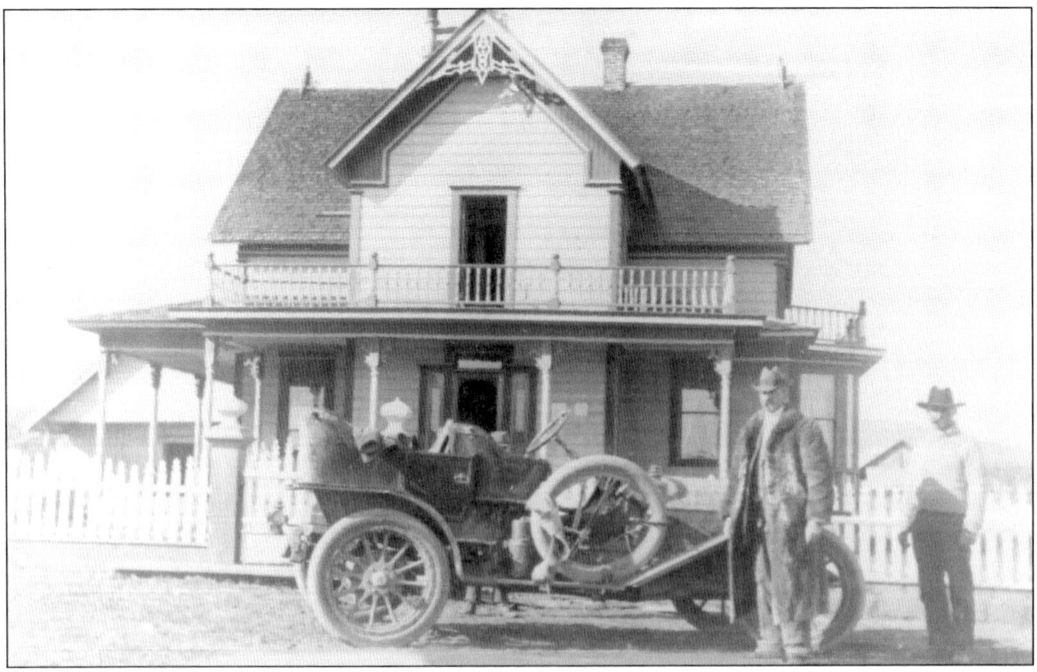

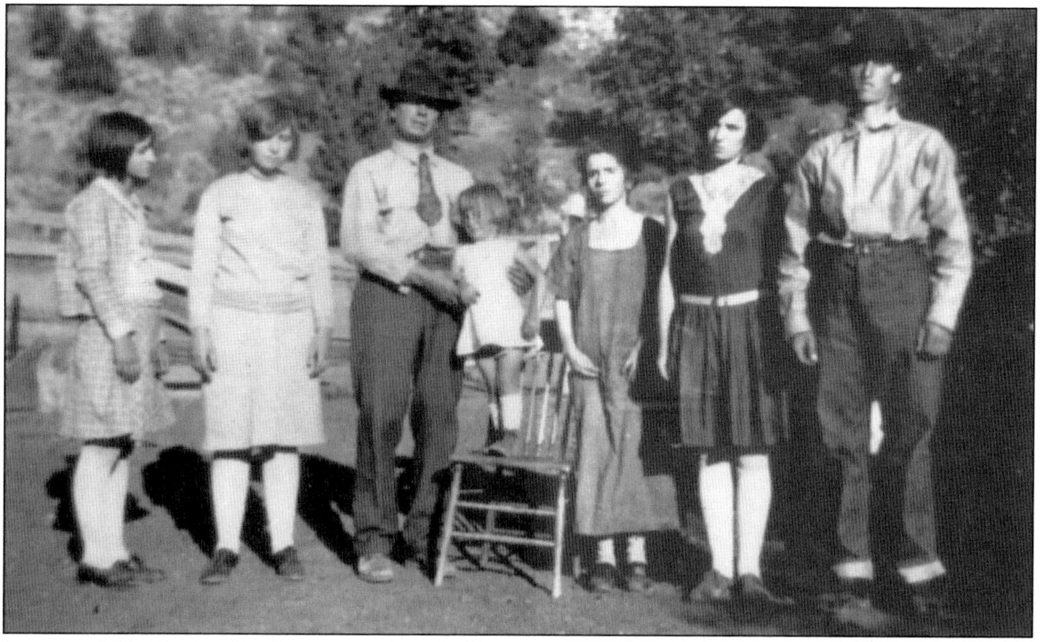

James and Ida Torrico Beoletto moved to the Post area near Conant Basin in 1913 and homesteaded. Family members were photographed at their ranch about 1930. They are, from left to right, Elizabeth, Lena, James, Frances, Ida, Flora, and John. They increased their holdings by purchasing nearby homesteads. A neighbor murdered James in 1935, and Ida died in 1936. Their son John bought out the other heirs and operated the ranch. (Courtesy of Flora Beoletto Gillmor.)

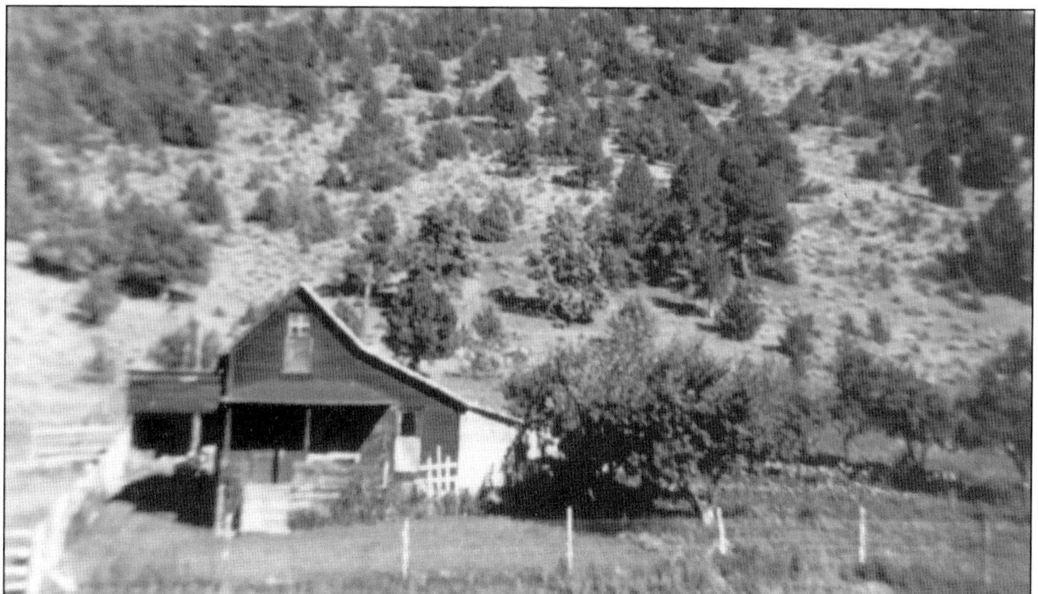

This is a view of the James Beoletto homestead cabin on Lucky Creek. After his father was murdered, John Beoletto took over management of the ranch and further increased his holdings. The ranch is still within the Beoletto family, as Tom and Beverly Beoletto Wolverton operate it. It is one of the few family ranches in the Upper Country that is still operated on a generational basis. (Courtesy of Flora Beoletto Gillmor.)

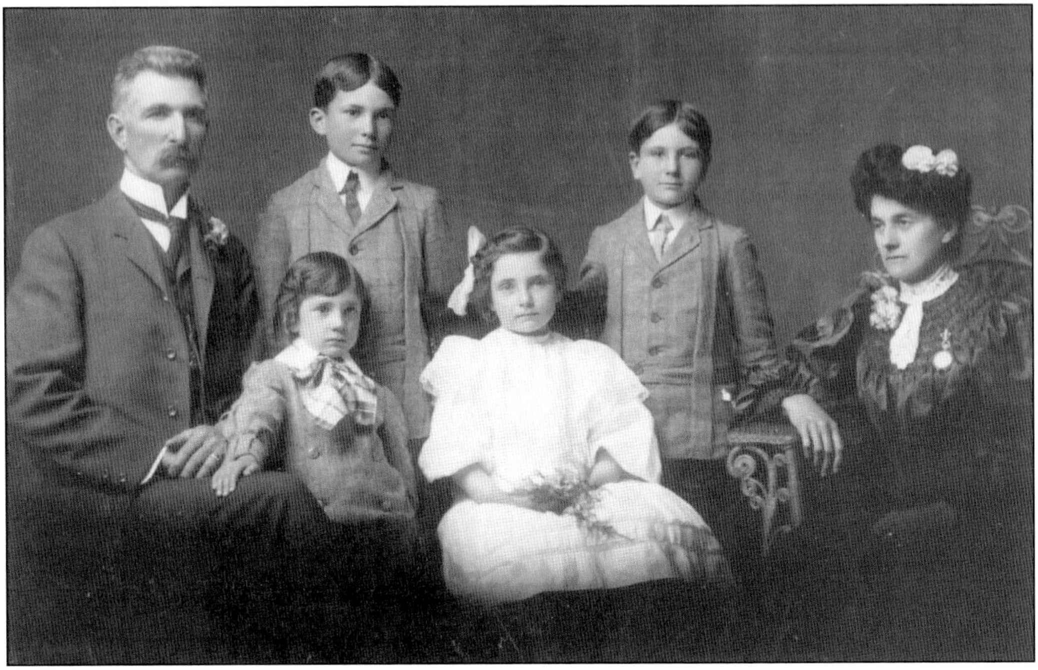

Hugh and Mary Fogle Lister raised their family on Beaver Creek. They are, from left to right, (first row) Hugh, Vernon, Violet, and Mary; (second row) Lawrence and Robert. Hugh's parents were among the earliest settlers in the Upper Country. Hugh bought the Love Bailey Ranch on Beaver Creek in 1908, and the family managed the ranch for several years.

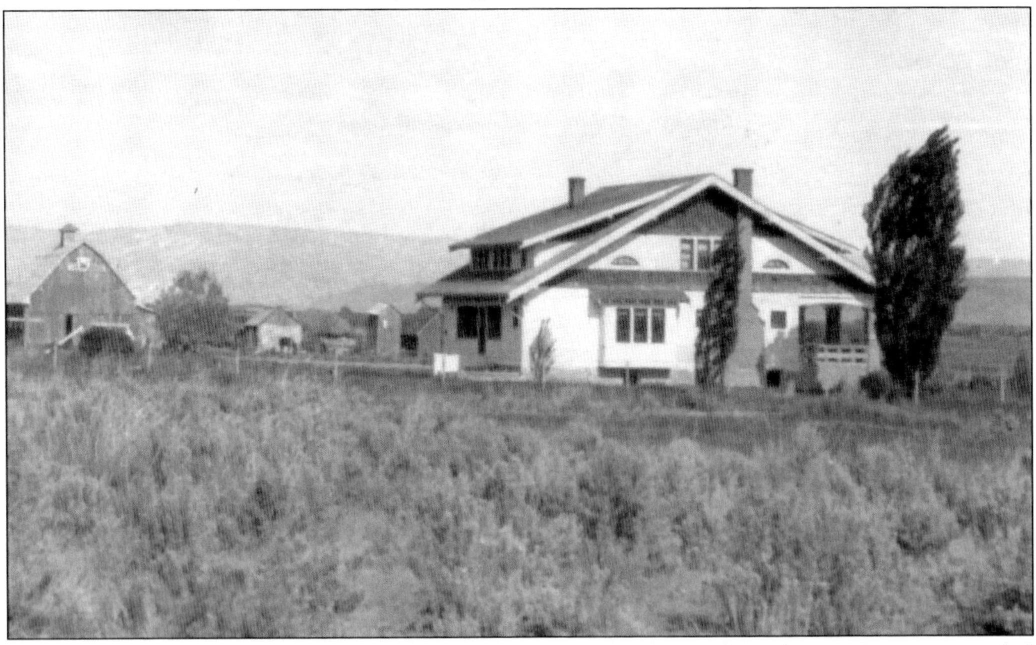

This ranch house was the headquarters for the Lister Ranch. Hugh and Mary Lister expanded the ranch, and their son Robert took over operations in later years. The Lister family sold the ranch in 1976. The Beaver Creek Cemetery is located near the ranch. Today, the ranch is the headquarters for a large syndicated ranch.

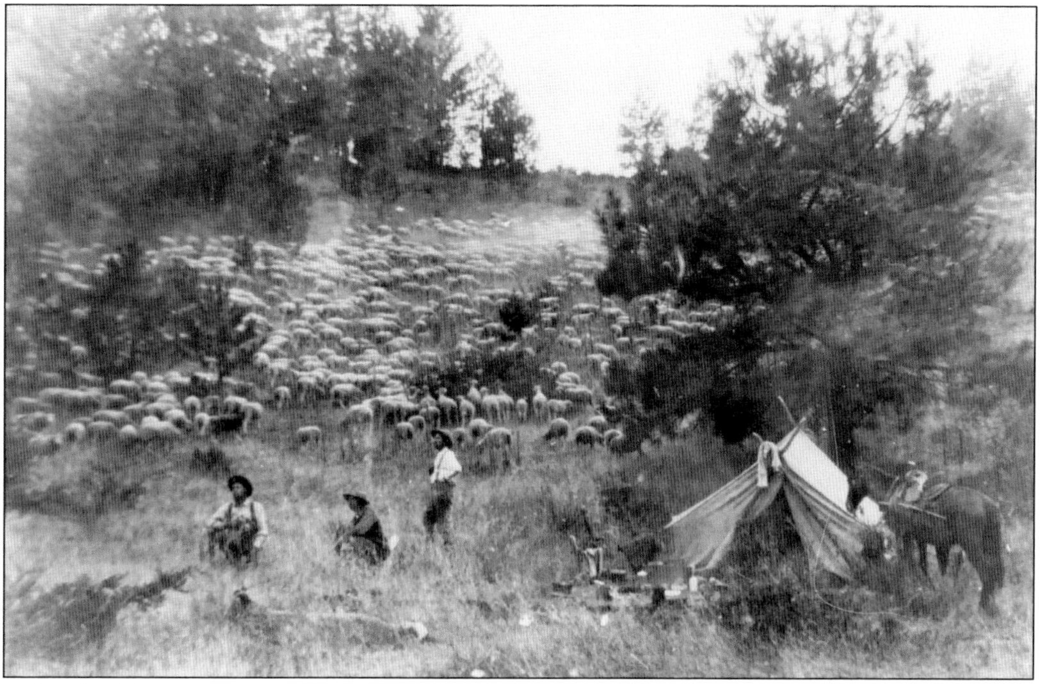

A band of sheep is grazing on upper McKay Creek about 1900. This band belonged to Tom Houston. The men in the photograph are unidentified. Typically, a single sheepherder stayed with the sheep and moved them to different pastures. A herder would normally set up a tent for his camp and was accompanied by a well-trained sheepdog that could move bands and protect them from predators.

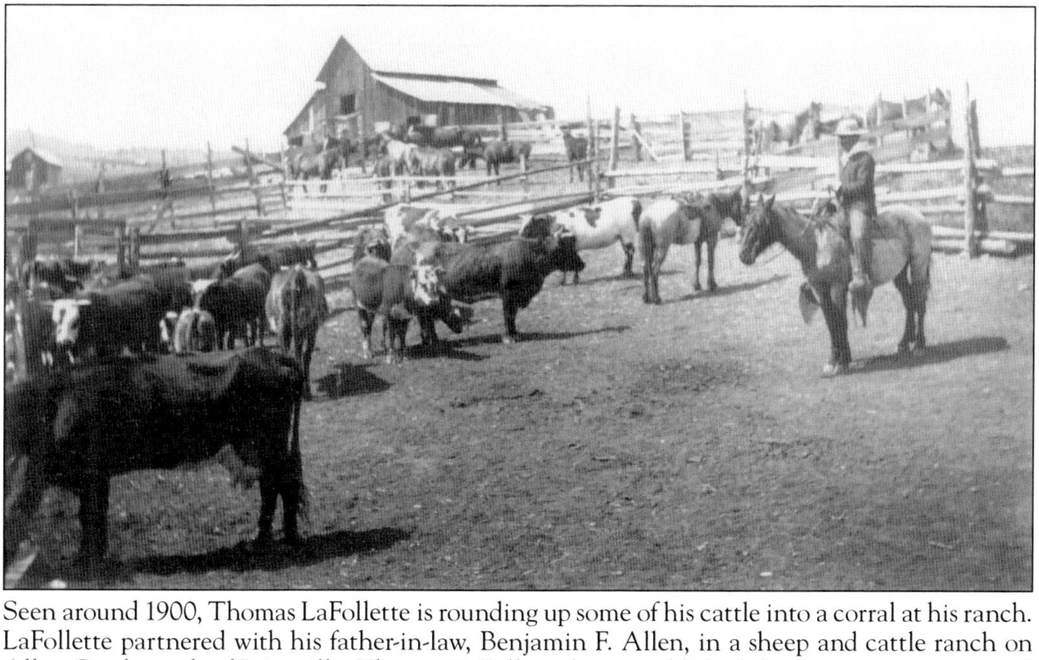

Seen around 1900, Thomas LaFollette is rounding up some of his cattle into a corral at his ranch. LaFollette partnered with his father-in-law, Benjamin F. Allen, in a sheep and cattle ranch on Allen Creek north of Prineville. Thomas LaFollette later established the first nursery in central Oregon at Powell Butte.

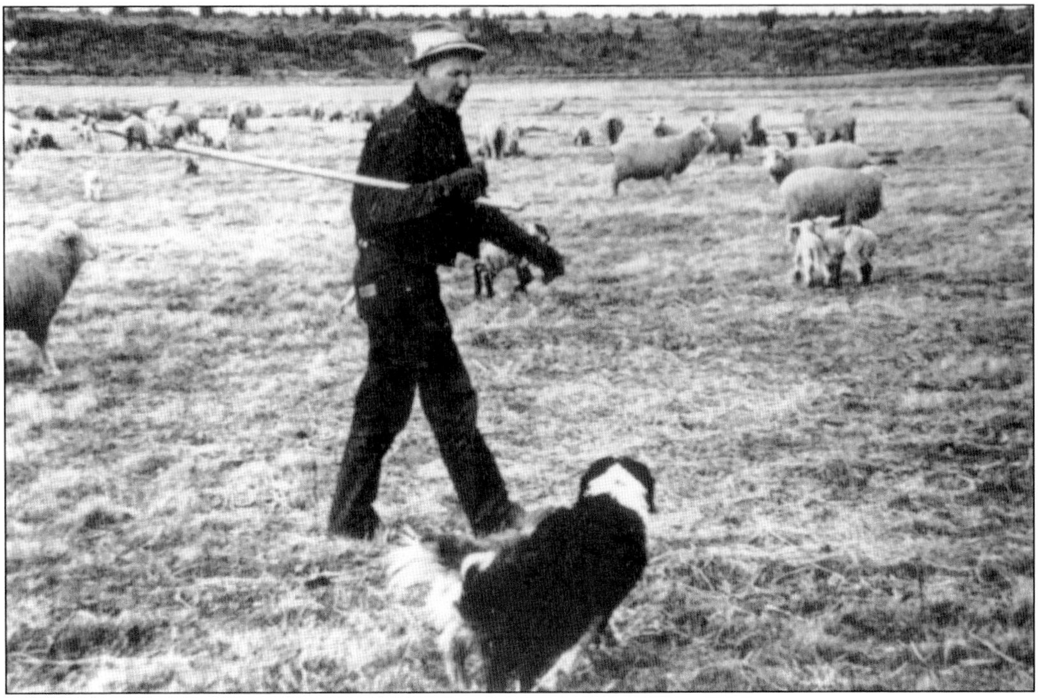

Jack Shumway is tending to his sheep at his ranch on Dry River southwest of Powell Butte. He moved to Powell Butte shortly after World War I. He and a friend were persuaded that central Oregon had opportunities, and they purchased 80 acres apiece. Jack first raised potatoes and farm crops. He expanded his ranch to include cattle and sheep. He eventually accumulated over 15,000 acres and had an extensive sheep operation. Several years after his death, the Shumway Ranch was sold to a developer, and it is now the site of Brasada Ranch.

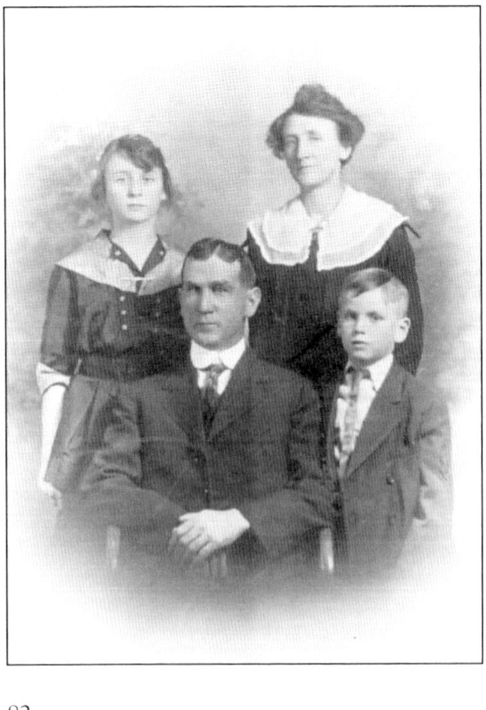

Claude and Mary Wiltse Dunham operated a ranch on Bear Creek. Pictured are, from left to right, Vera, Claude, Mary, and Clifton. Claude's family moved to central Oregon in 1884 when he was four year old. In 1906, he and his brother Harvey purchased a ranch near Taylor Butte on Bear Creek. Claude and Mary operated the ranch on Bear Creek, and Harvey established a ranch on upper Crooked River east of Post. Claude and Mary lived on the ranch until it was sold in 1946. Claude served as a county commissioner for eight years. Mary was selected as Crook County pioneer queen in 1960.

Frank and Lora DeLore McCullough had a long pioneer heritage in central Oregon. Lora had grown up near Suplee, and Frank grew up near Mount Vernon, Oregon. They were married in 1923 and spent their early married life ranching near Mount Vernon. During the Great Depression, Frank worked for legendary Bill Brown on the High Desert as a horse buckaroo. They bought a ranch east of Post in 1936 and expanded their holdings to include the Pine Creek Ranch in 1960. Eventually, the ranches were divided between their three sons. Lora was selected as a Crook County pioneer queen in 1977.

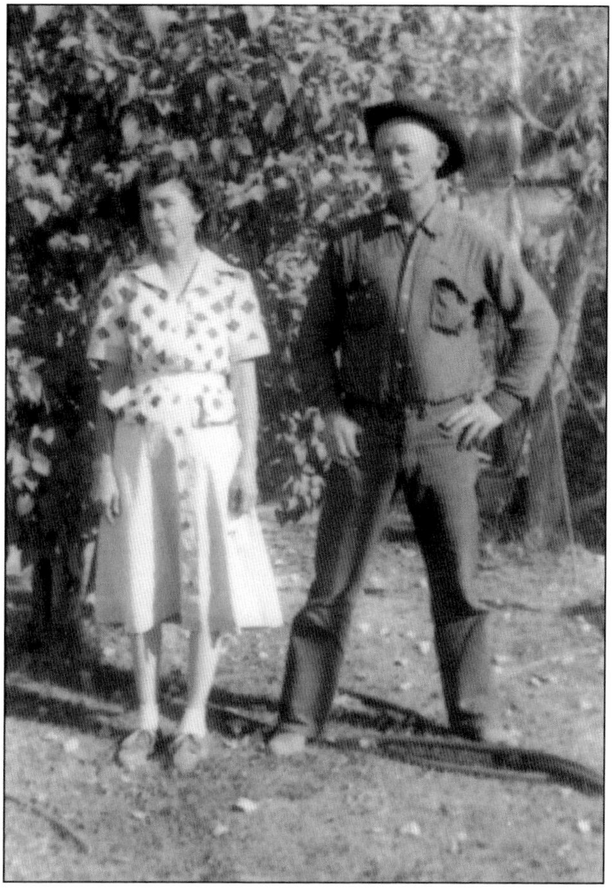

The William Foster family lived at Paulina for many years. From left to right are Mary Faulkner Foster, Van Foster, and William W. Foster. William Foster was among the early settlers in the Paulina vicinity and was known as "Uncle Billy" to local ranchers. William was an invalid for several years as a result of complications of typhoid fever.

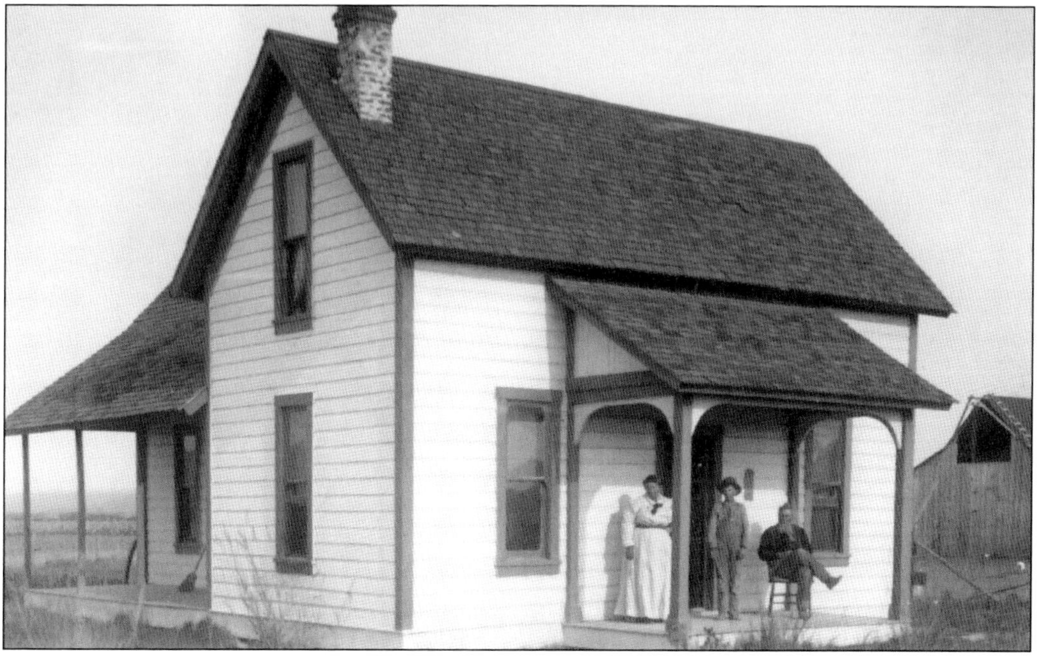

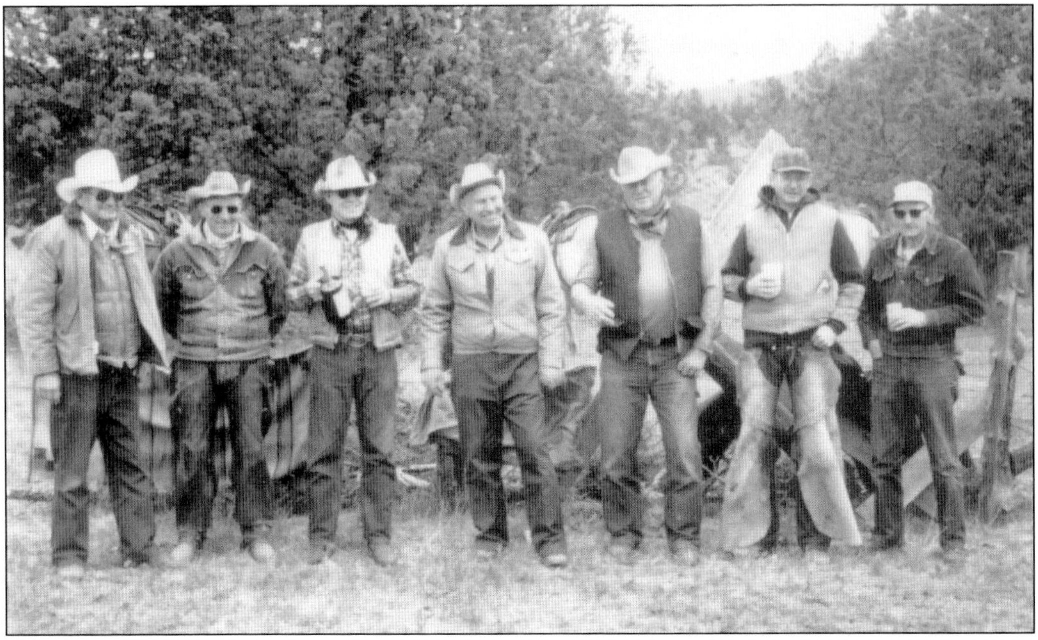

This is a group of Post area ranchers on a joint cattle roundup in 1986. The tradition of neighbors assisting in roundups and branding continues from pioneer days to the present. They are, from left to right, Jack McCullough, John Gage, Miller Tweedt, Don Brummer, Joe Herin, Don McCullough, and Tom Davis.

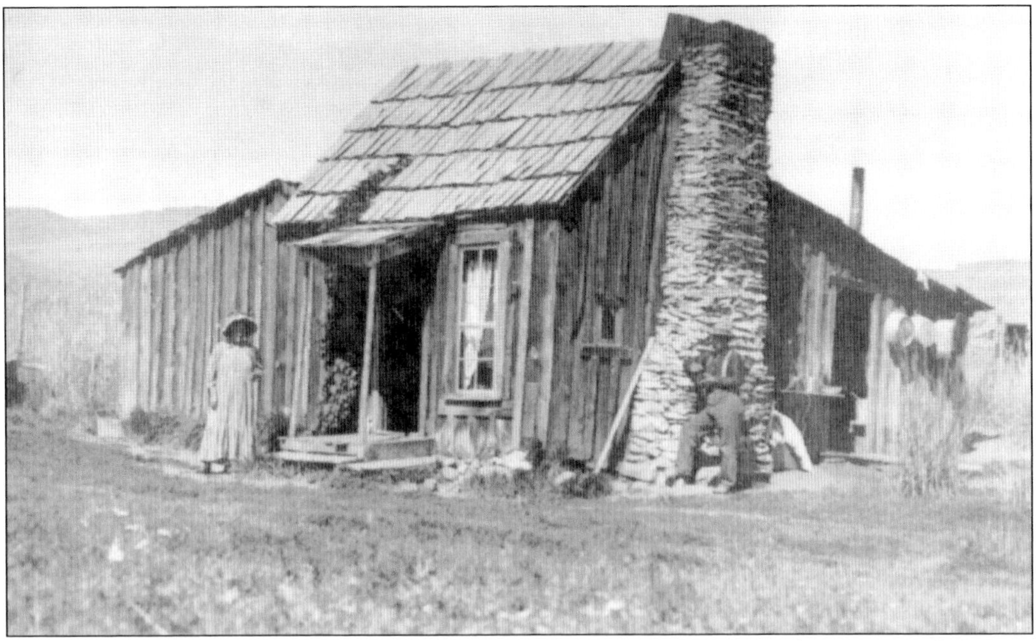

Near the turn of the 20th century, there was a large influx of homesteaders to central Oregon and Crook County. Many people from across the nation and from other countries came to file on one of the last major homestead surges in the country. This is the homestead house of Marcel and Mary Senecal. Mary is on the left near the porch, and Marcel is by the chimney. The house was near the site of the Suplee Post Office.

Alice Day Pratt is on a horse near her homestead by Friar Butte just southeast of Post. Alice came to try her luck at homesteading as a single woman. She raised chickens and had dairy cows. To supplement her income, she also taught in local country schools. She became a well-known author of children's books in her later life and also wrote of her homestead experiences. Like most early homesteaders, she eventually relinquished her claim, as she could not sustain a profitable farm.

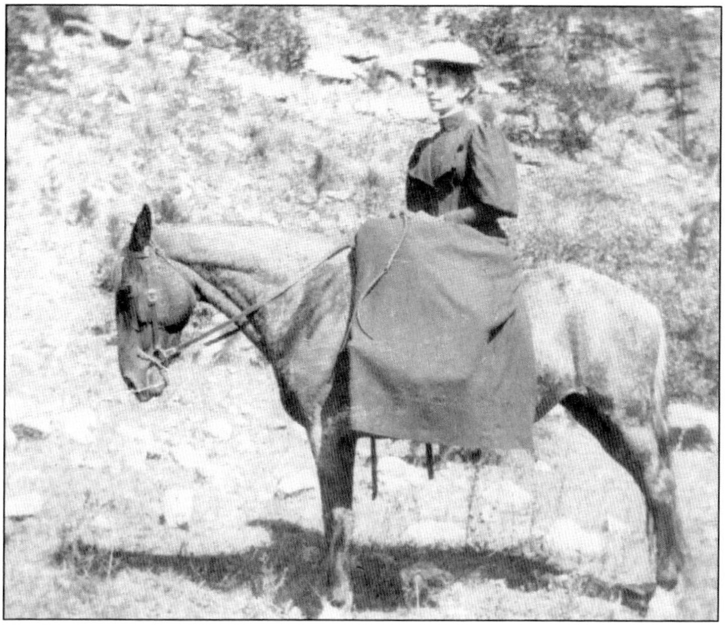

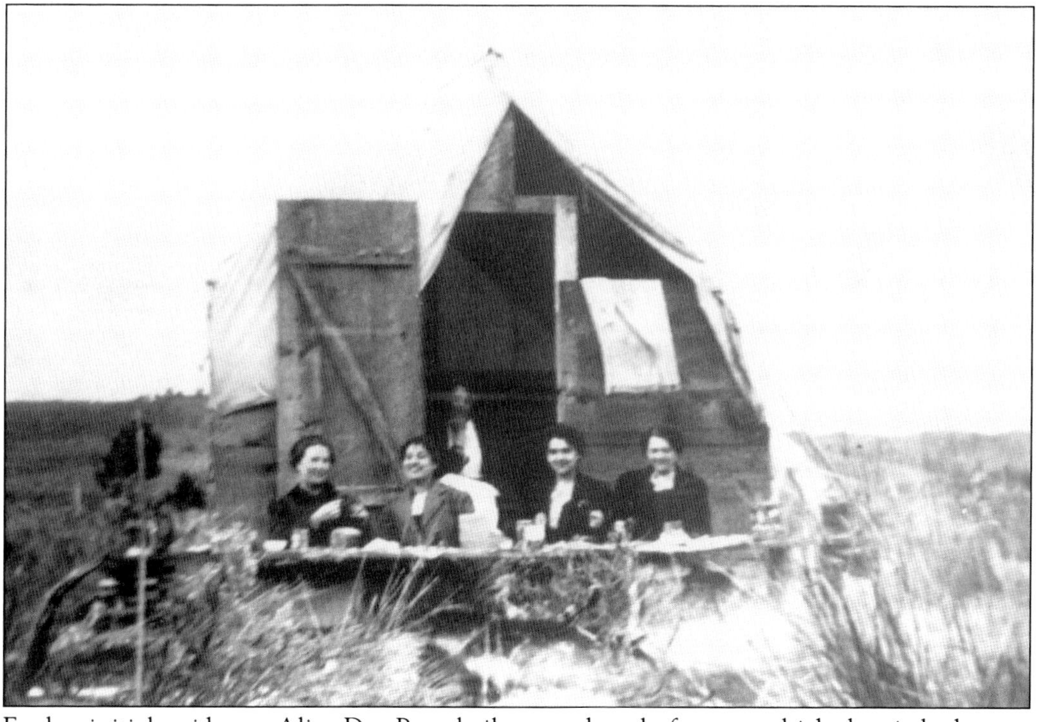

For her initial residence, Alice Day Pratt built a wooden platform on which she pitched a tent of canvas. Unidentified local teachers are eating supper at her primitive cabin. Pratt eventually finished her wooden cabin with walls and a roof. The cabin is still standing but is in a very dilapidated state.

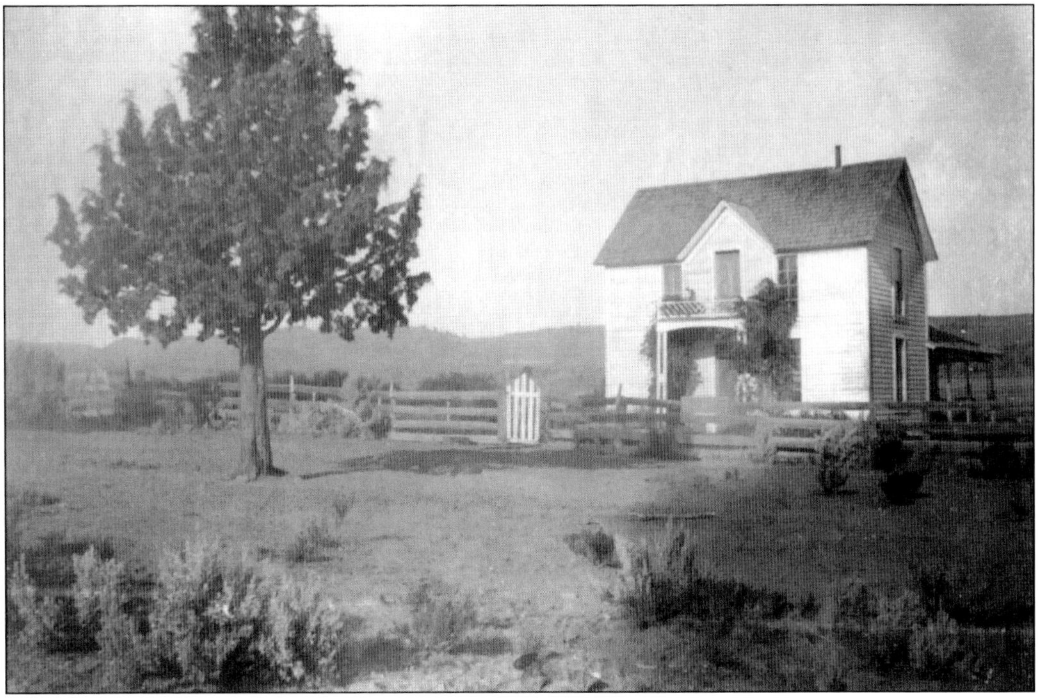

The George Wiley house, seen in 1885, is located on Newsom Creek about five miles southeast of Post. George Wiley was among the early settlers near Post, coming prior to 1880. This was one of the first houses built along Newsom Creek. The house has had various owners through the years and is still being used as a house today.

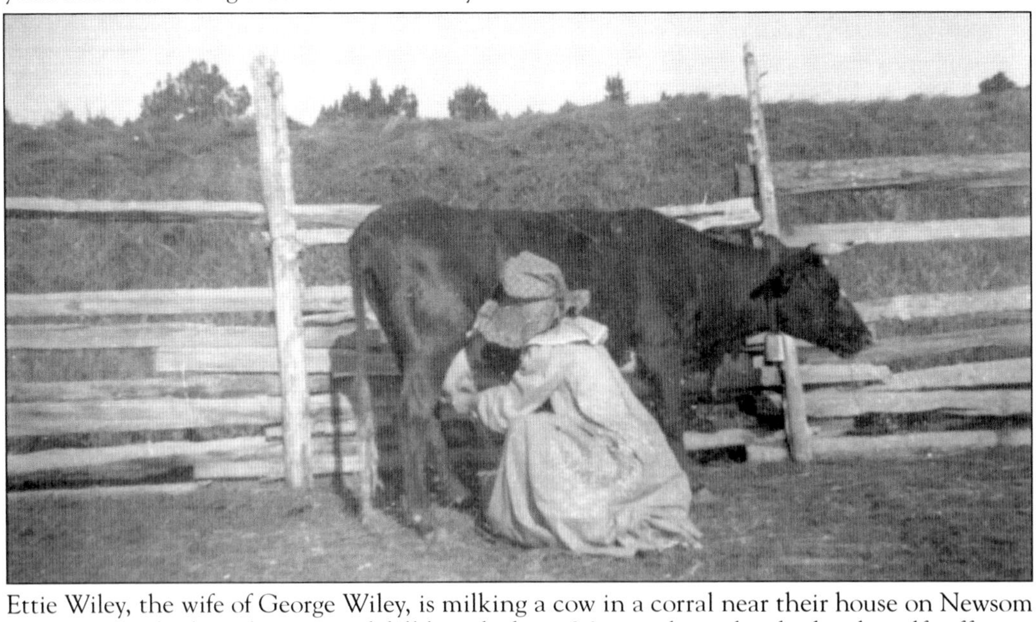

Ettie Wiley, the wife of George Wiley, is milking a cow in a corral near their house on Newsom Creek. Note the large bonnet and full-length dress. Most early settlers had to be self-sufficient and usually produced most of their own produce and dairy products, such as milk and butter. As fruit was a very desired crop for domestic use and it took a few years to produce, orchards were usually among the first plants to be established.

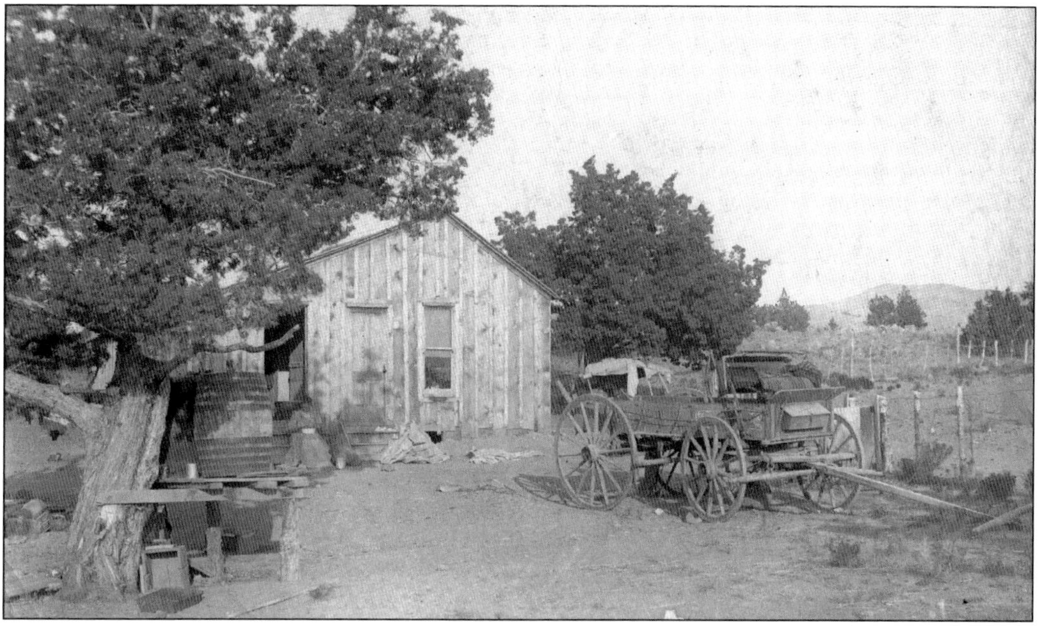

Joe Gerardo homesteaded on Williamson Creek near Bear Creek Buttes in 1905. This is a typical dryland homestead. Water was scarce and had to be hauled from springs, sometimes located far away, to provide domestic water. Note the water barrels at left. Joe Gerardo later operated a butcher shop in Prineville.

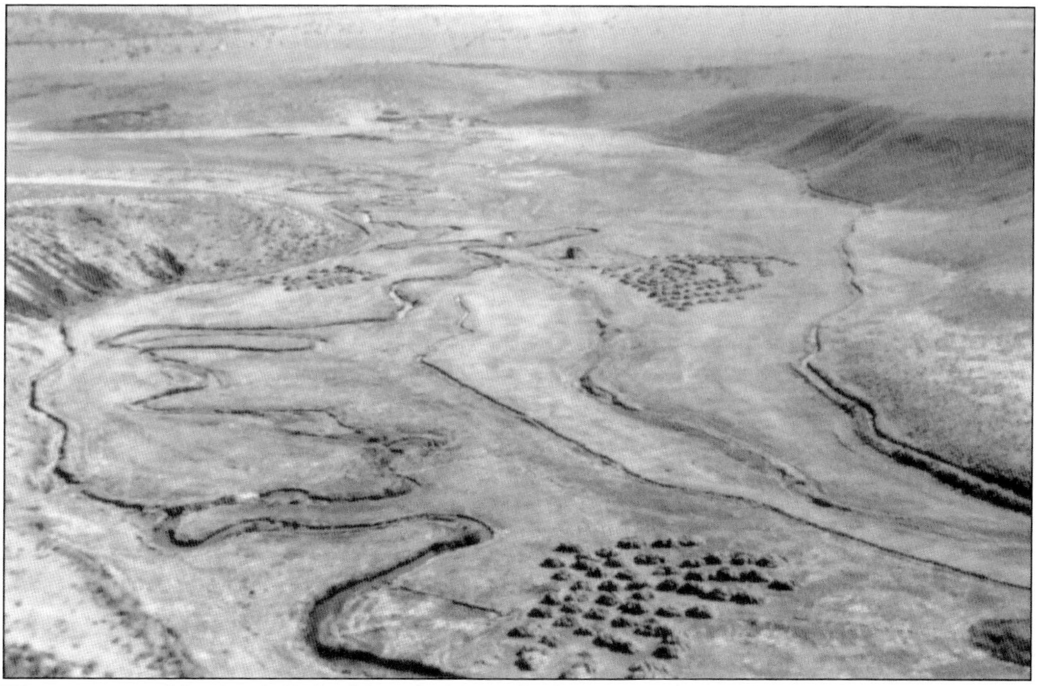

This is a view of the South Fork of Crooked River looking east. The ranch in the center background is the Hackleman Rafter Q Ranch. Seth Rodman originally established the ranch in the mid-1870s. Some of the first farming in the county was to grow forage for livestock. Note the piles of hay in the fields.

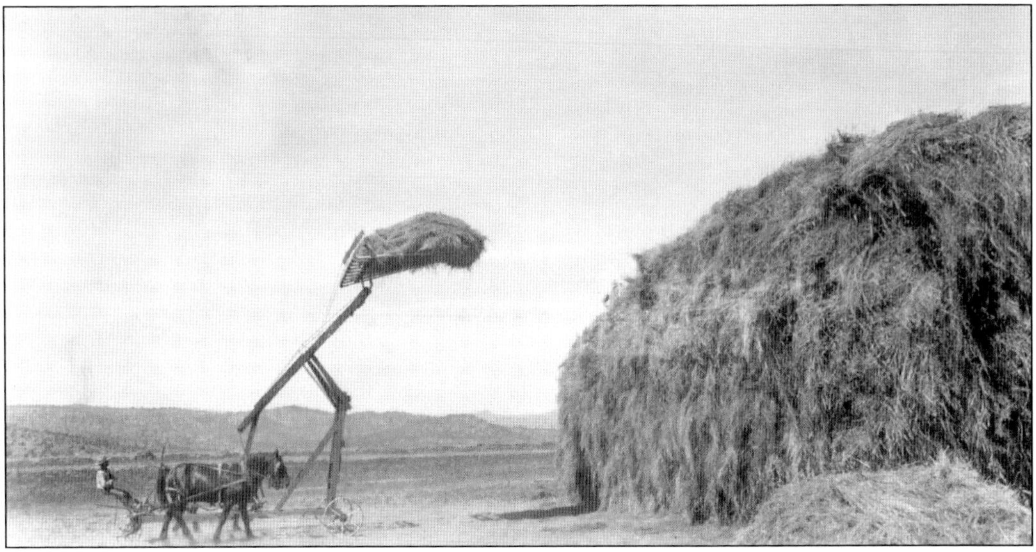

Hay is being stacked with a buck rake in lower Crooked River Valley about 1905. Most of the hay harvested was stacked in large loose piles, as seen in this photograph. Most early growing of forage for harvest was done in areas where water was available, such as along creeks or streams. Some dryland crops, such as rye, were also grown for use in feeding livestock during the winter.

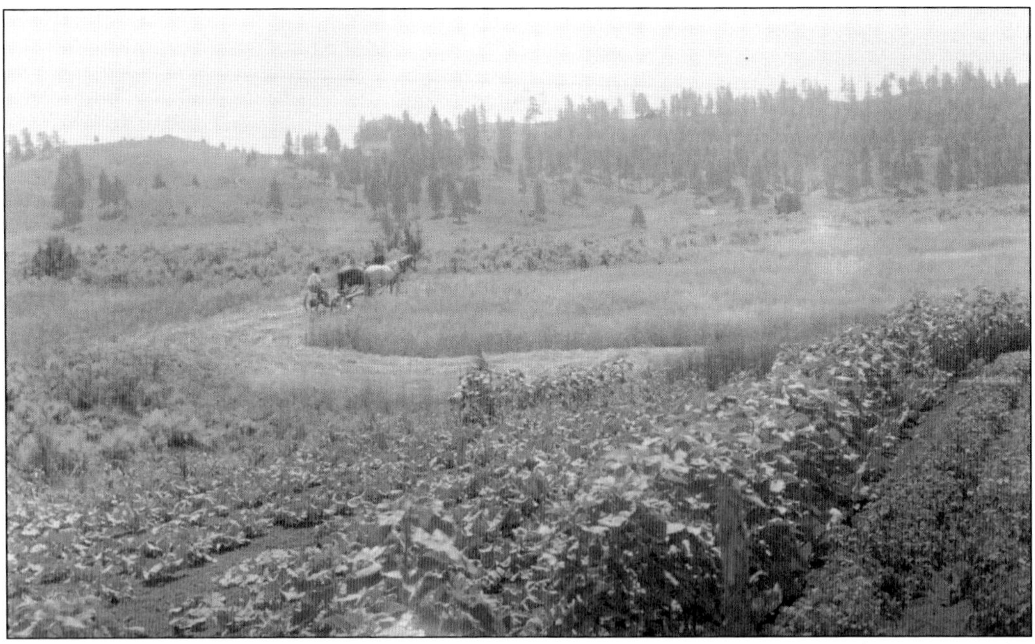

In 1905, John Knox is harvesting hay at his ranch near Conant Basin, west of Post. Note the plentiful garden in the foreground. Farming became a major part of ranching operations, as winters often were snowy with severe weather and forage for winter feeding was necessary. Gardens provided vegetables and fruits for domestic use.

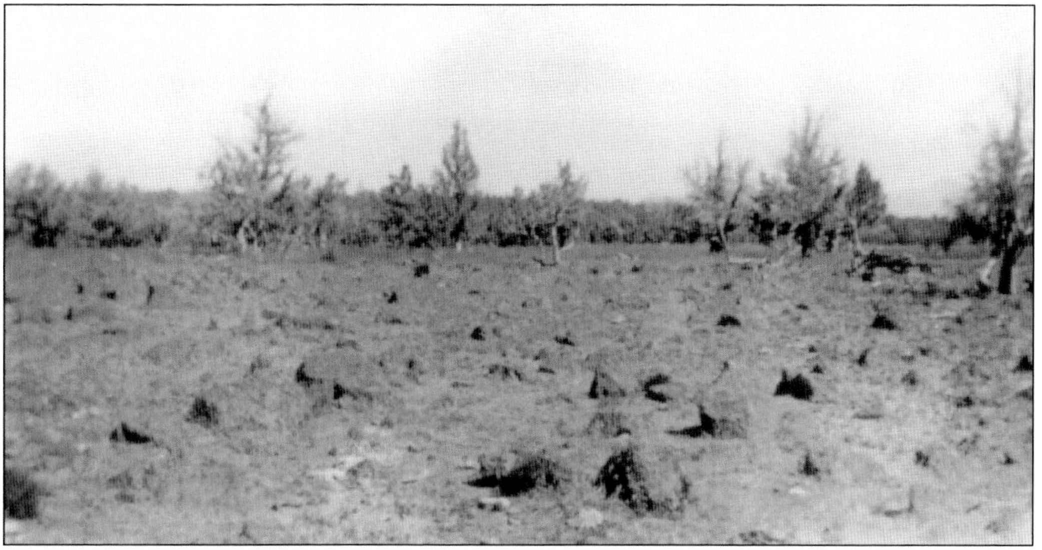

Early homesteaders faced many obstacles in farming the arid region of central Oregon. Land had to be cleared of numerous rocks, such as those seen here near Powell Butte. There was plenty of flat land and rich soil, but preparing the land for farming was backbreaking work. Wagons or sleds were loaded with rock that was then transported to the edges of fields and piled.

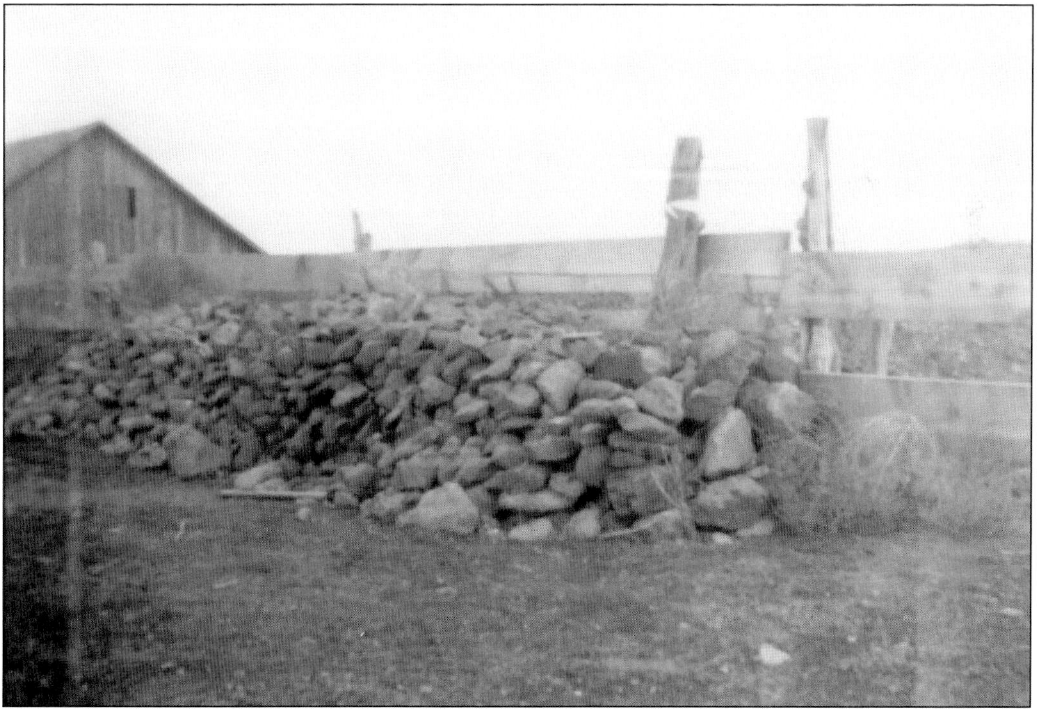

This is a pile of rocks gleaned from a field near Powell Butte by an early homesteader. Throughout the region, piles or rows of rocks are still visible reminders of the arduous task of preparing the land for farming.

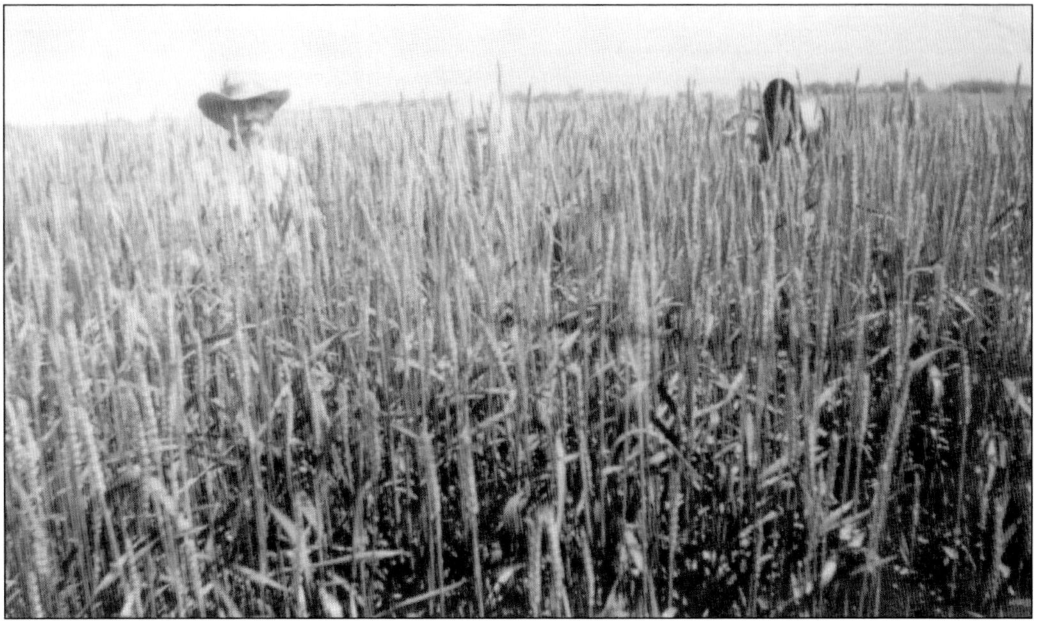

Elanson Bussett stands in a field of winter wheat that he has grown on the lower western slope of Powell Butte about 1907. Most early homesteaders had to grow crops that were not irrigation dependent to make a living. Winter wheat could be planted in the fall, and winter moisture allowed it to grow in the spring and early summer. It was the predominant crop for early homesteaders.

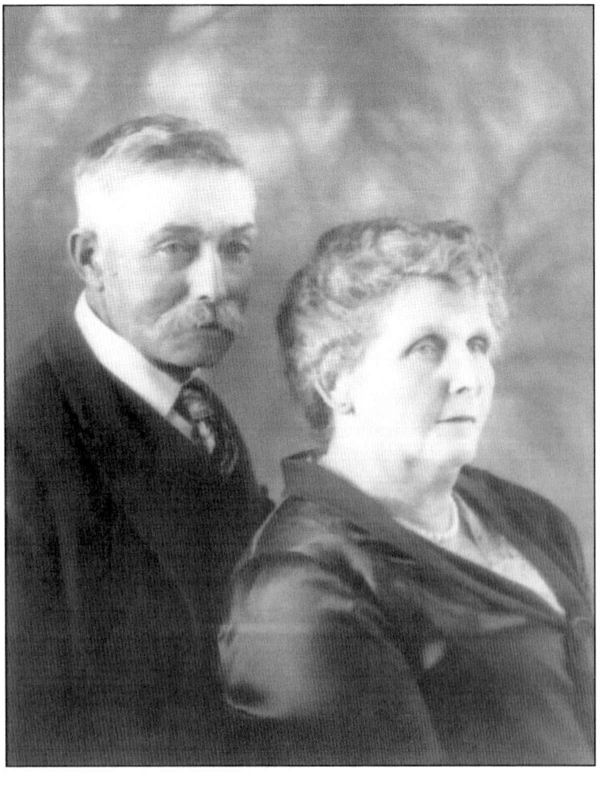

Elanson and Nellie Brown Bussett were among the earliest homesteaders in the Powell Butte vicinity. They built a rough wooden house in 1904. Elanson and his sons cleared the land for farming winter wheat, and Nellie spent time hauling water by horse and wagon from springs at the base of Powell Butte. Elanson and Nellie operated their farm until 1935, when their son Lloyd bought it.

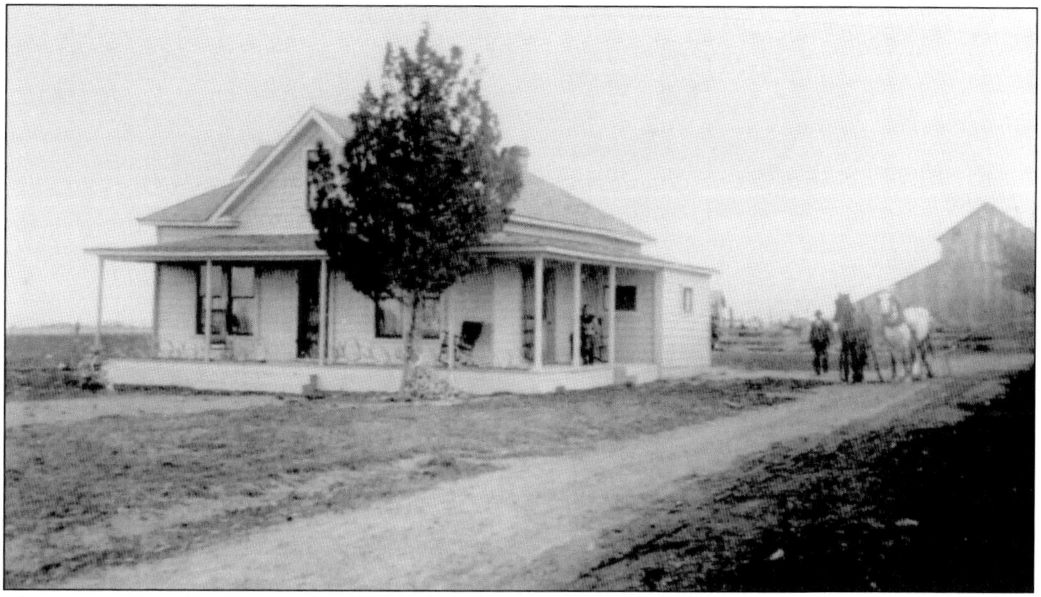

Elanson and Nellie Bussett built this farmhouse near Powell Butte. Their original house was constructed of rough lumber with single-board walls. This was one of the first sturdily constructed houses in the Powell Butte farming community. The Bussett place was the only place to stop between Bend and Prineville, and travelers often dropped in to share a meal or get overnight lodging at their home. When irrigation water arrived in Powell Butte in 1908, they expanded their holdings and built this home near the irrigation ditch.

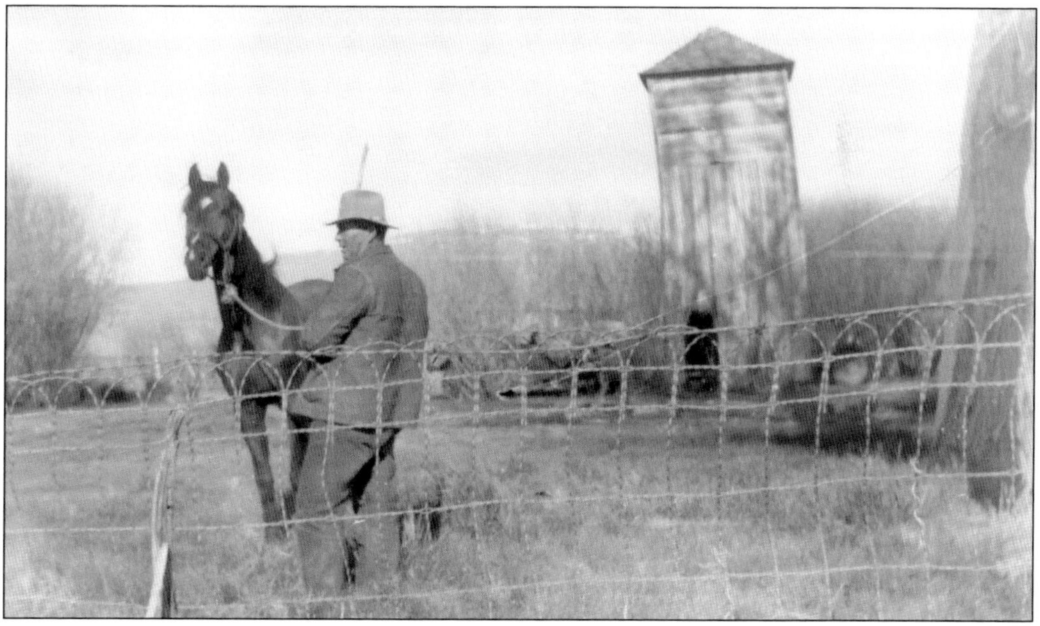

Claude Butler is holding the reins of a horse at his farm in the Lone Pine vicinity on lower Crooked River. The fertile ground and plentiful water of the lower Crooked River led to the development of several farms in the vicinity. Claude's parents, Victor and Olive Rodman Butler, were among the earliest settlers. Claude and his wife, Gladys Wimp Butler, expanded their ranch and farm to include over 2,700 acres.

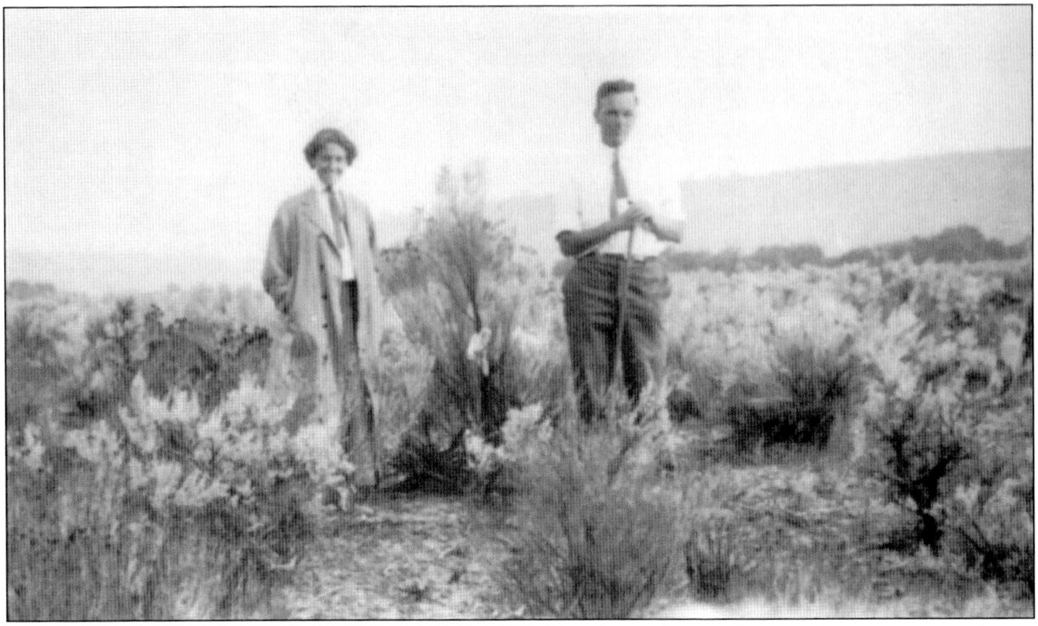

Dorothy and Henry "Hal" McCall came to central Oregon in 1912 and began farming on the lower Crooked River just east of O'Neil. Dorothy was the daughter of wealthy "copper king" Thomas Lawson, and Hal's father was the governor of Massachusetts. Hal was a graduate of Harvard and was a prominent baseball player during his college years. Hal brought Holstein cattle to the ranch and introduced the foundation for the dairy industry in central Oregon. Dorothy and Hal's son Thomas "Tom" later would become the governor of Oregon, serving from 1967 to 1975.

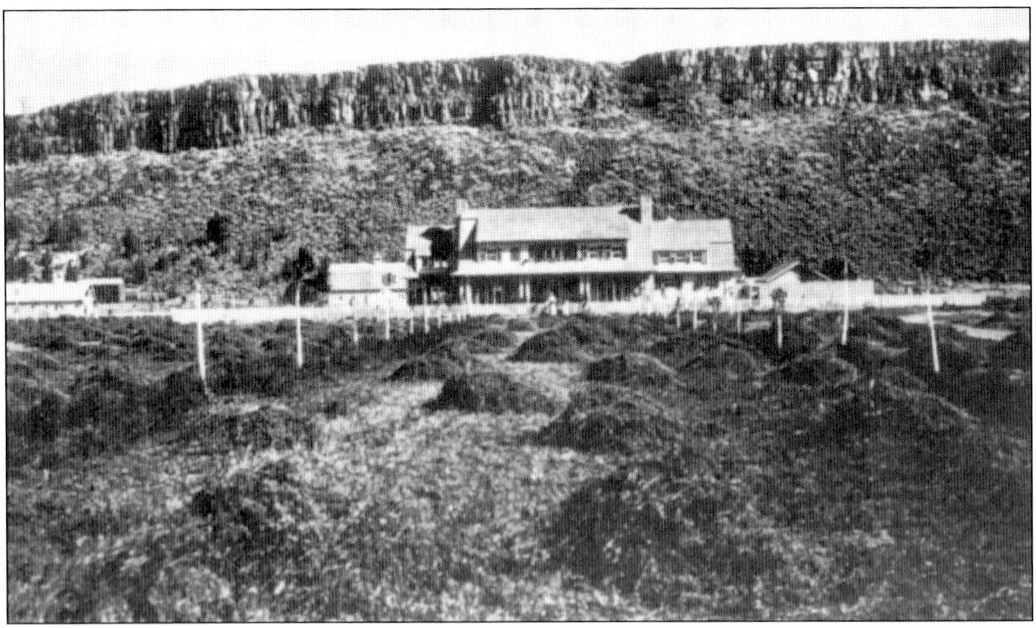

The Henry and Dorothy McCall ranch on lower Crooked River was known as Westernwold. Dorothy's father, Thomas Lawson, built the house as a present for the young married couple. Dorothy McCall wrote a book titled *Ranch Under the Rimrock*, in which she related their experiences on the ranch. The house is still being utilized as a residence.

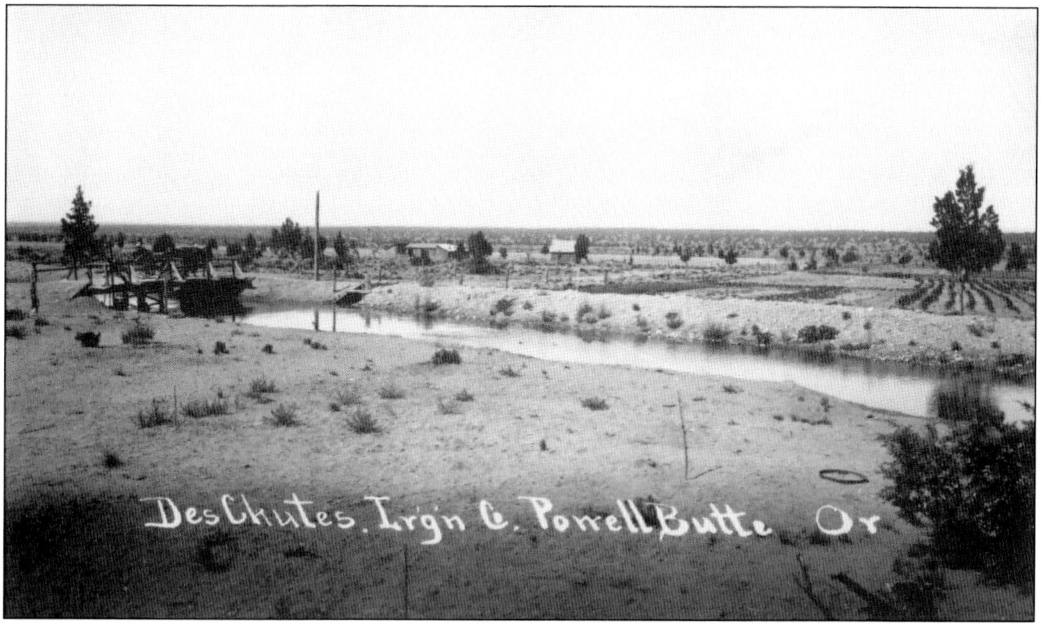

Irrigation water arrived in the Powell Butte vicinity in 1908 when a canal was constructed from Bend to Powell Butte via Alfalfa. Water was diverted from the Deschutes River and flowed for several miles. The arrival of water changed farming dependence on winter wheat to a variety of crops. This is the Deschutes Irrigation Company canal at Powell Butte. The Guy Sears farm is on the far side of the canal. Later, the canal became part of the Central Oregon Irrigation Company.

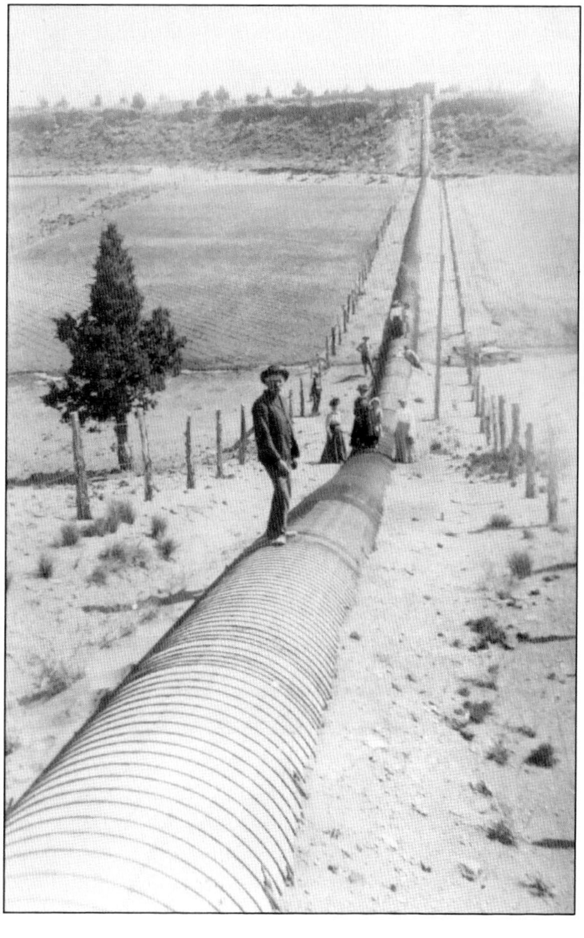

Water delivery to the farmlands near Powell Butte required that a siphon be built across Dry River as it impeded water flow northward. A wooden pipe, about four feet in diameter, was laid through Dry River and allowed the water to plunge down into Dry River and up onto a flume and then on to the plains northward. Guy Sears is standing on the pipe, and his family is in background. The siphon is now gone, but the flume is still in place and is part of a golf path for Brasada Ranch.

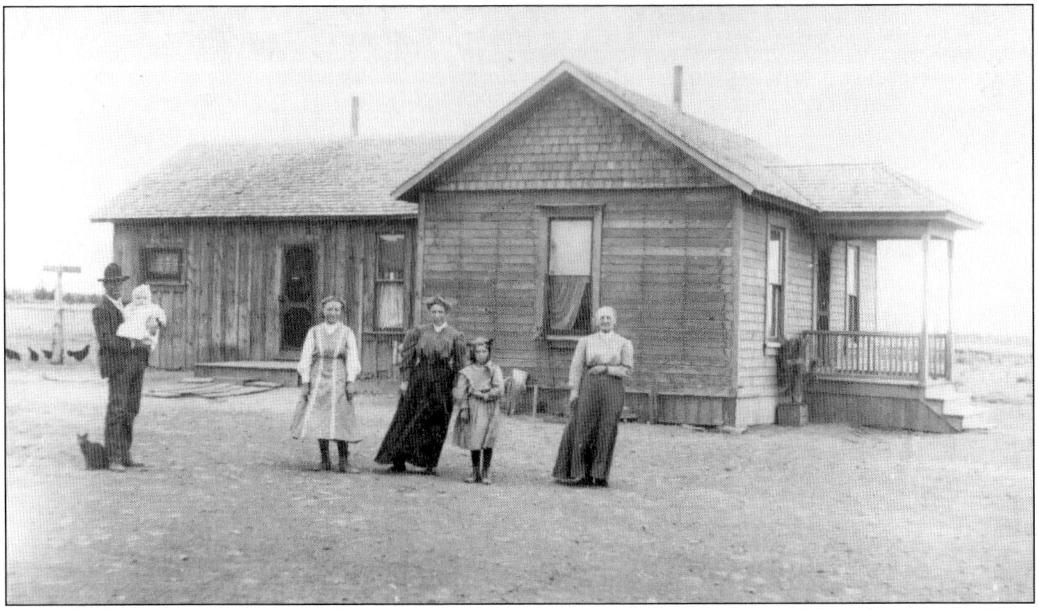

Guy Sears established a farm at Powell Butte about 1909. Seen in front of their house are, from left to right, Guy holding Doris, Orisa, Nellie, Ada May, and Sarah Wilson Pauls. The family moved to Powell Butte to farm in 1905. Living near the right-of-way of the 1908 irrigation canal, they were among the first in Powell Butte to irrigate with water from the canal.

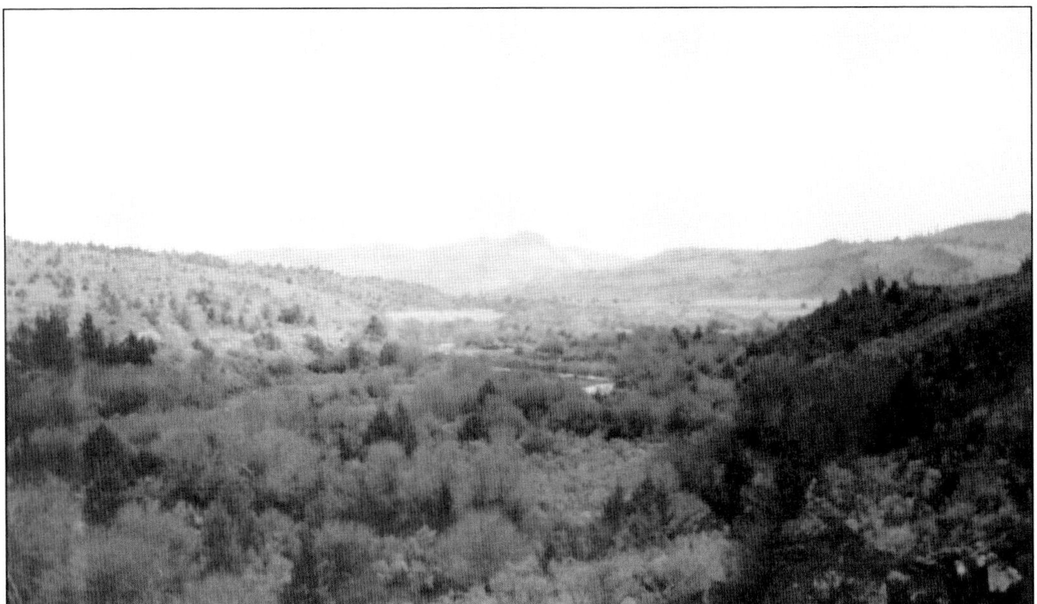

This is a view looking east upstream on Ochoco Creek about six miles east of Prineville. Farm fields can be seen along the creek in the background, and the stream is lined with willows. This is the site of present Ochoco Dam and Reservoir before construction began.

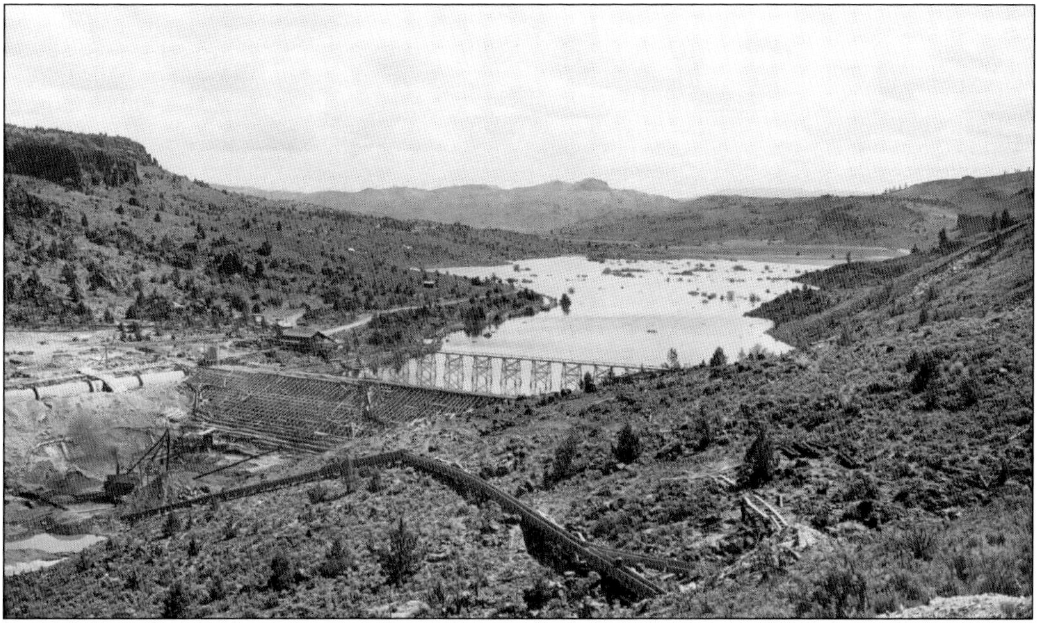

Farmers in the Ochoco Valley and north to McKay Valley needed irrigation water to diversify crops and formed together to propose the construction of Ochoco Dam five miles east of Prineville. Actual construction began in 1917 and was completed late in 1918. The dam was constructed by sluicing fill material from the surrounding hillside down to wooden forms and then compacting the fill. The concrete outflow for the canal is on the left.

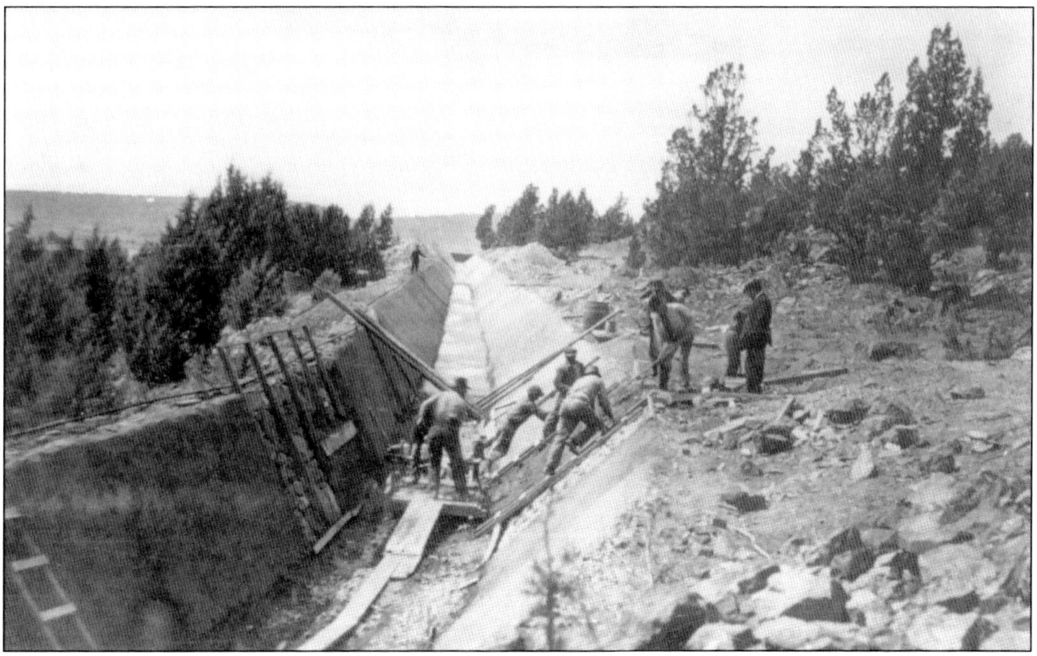

A crew is constructing the irrigation canal from the outlet at Ochoco Dam in 1918. Once completed, the canal system provided irrigation water to numerous farms in the Ochoco and McKay Creek valleys. The farming system completely changed with irrigation water providing the opportunity to diversify crops.

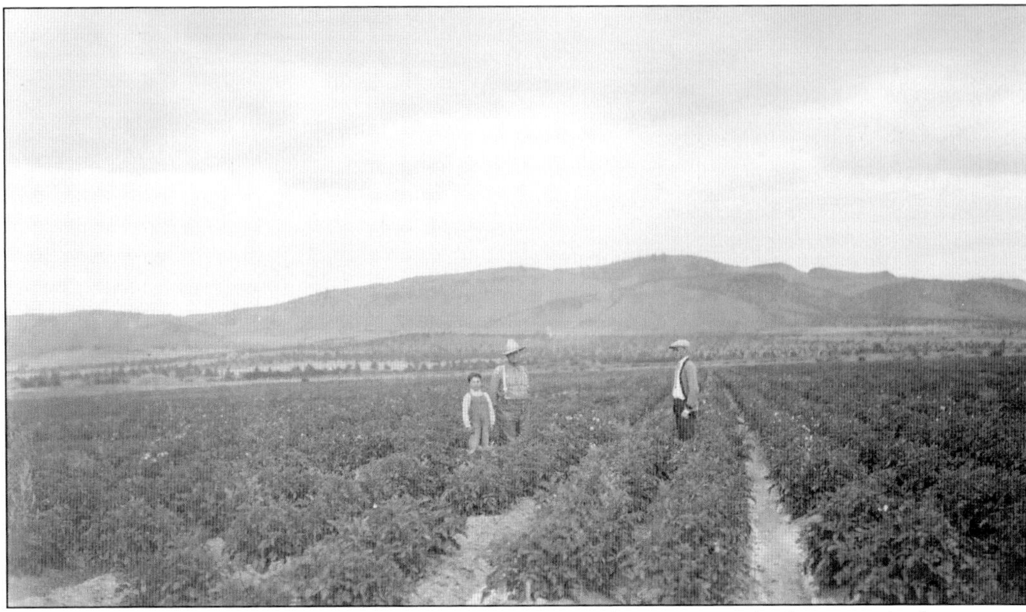

Potatoes soon became the predominant crop in central Oregon with the arrival of irrigation systems. This is a field of Netted Gem potatoes on the Sleasman farm at Powell Butte. For many years, potatoes were the main cash crop in Crook County, and most farms had underground storage buildings for the potatoes.

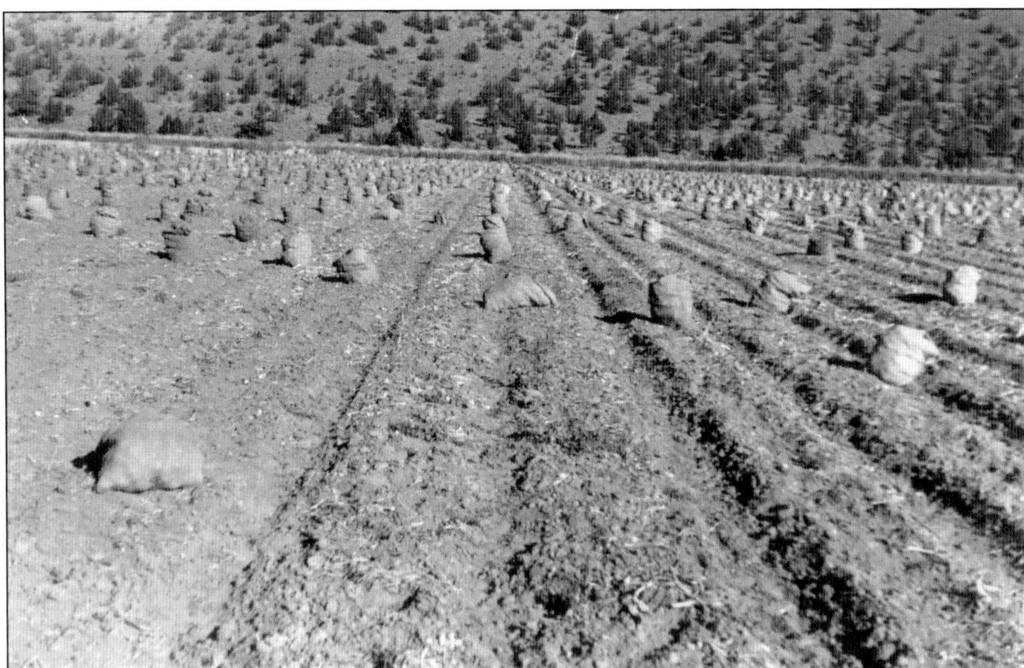

This is a field of potatoes being harvested on lower Crooked River about 1915. The potatoes would be dug up by machine and bagged in burlap sacks by field workers as shown in this photograph. Wagons or trucks would then come by and collect the bags of potatoes and haul them to storage or to market.

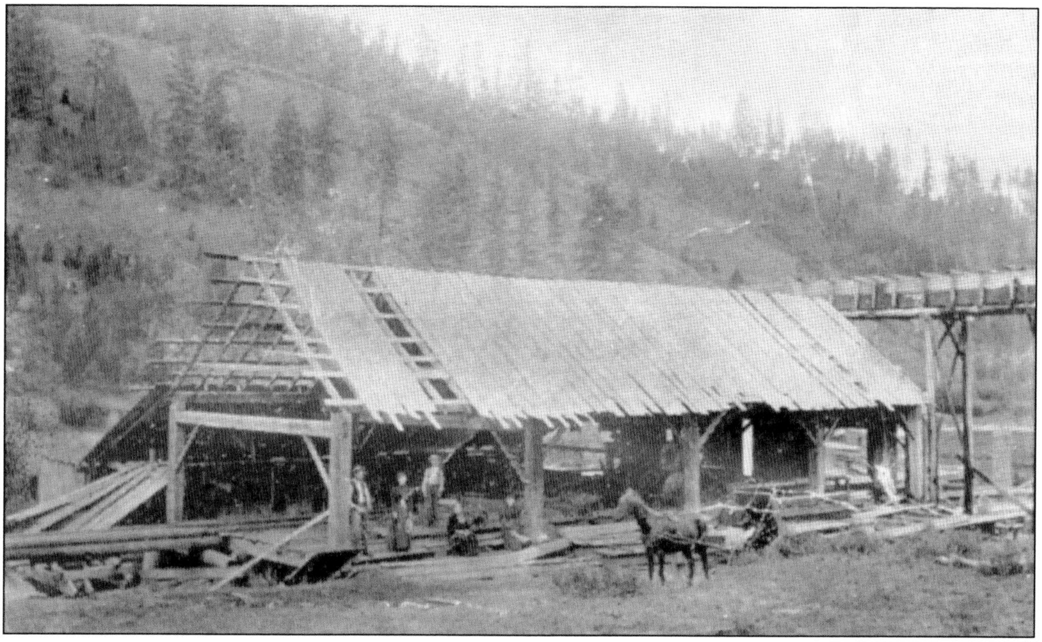

The Birdsong and Demaris sawmill was located near Stein's Pillar on Mill Creek. Since settlers needed lumber to build homes, sawmills developed early in central Oregon. This mill was one of the earliest to be established, around 1900. It provided lumber for local use. Note the flume to the right of the building. It was used to float logs from a point on Lemon Creek. The initial use of the flume led to logs gaining too much speed, and the first log broke through the siding and nearly destroyed the crew bunkhouse. William Birdsong and John Demaris operated the mill.

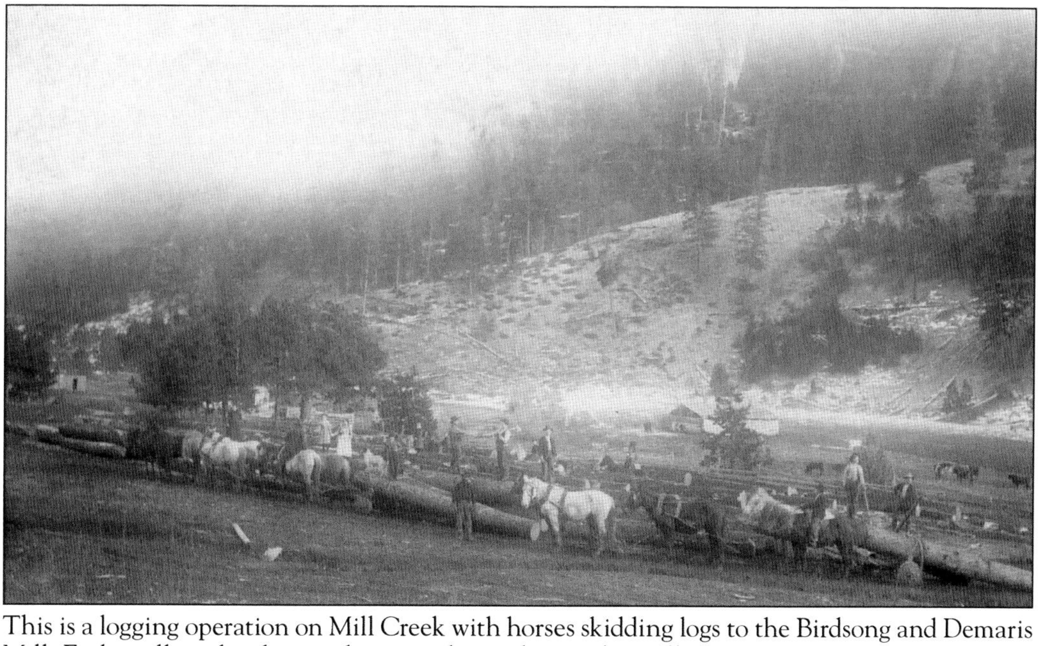

This is a logging operation on Mill Creek with horses skidding logs to the Birdsong and Demaris Mill. Early mills utilized trees that were located near the mill site, and logs were often moved short distances. A close look reveals that several logs have been skidded to the middle ground, and several people are posing.

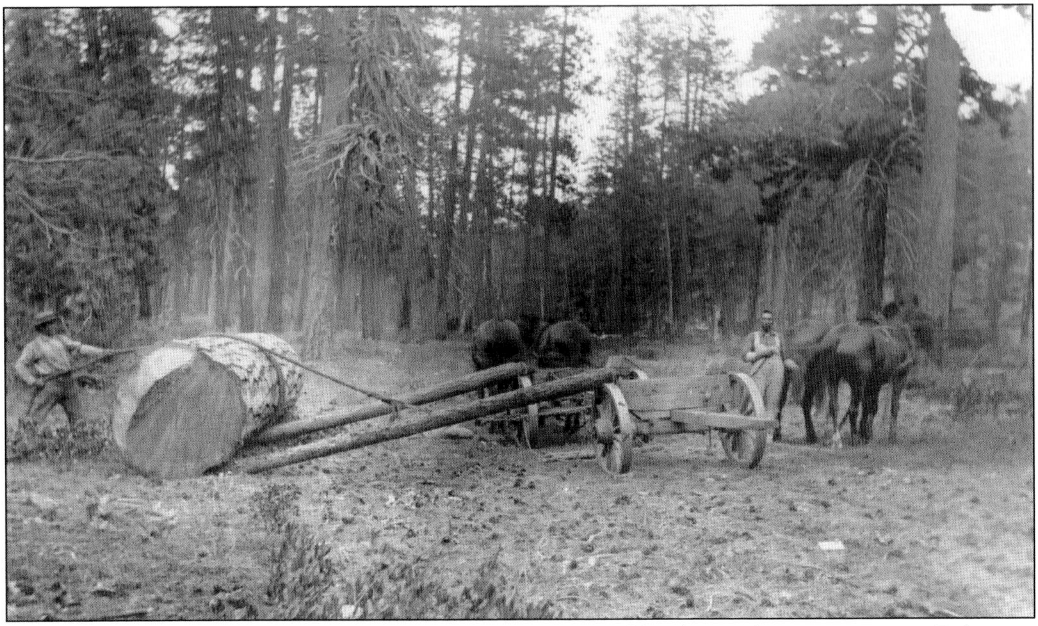

This photograph and the one below show a sequence of loading a log on a wagon. Poles are placed on the wagon to the ground, and a rope is wound around the log and horses pull the log up onto the wagon for transport to the mill. This c. 1905 operation is on McKay Creek near the Demaris Mill.

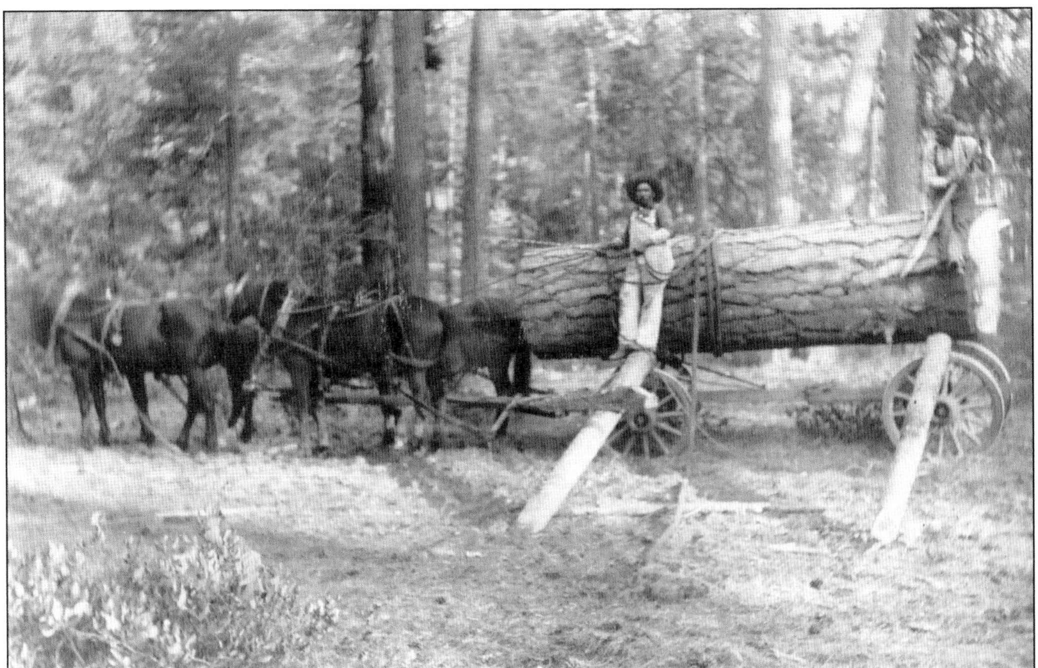

This photograph shows the log hoisted onto the wagon with the poles on the side. The log is about 16 feet long and roughly 30 inches in diameter. Since early mills cut logs into lumber by circular saw, this was about the maximum diameter log that could be cut. Early mills were either water powered or steam powered.

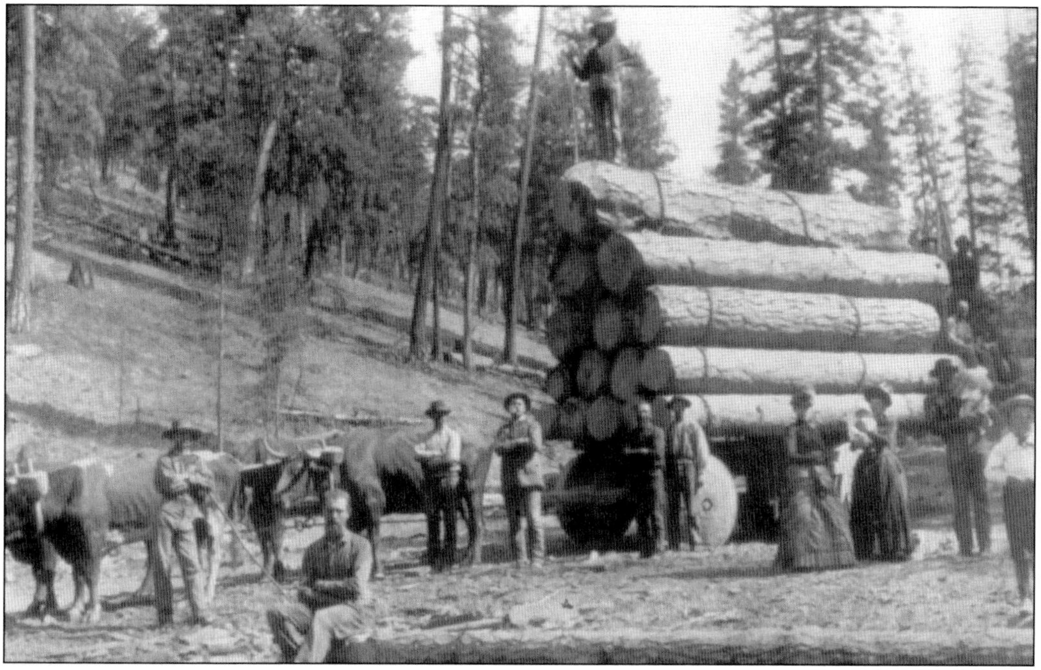

A large load of logs is on a wagon pulled by oxen on Ochoco Creek about 1900. Note the solid wooden wheels. The logs were loaded similar to the fashion shown on the previous page, but were rolled from a hillside to allow higher stacking. This was obviously a festive day, as women and children are present.

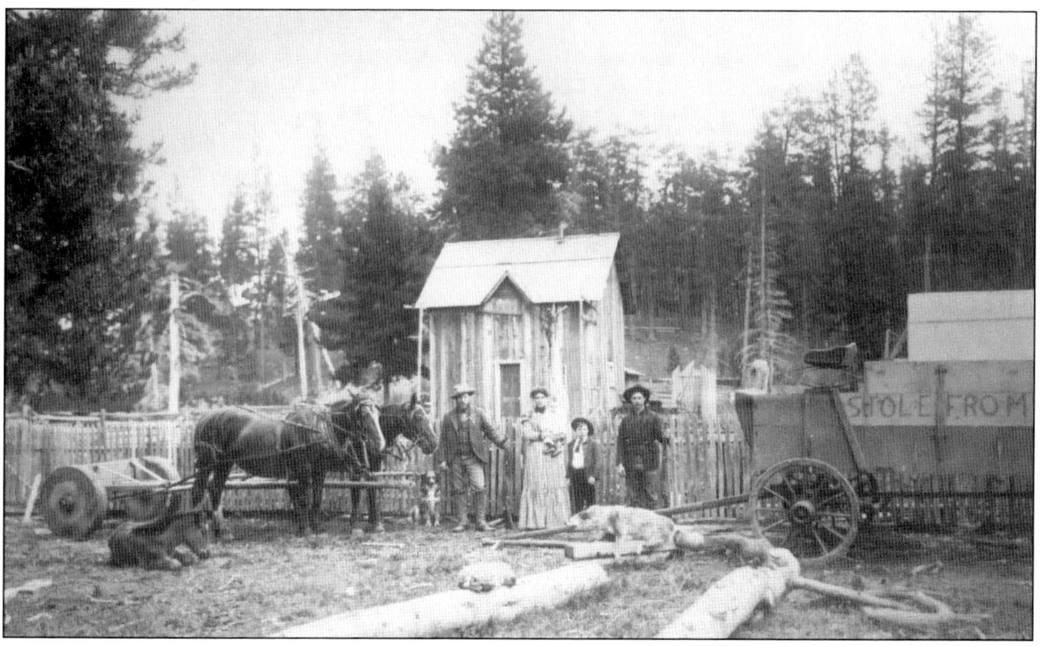

Pioneer homes required roofing as well as lumber for construction. William "Bill" Childers established a shake mill for splitting bolts of wood into roofing shakes near Big Summit Prairie about 1900. The wood most commonly used for shakes was western larch, as it has straight grain that allows for easier splitting. The building at rear appears to be quite tall and narrow.

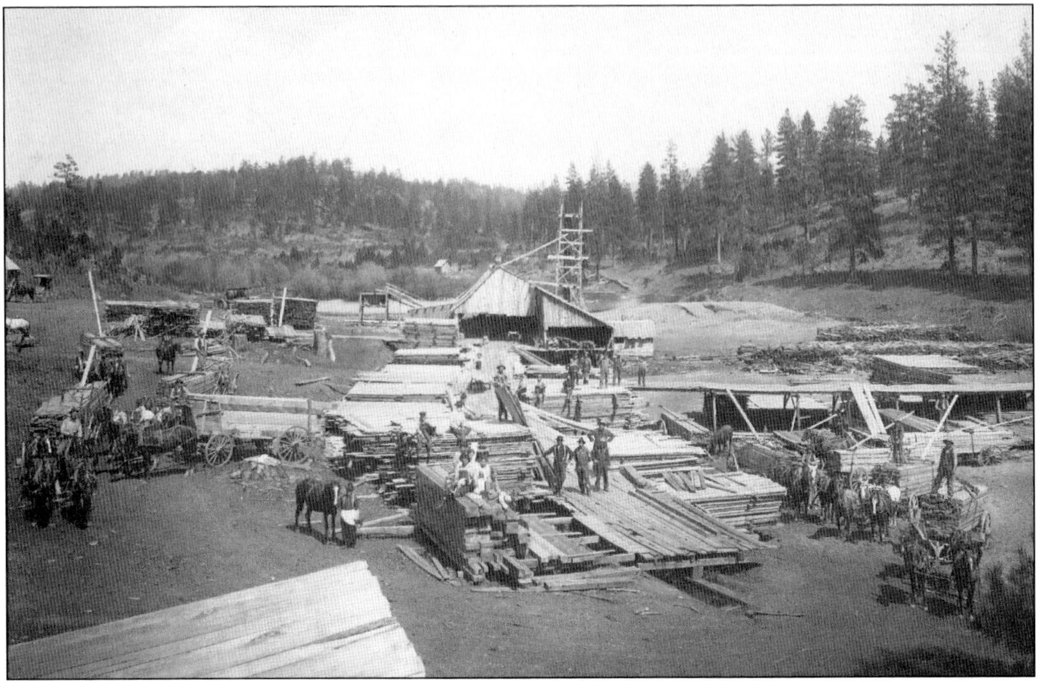

The Hawkins Brothers Mill on Ochoco Creek was built at the mouth of Duncan Creek about 1906. This was one of the first mills on upper Ochoco Creek and was a busy enterprise, providing lumber for numerous homestead houses and mining operations. A variety of activities are being conducted in this photograph, including loading of wagons with lumber. James and William Hawkins operated several mills in central Oregon in various locations.

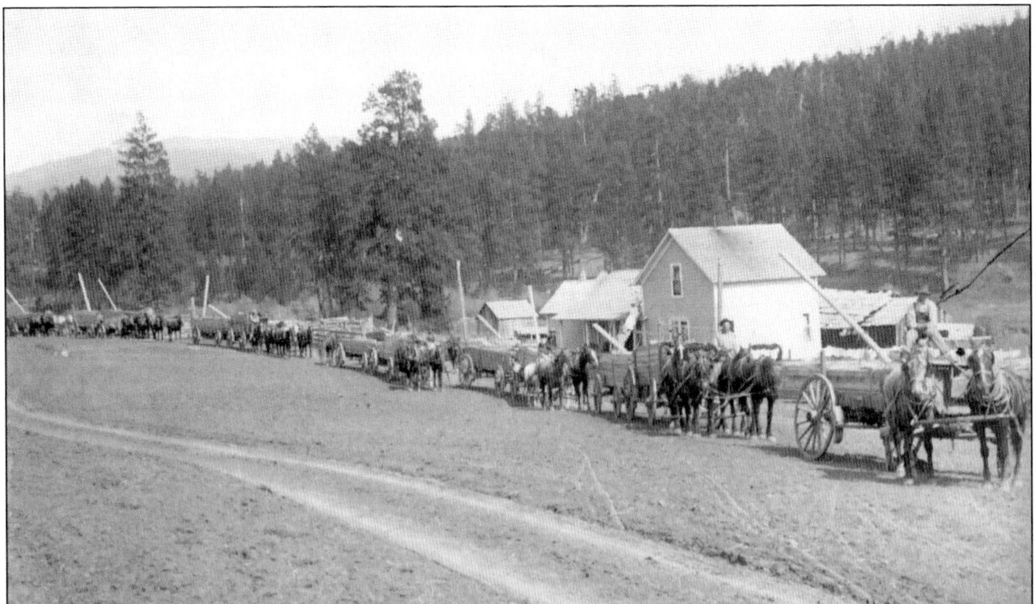

Several wagonloads of lumber are being transported by horse-drawn wagons down Ochoco Creek from the Hawkins Brothers Mill in 1905. The wagons are in front of the Isaac "Ike" Blevins Ranch. This was an unusually large delivery of lumber.

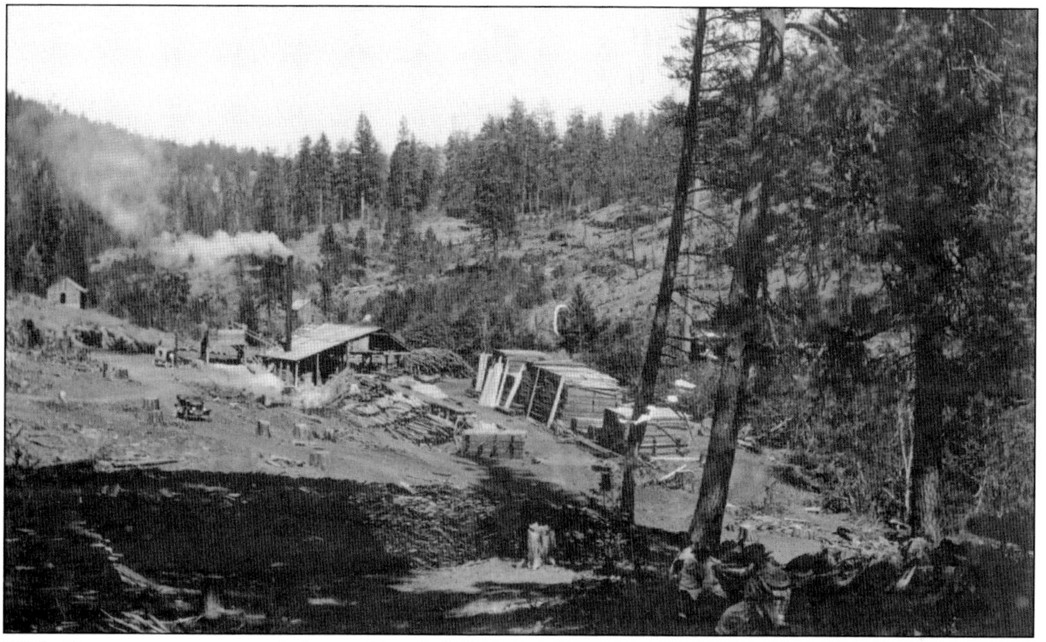

Walt Demaris constructed this mill on McKay Creek about 1910. He operated a number of mills at various times on McKay Creek and Allen Creek. At least two of his mills burned down. He later partnered with Ernest McKenzie in a mill operation on McKay Creek. The mill ceased operations in the mid-1920s.

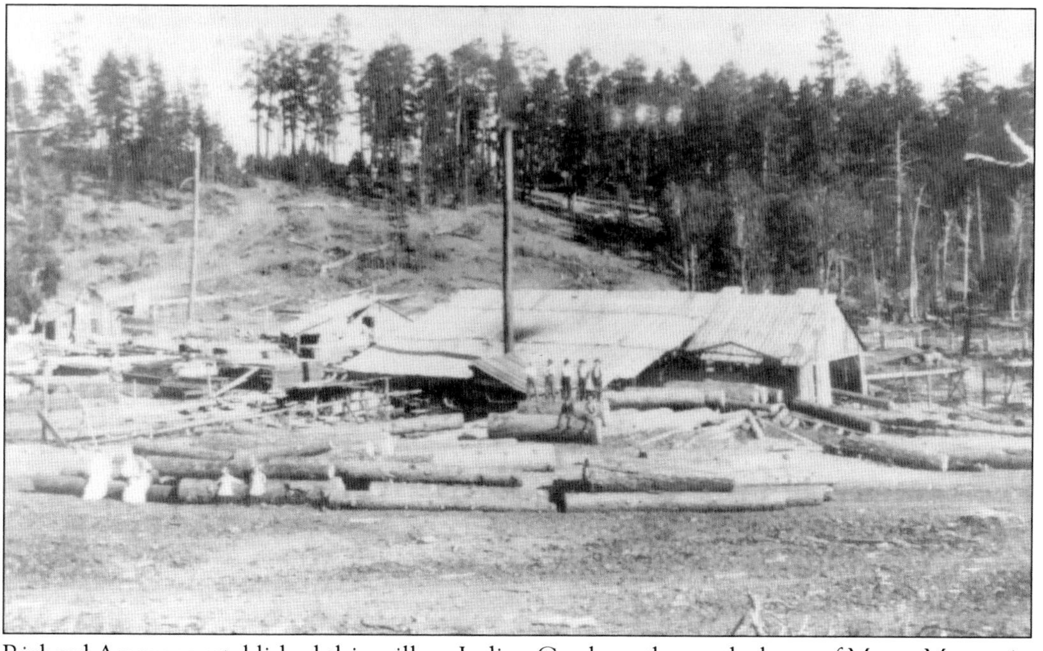

Richard Ammons established this mill on Indian Creek on the south slopes of Maury Mountain about 1912. He had come to central Oregon and worked for the Hawkins Brothers Mill. He married Nora Birdsong and partnered with his father-in-law, William Birdsong, in mill operations until operating his own mill at this site. It provided lumber for homesteaders who settled to the south of the Maury Mountains. He later sold the mill.

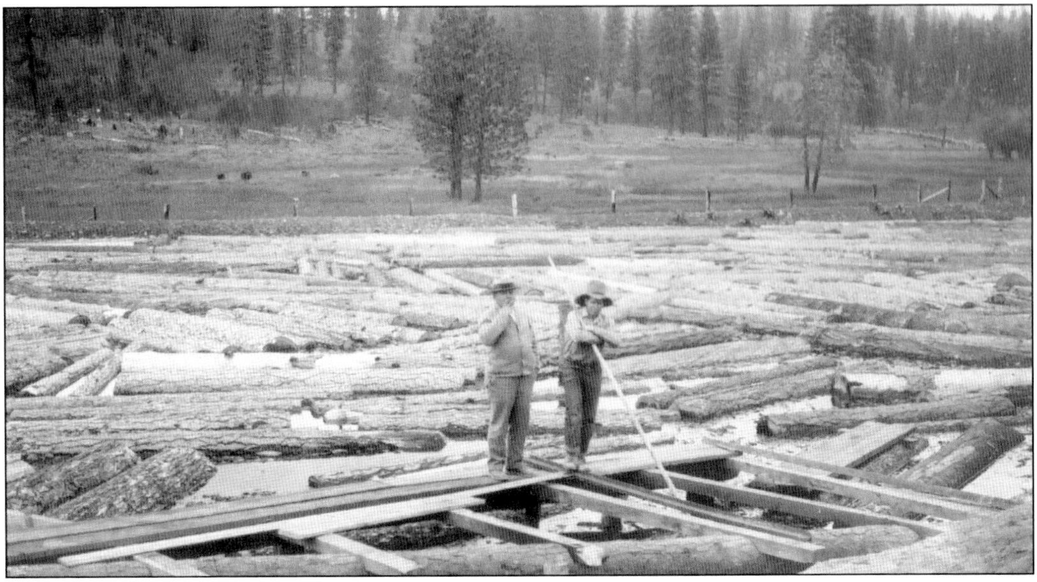

C.W. Woodruf (left) and Lain Smith (right) are standing on a log in the millpond at the Smith Brothers Mill on Ochoco Creek about 1929. Alonzo "Lon" and Thomas "Tom" Smith owned this mill and had operated the mill at various other locations. Woodruf was one of the early managers of the City of Prineville Railroad, and Lain Smith was the brother of Tom and Lon.

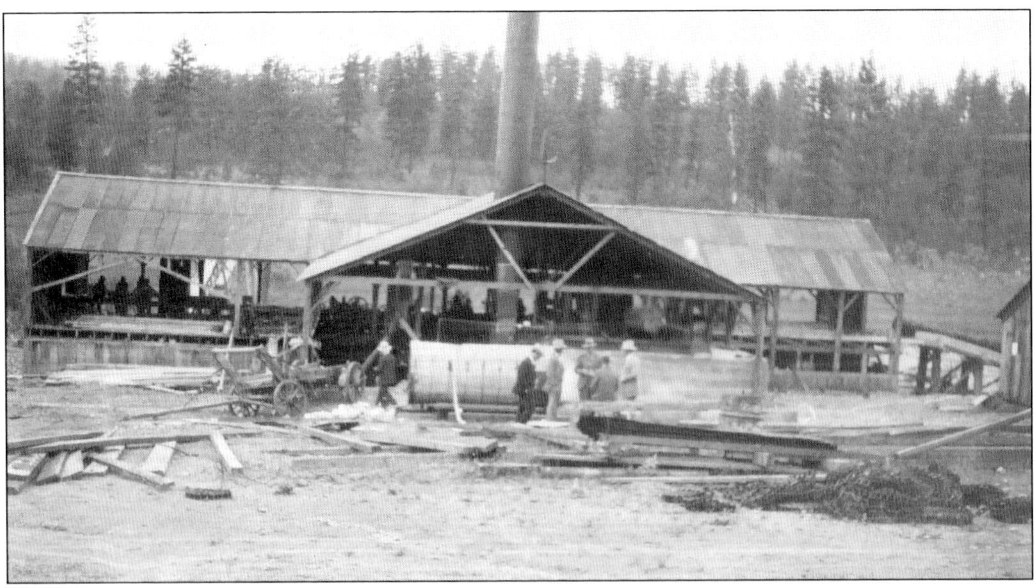

This is the Smith Brothers Mill on Ochoco Creek about 1929. The mill operated from 1928 until 1935. It utilized both private and federal timber for its milling operations. One of the first federal timber sales was to the Smith Brothers Mill. The mill was located about two miles west of Ochoco Ranger Station. Remnants of the old mill are still visible along the old Ochoco Highway.

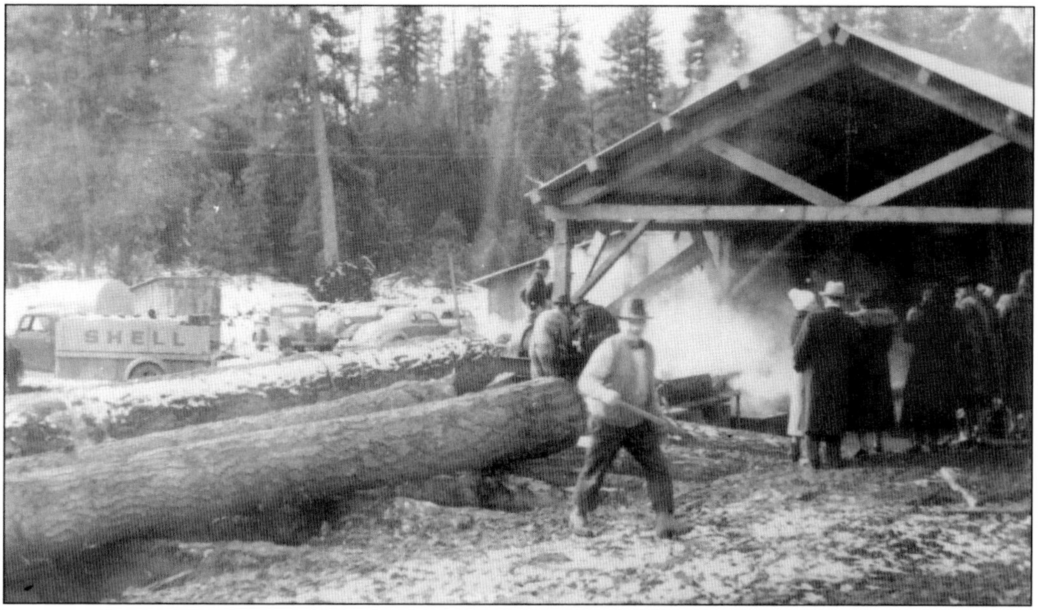

Large mills did not arrive in Crook County until the late 1930s. One of the early large mill operations was Alexander-Yawkey. It was a Midwest-based company that had purchased large tracts of timber in the forested mountains north of Prineville. Pictured here is the first day of operation of a mill the company had built on upper McKay Creek in 1937. A planing mill had been constructed in Prineville that later became a major mill operation.

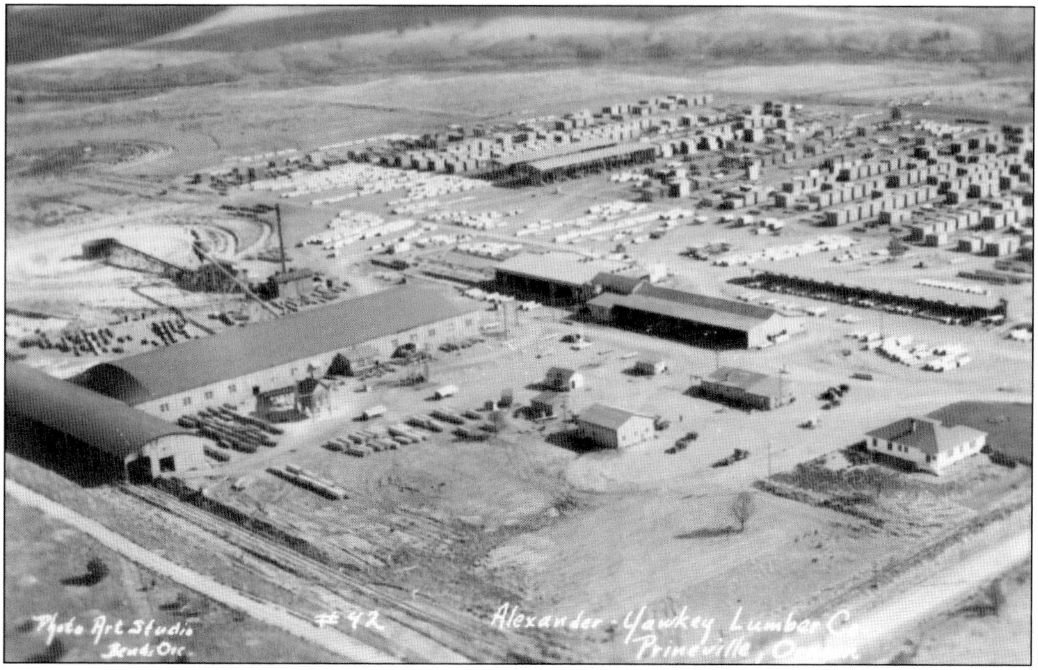

This is an aerial view of Alexander-Yawkey Mill just north of Prineville in 1945. The mill became one of the largest in Prineville and operated on three eight-hour shifts. Lumber was processed, dried in kilns, and then shipped out by rail on the City of Prineville Railroad. The mill operated until the company depleted its own timber supply and closed operations in 1959.

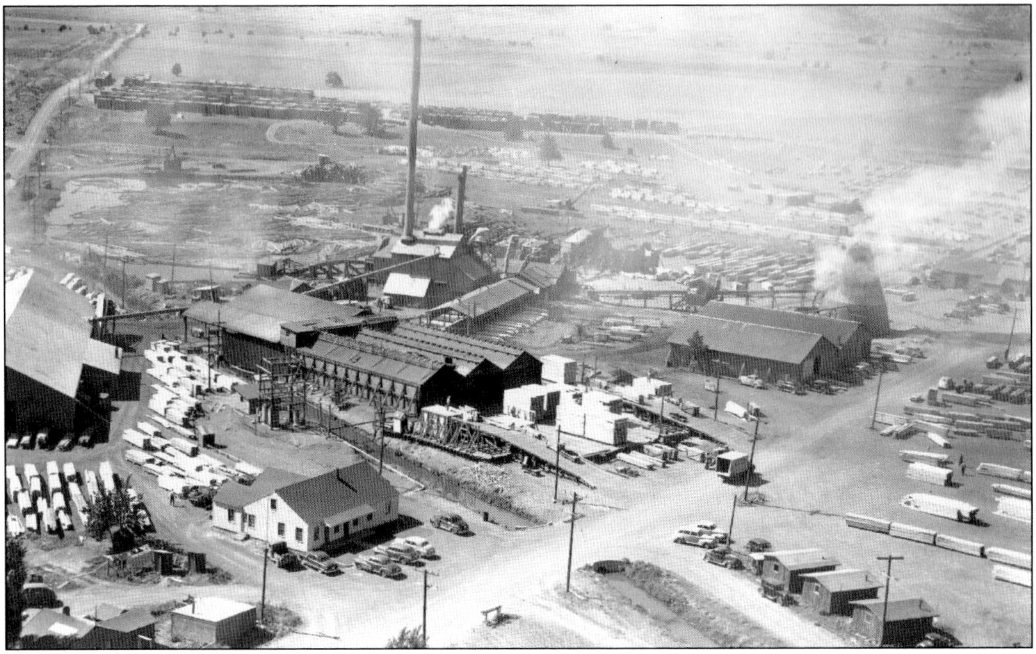

This is an aerial view of Pine Products Mill about four miles northwest of Prineville. The mill was originally started by the Davidson Brothers in 1925 but ceased operations during the Great Depression. W.J. "Pop" Forsythe and Howard Crawford reopened the mill in 1935, but it burned the following year. They rebuilt it and added a molding plant. The mill ceased operations in 1992.

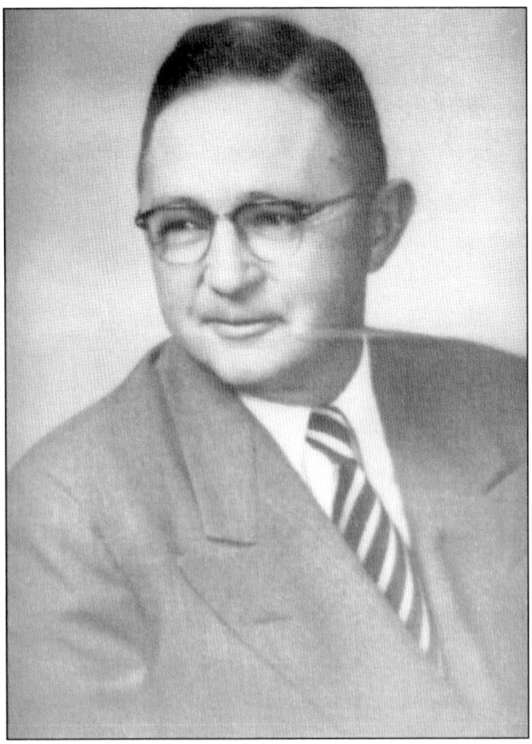

Ward Rhoden took over management of Pine Products Mill. He developed it into one of the leading mills in Prineville. Rhoden was active in local affairs and was a strong supporter of athletics. Eventually, his son Jack took over management of the mill.

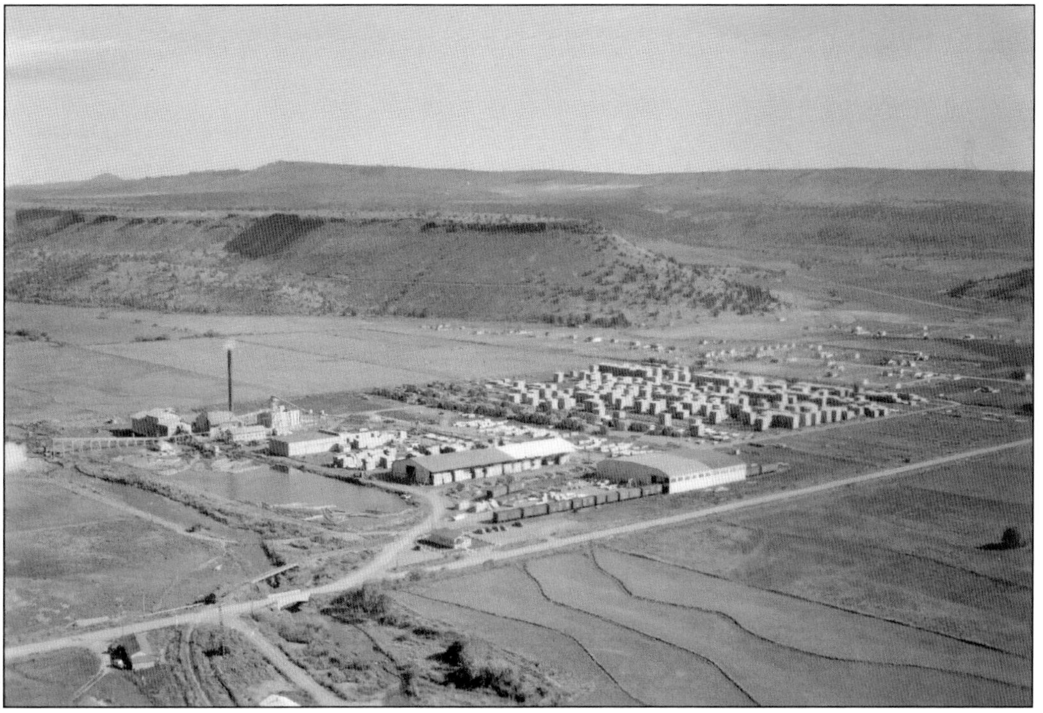

This is an aerial view of Ochoco Lumber Company just southeast of Prineville in 1949. The company built the mill in 1938 with machinery obtained from a mill in Sand Point, Idaho. The company managed its own timberlands as well as purchased federal timber to supply the mill. It was the last major mill to operate in Prineville and ceased operating in 2001, but the Ochoco Lumber Company continues to manage company-owned lands.

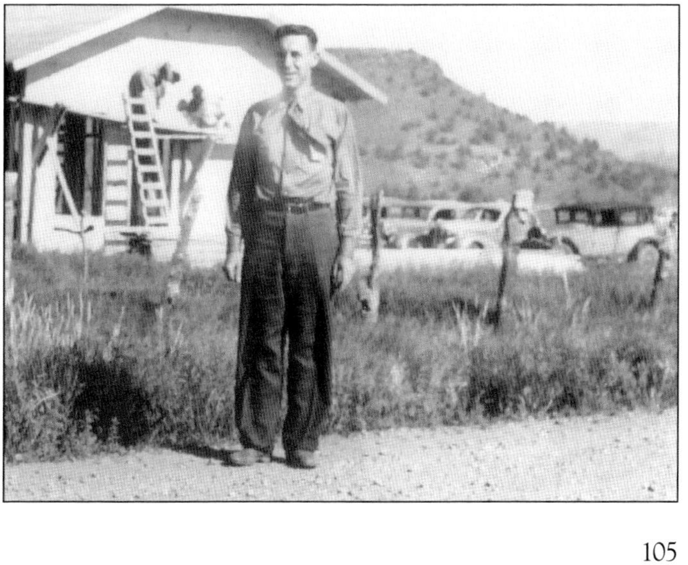

Stuart Shelk started as an office manager for Ochoco Lumber in 1938. He was promoted to general manager in 1944. He successfully managed the mill over the next 30 years and made it one of the most profitable and productive in the Northwest. He retired in 1976, and his son John took over management of the mill. A declining federal timber supply and difficult economic times resulted in the mill closing in 2001.

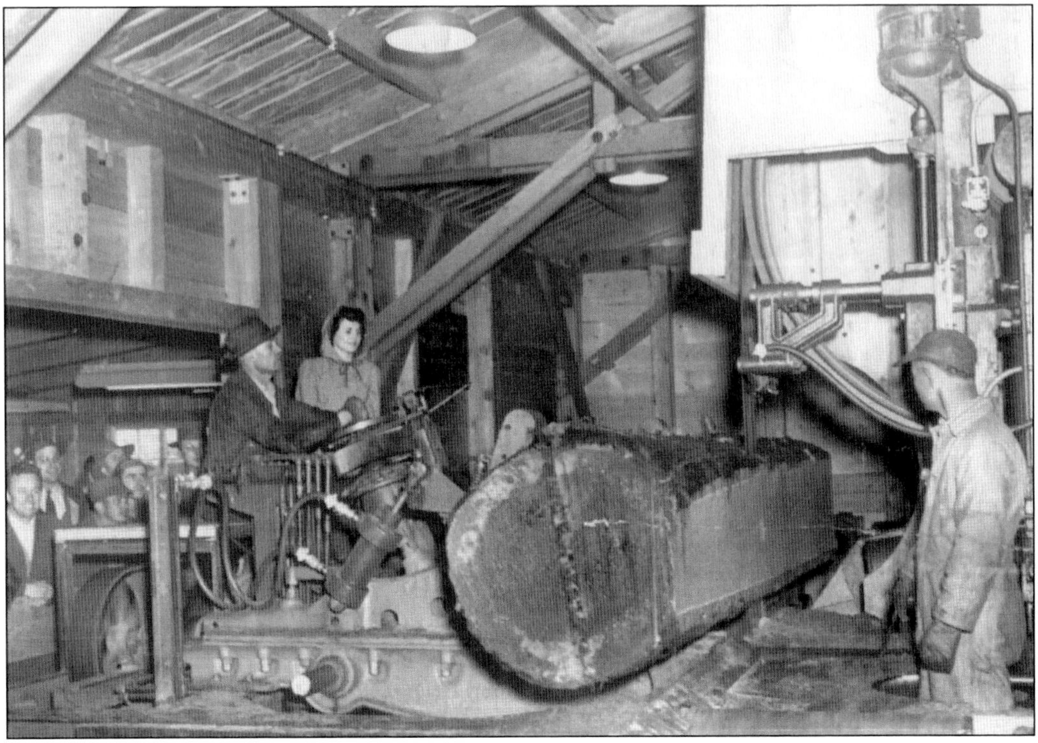

Hudspeth Sawmill celebrated opening day in Prineville in 1947. Standing on the head rig is Floreine Hudspeth, the wife of John Hudspeth, who can be seen at lower left. He and his brothers Claude and Fred established the mill, which soon became one of the largest lumber suppliers in the region. The mill operated until the late 1980s.

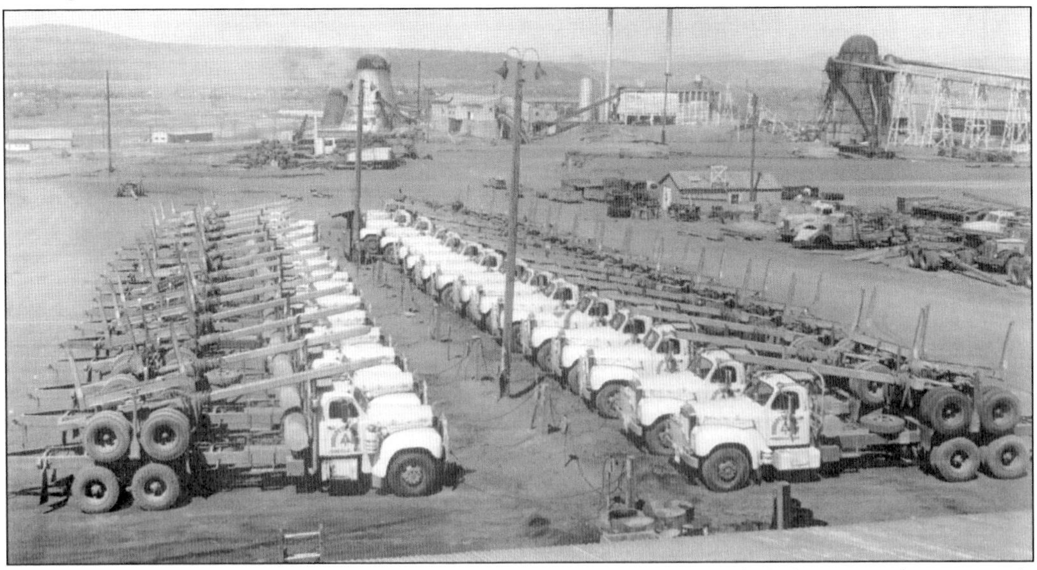

Hudspeth Pine Inc. had a large network of logging operations that included contract logging with small operators as well as its own operations. The company had a large fleet of logging trucks, as seen in this 1959 photograph of trucks lined up at the truck yard at the mill. It was common to see the powder-blue log trucks passing through the streets of Prineville en route to the mill.

Five

Government Administration

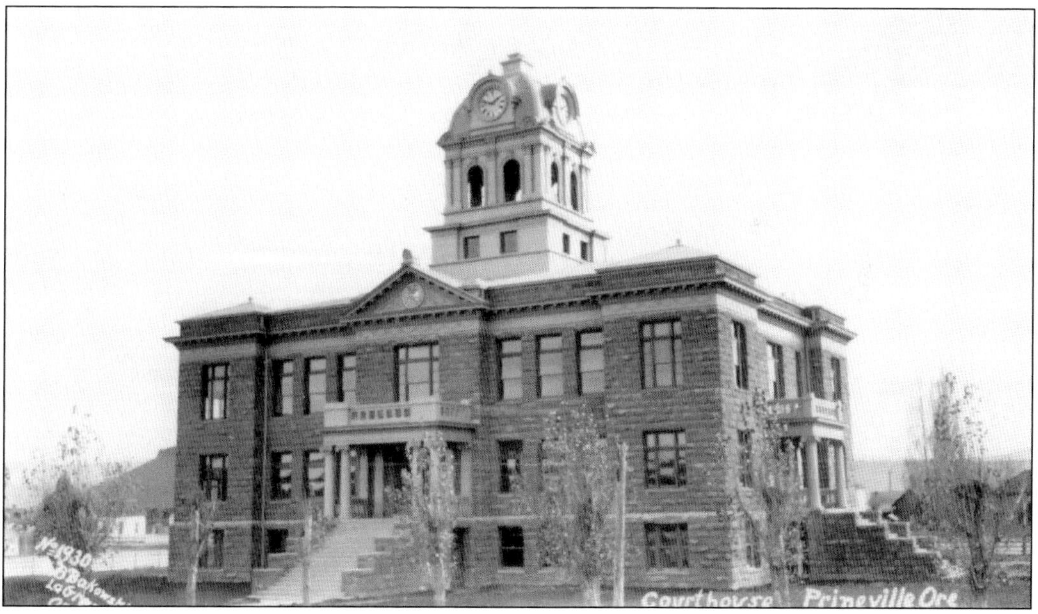

It was determined that Crook County needed a new courthouse in 1908. Plans for a grand stone building were developed, and after the original contractor was dismissed, local builder John Shipp constructed the three-story building with a clock tower. The original building had stairwells on three sides. Two of the stairwells were removed in a remodel in 1941. The building was completed in 1909. It became the center of county government but also created tension among outlying communities such as Madras, Redmond and Bend. Townspeople protested that Prineville had built a "Taj Mahal" at the expense of their communities; the end result was to create new counties out of Crook County.

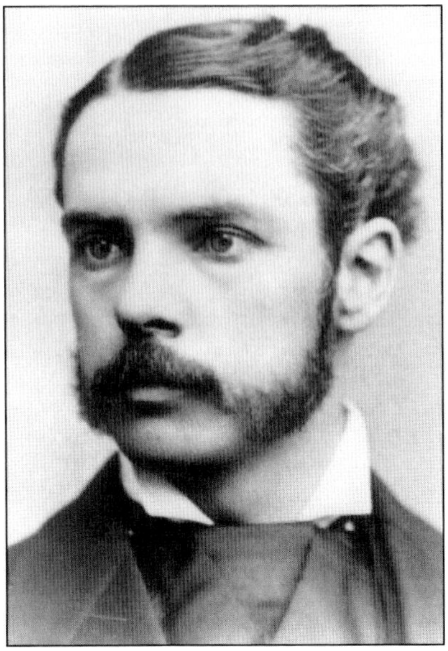 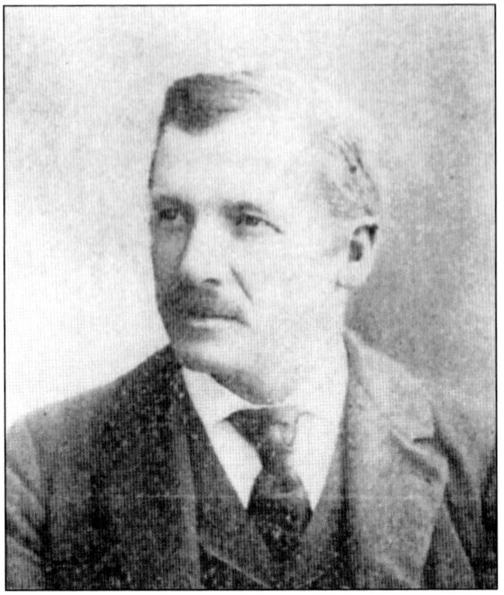

The first election for newly created Crook County was held in 1884. Prior to that time, the Oregon governor appointed officials to serve in county political positions. The first appointed county judge was George Thompson, a Hay Creek rancher. The first elected county judge was F.A. McDonald (left). The first elected county clerk was Almond Chester Palmer (right). Palmer was also an editor of the *Deschutes Echo* newspaper. These two men were important in the development of early county government.

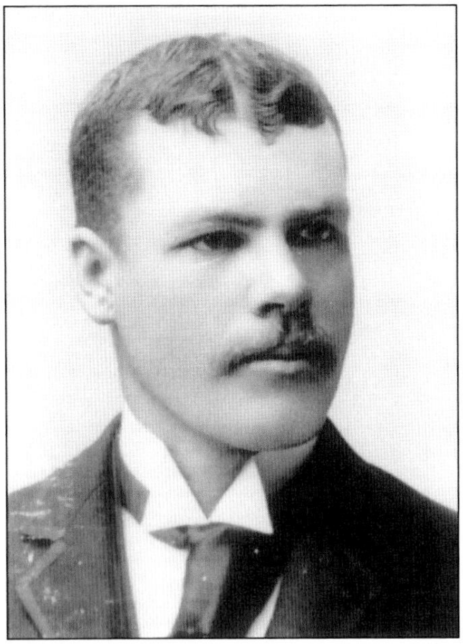 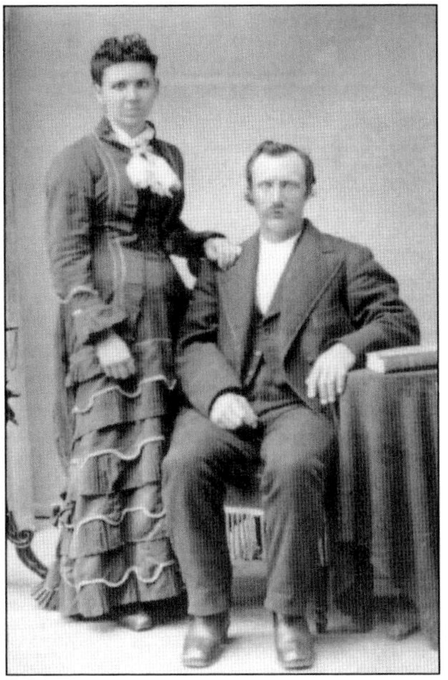

Charles Cartwright (left) was one of the first appointed county commissioners in 1882 when the county was first created. He was a ranch owner at Hay Creek Ranch, which was about 30 miles north of Prineville. James Garrett (right) was one of the first elected county commissioners in 1884. He is pictured with his wife, Mary Ellen. He also was a rancher in the Hay Creek vicinity. Early county government officials had a difficult task of organizing and financing county activities. One of their main objectives was to remove the use of vigilante justice.

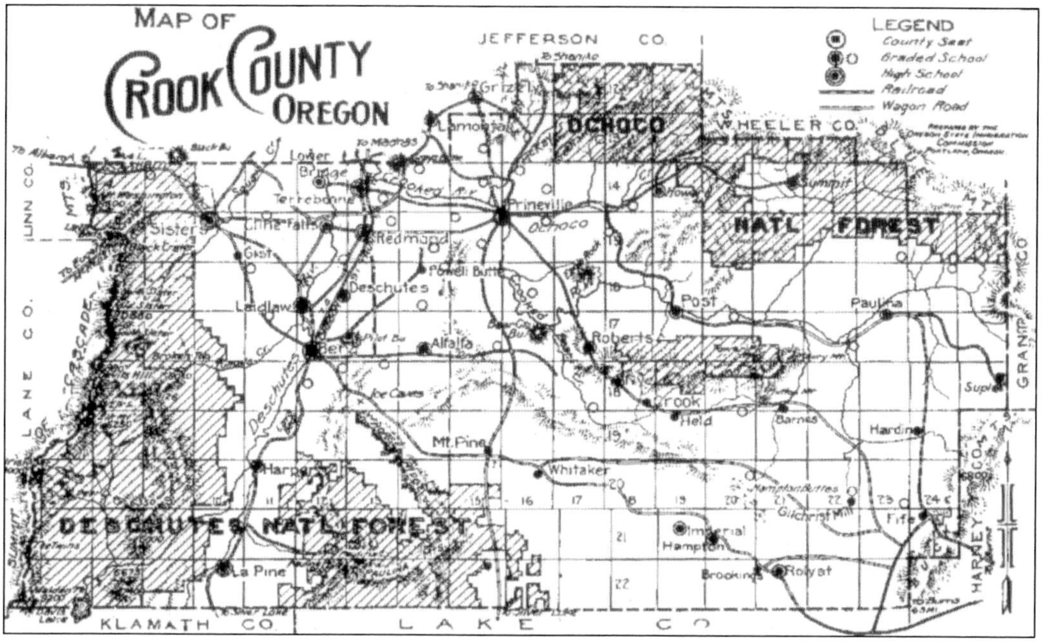

The residents of northern Crook County petitioned to have a new county created from Crook County in 1914. As a result, an election was held, and Jefferson County was created from Crook County. This is a map of Crook County in 1915. The county boundaries only remained in this configuration for one year as Deschutes County was created from Crook County in 1916.

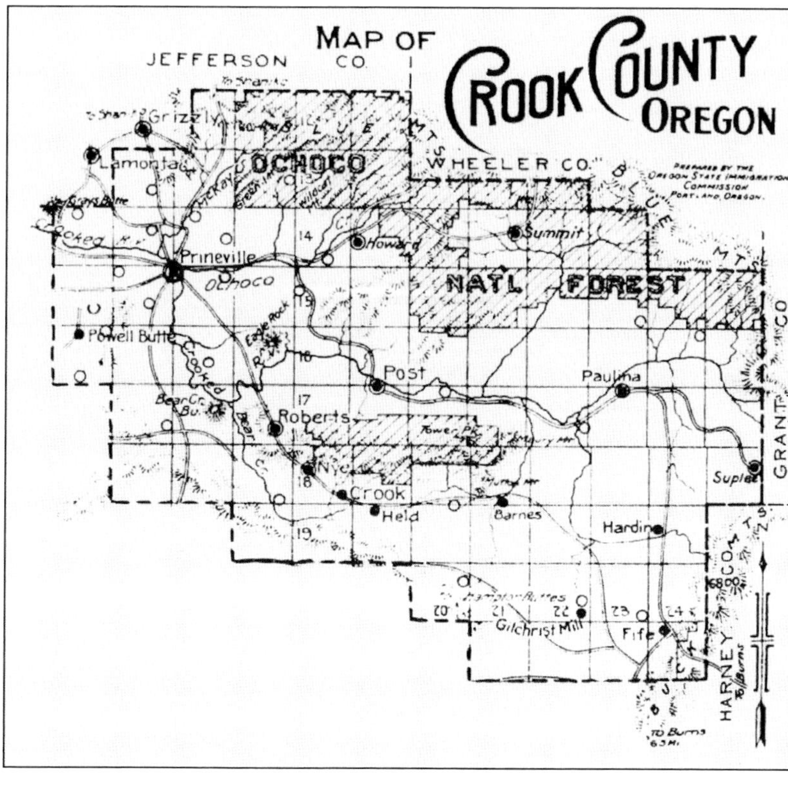

This is a map of Crook County in 1918 shortly after the creation of Deschutes County in 1916. The once large county was reduced to its current boundaries. Deschutes County was the last county to be created in Oregon. Note that the Ochoco National Forest constitutes a significant portion of the county.

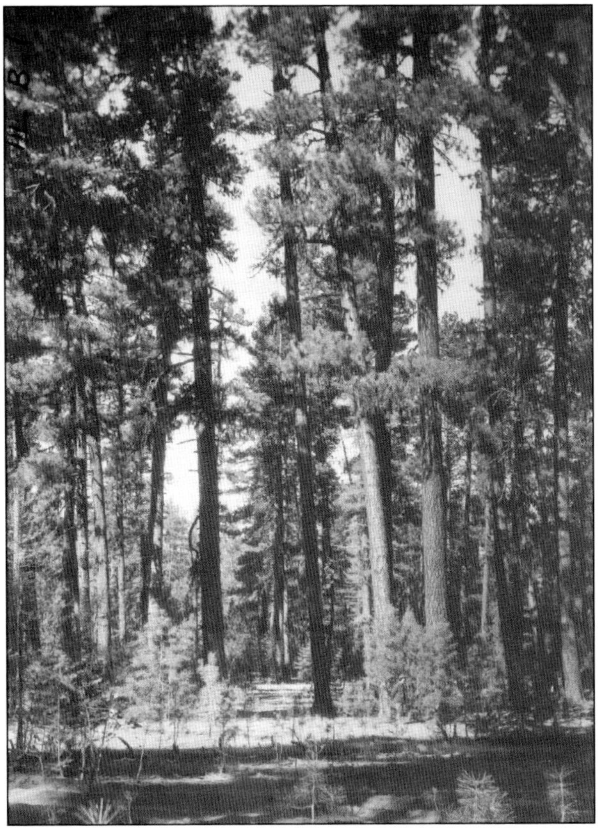

Crook County has large reserves of ponderosa pine forest. This is a photograph showing the large pine stands of the forested area. The forested lands remained in federal government ownership and were mostly used for grazing the lush grasses under the pine canopies in the early years. The Ochoco National Forest was established in 1911 and headquartered in Prineville. It had previously been part of the Deschutes National Forest, which also was headquartered in Prineville.

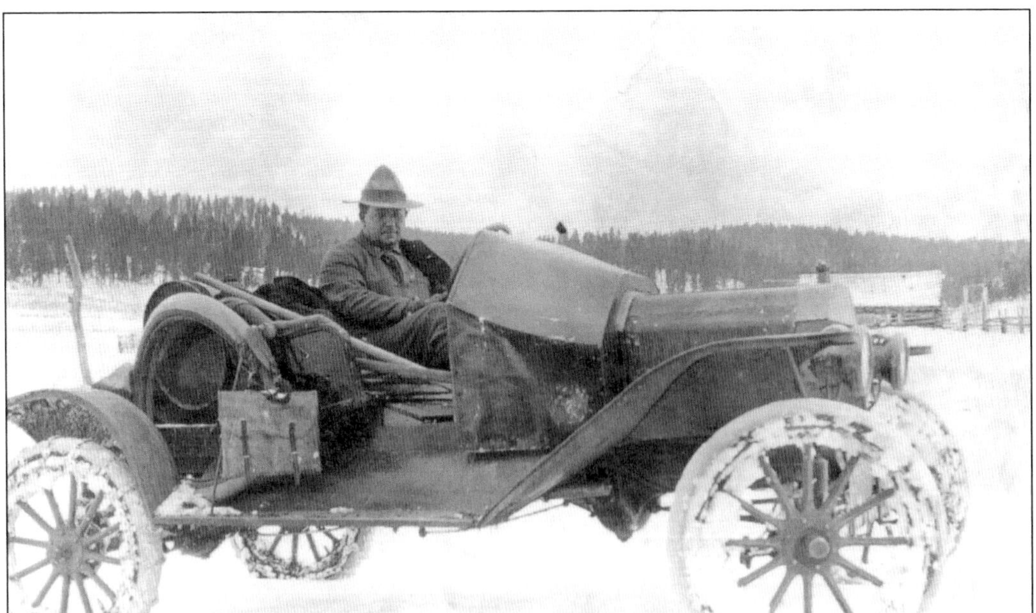

One of the early forest supervisors of the Ochoco National Forest was Homer Ross. He is seen here in an early automobile that he has outfitted with a fire pump unit. This was one of the first motorized firefighting units utilized by the Forest Service.

Cyrus "Cy" Bingham was an early forest ranger on the Ochoco National Forest. He had worked in several units of the Forest Service prior to working for the Ochoco forest. He was a very large man at six feet, five inches tall and weighing over 300 pounds. He later became the forest supervisor of the Malheur National Forest and a sheriff of Malheur County. Bingham Prairie north of Prineville is named for him.

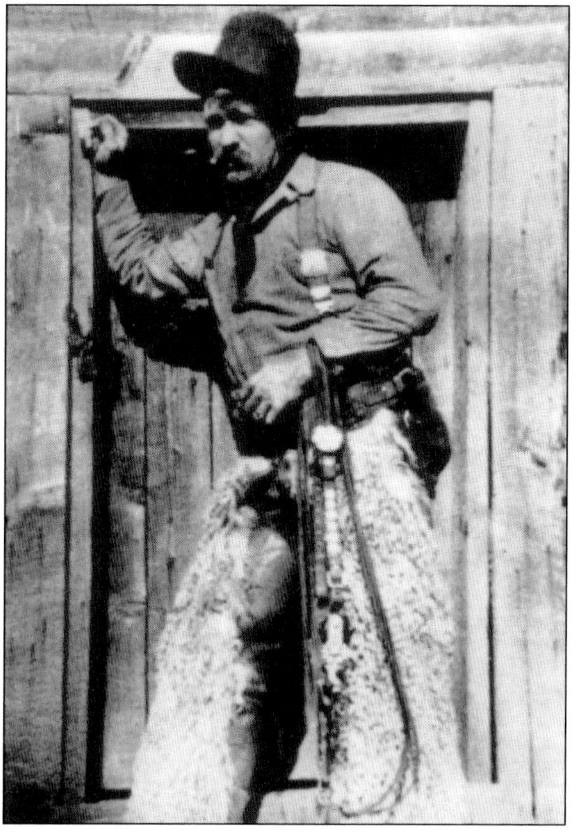

Remote ranger stations were established in the Ochoco National Forest to administer public lands. This is Divide Ranger Station, located on the mountain summit about 20 miles north of Prineville, in 1914. Early rangers utilized stations while monitoring grazing on the forest and conducting daily actives. Usually, the stations were about a one-day horse ride from each other.

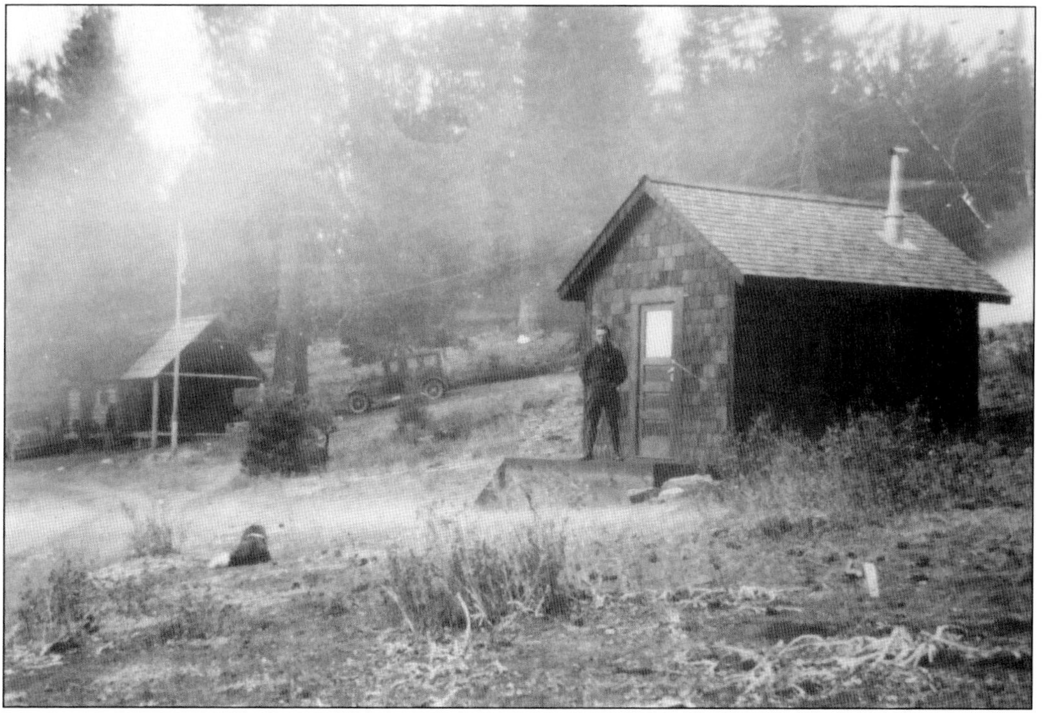

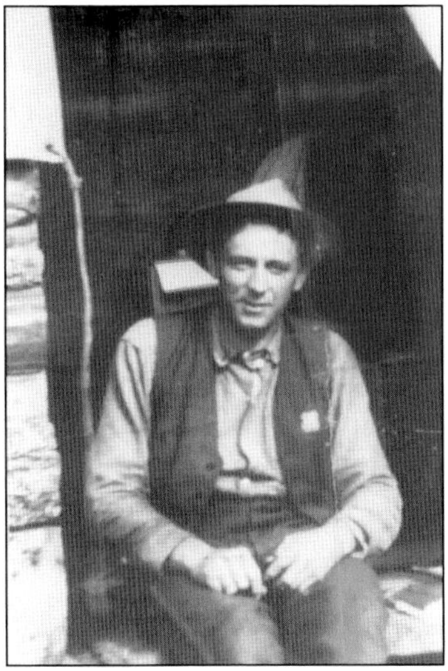

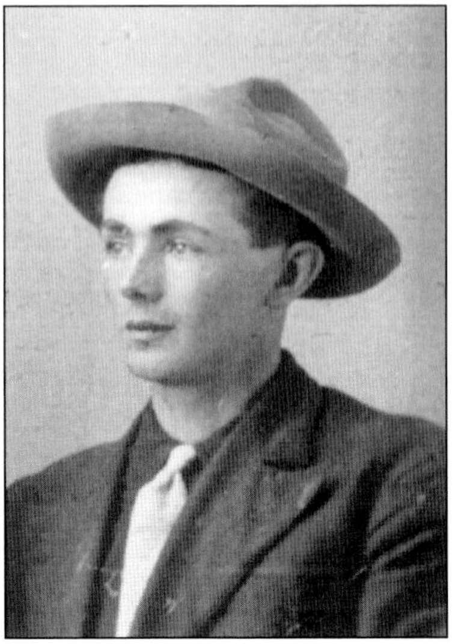

Clyde C. Hon (left) was an early forest ranger at Ochoco Ranger Station, located about 25 miles east of Prineville. Many of the early rangers operated ranches near the forest and were hired because of their knowledge of local ranchers and residents. Hon had a ranch on upper Ochoco Creek. Charles Congleton (right) was the first ranger at Rager Ranger Station, about 70 miles east of Prineville. He later established a ranch near the community of Paulina. Early rangers were often required to ride the forest range, and work included installing phone lines and fighting fire in addition to monitoring grazing permits.

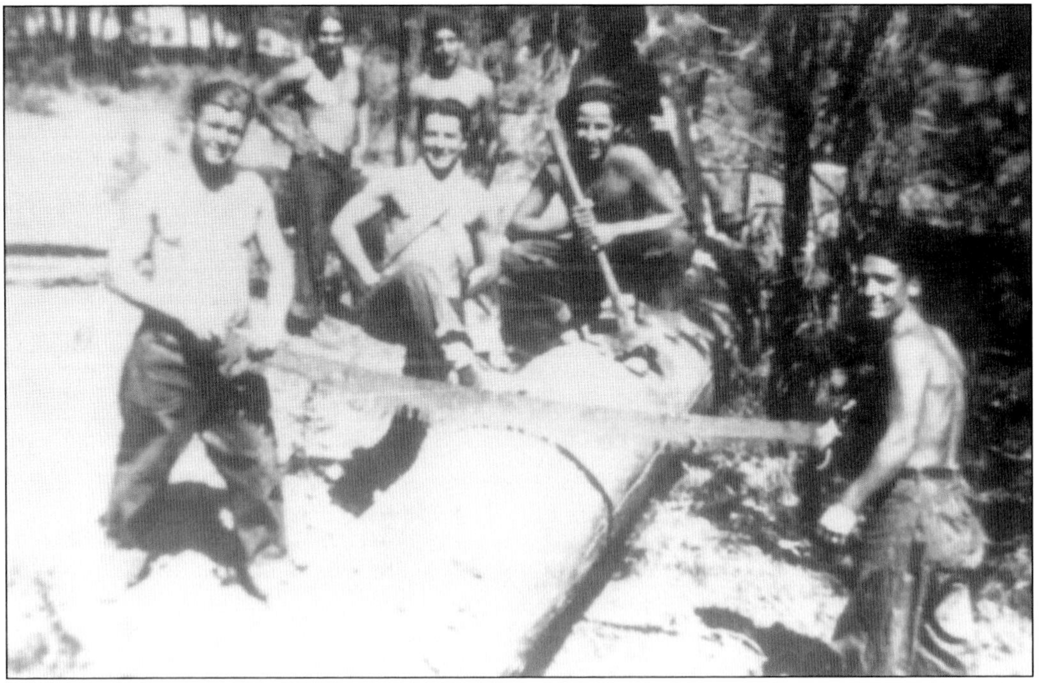

During the Great Depression, Civilian Conservation Corps (CCC) camps were established in the Ochoco National Forest. One of the main camps was located at Ochoco Ranger Station and was known as Camp Mill Creek. Young men from all over the nation were hired to do nature conservation work. This is a group of CCC men working at Camp Mill Creek in 1935.

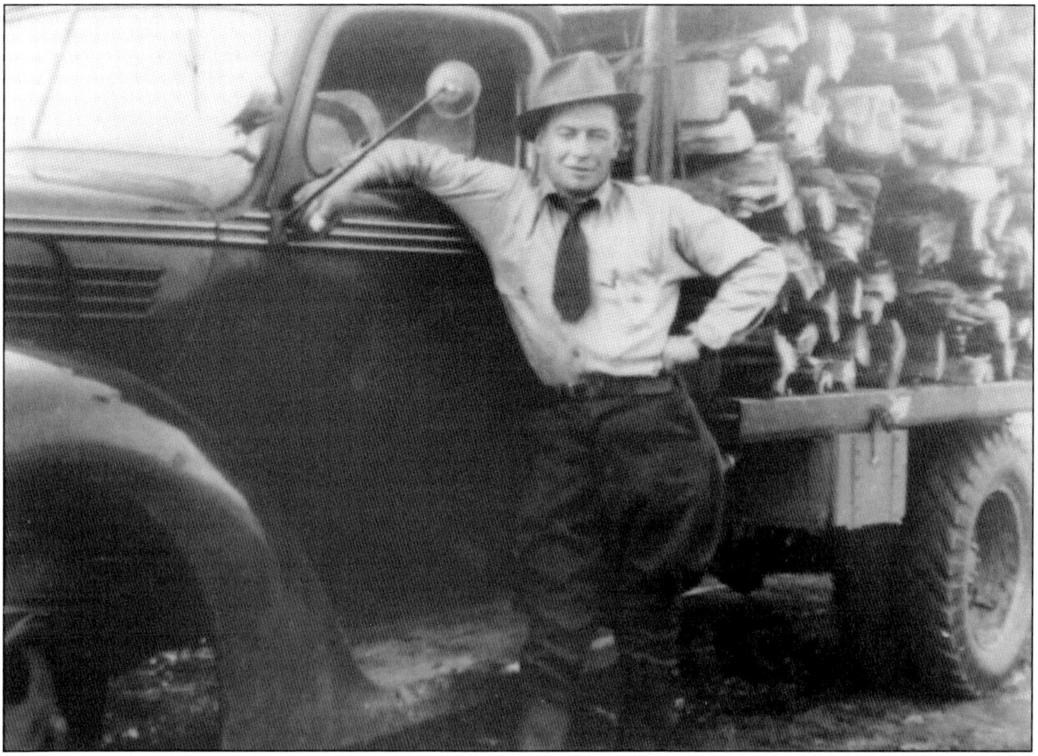

Public rangelands in Crook County were first administered by the General Land Office and then managed by the Taylor Grazing Act. This agency later became the Bureau of Land Management (BLM). The BLM administers large tracts of federal rangelands in the county with Prineville District's headquarters located in Prineville. Joe Urbanek, shown in this 1940 photograph, started work for the Taylor Grazing Act lands when they were first administered locally. He worked for the government for over 45 years, concluding his career on the Prineville District of the BLM.

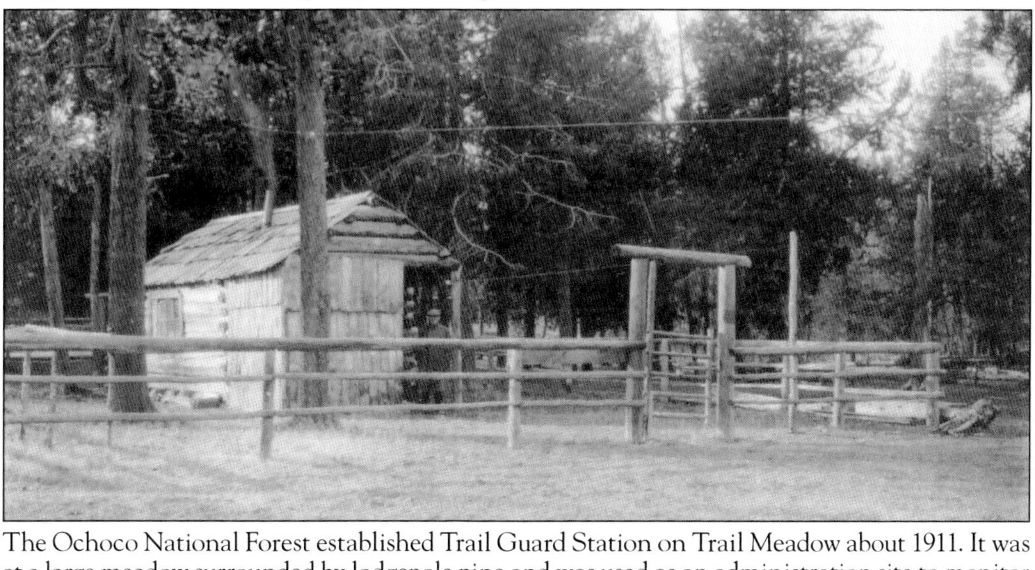

The Ochoco National Forest established Trail Guard Station on Trail Meadow about 1911. It was at a large meadow surrounded by lodgepole pine and was used as an administration site to monitor sheep on the upper ranges of the forest. It was only occupied from late spring until mid-fall.

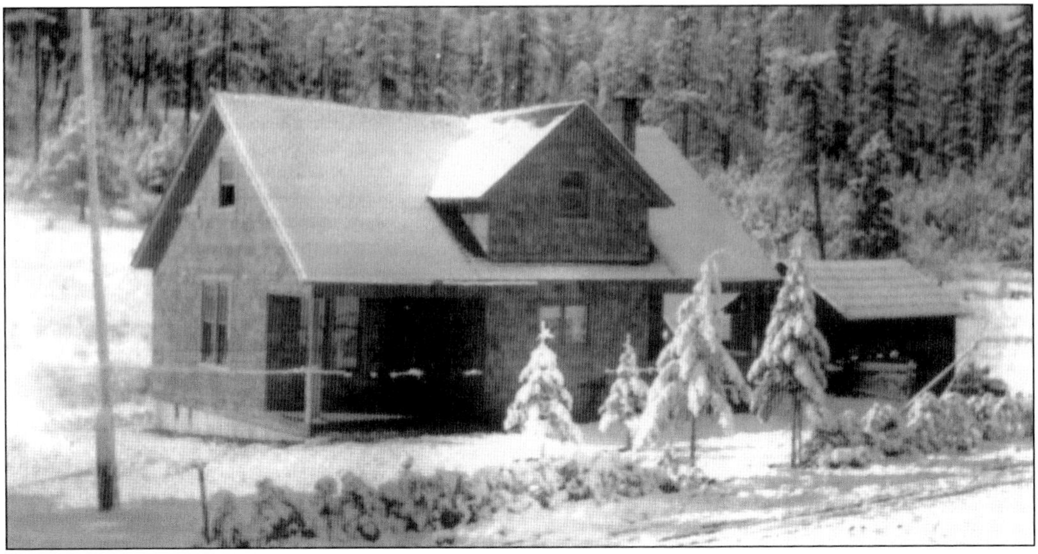

Maury Ranger Station was established on Maury Creek on the northeast end of Maury Mountain in the 1920s. This is a later building that became the main station on the Maury Mountains. It was removed in the 1950s.

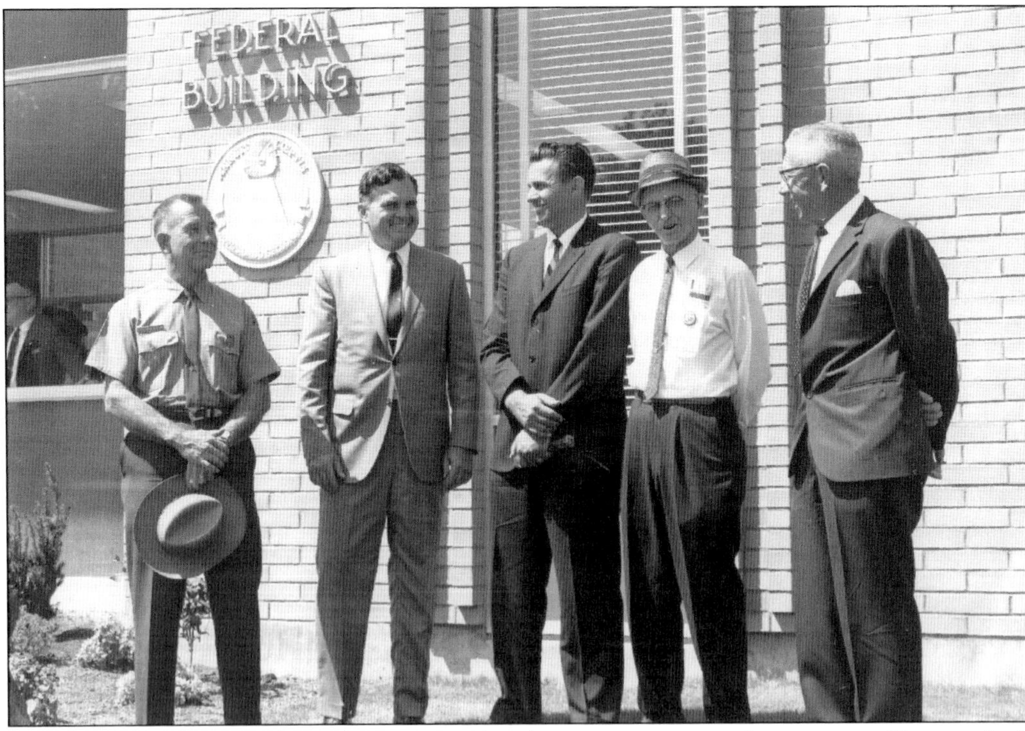

The post office has long been the center of local communications. A new post office was built in Prineville in 1966. The new federal building also housed the headquarters of the Ochoco National Forest. This photograph was taken at the dedication of the new post office and federal building. From left to right are Les Sullivan, Ochoco National Forest supervisor; Al Ullman, US congressman; Russ Vernon, Prineville mayor; Tex King, Crook County sheriff; and Ervin Grimes, Crook County judge.

Six

SOCIAL DEVELOPMENT

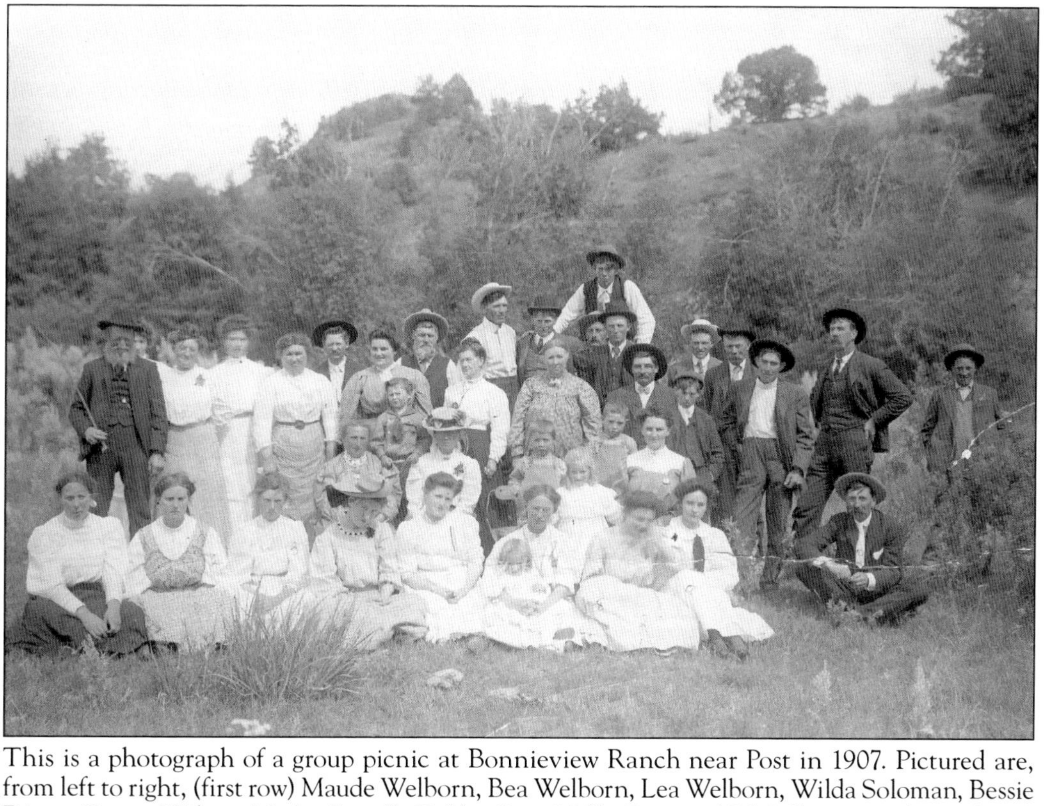

This is a photograph of a group picnic at Bonnieview Ranch near Post in 1907. Pictured are, from left to right, (first row) Maude Welborn, Bea Welborn, Lea Welborn, Wilda Soloman, Bessie Dinge, Grayce Wilson, Madge Rowell, Goldie Gray, Nellie Post, and Ed Gillenwater; (second row) Rebecca Ann Gray, Ida Wilson, Jack Welborn, John Welborn, Blanche Rowell, and Ollie Keene; (third row) Joseph Hunsaker, Pearl Gray Rowell, Lavicy Knox, Nora Smead, Jessie Gray, Harold Gray, Lilly Knox, Ida Welborn, Billy Post, Roy Brummer, Joe Gibson, Edward "Bake" Knox, and Albert Wilson; (fourth row) unidentified, Hiram Smead, Sam Dinge, Dirwood Quackenbush, two unidentified, Bill Keene, Otto Gray, Floyd Rowell, and Henry Gray.

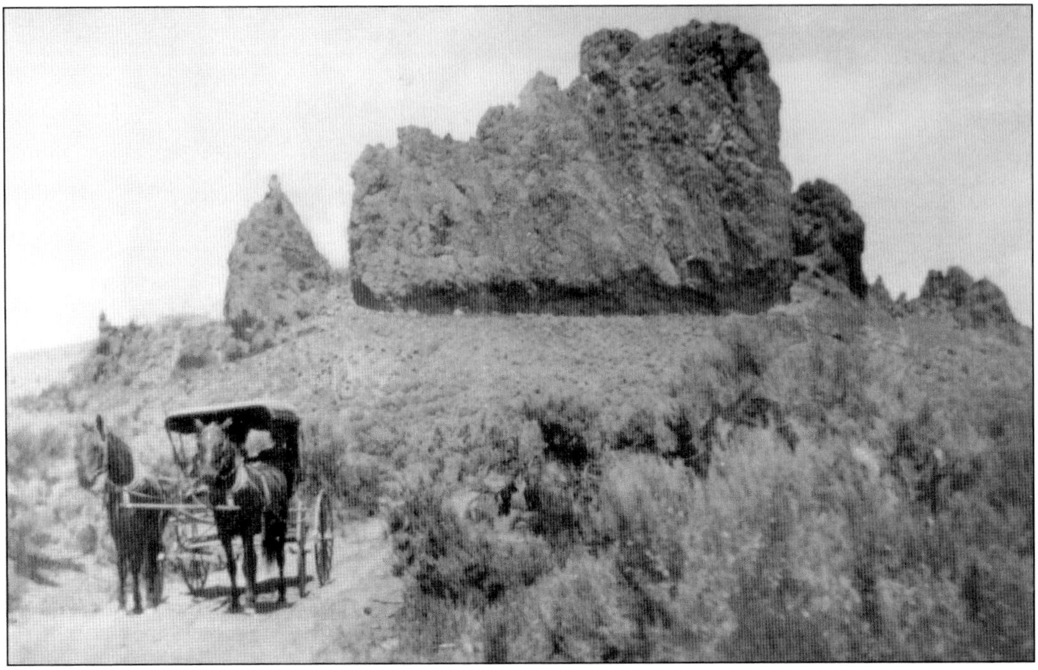

Homesteaders traveled this primitive dirt road down from Combs Flat to the Crooked River. This is a buggy with a prospective homesteader and a homestead finder traveling to view some potential land to file a claim on in 1911. Eagle Rock is in the background. Local entrepreneurs offered their expertise for a fee to help new settlers find a homestead site.

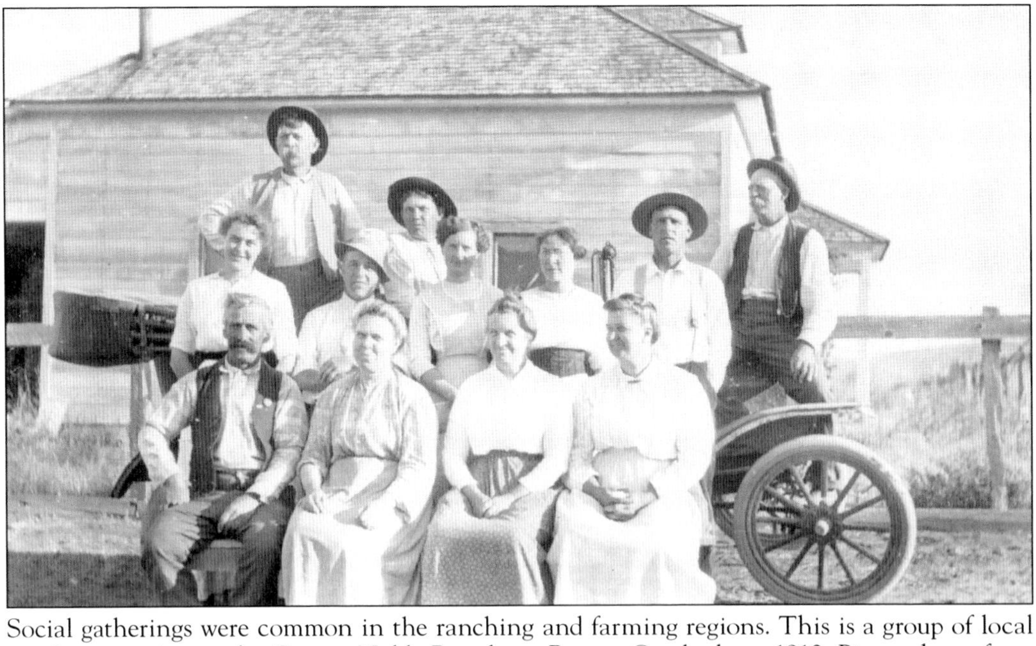

Social gatherings were common in the ranching and farming regions. This is a group of local ranchers meeting at the George Noble Ranch on Beaver Creek about 1910. Pictured are, from left to right, (first row) James Allyn, Sarah Noble Glenn Allyn, Martha Treichel, and Etta Noble; (second row) Varina Noble, two unidentified, Ollie Schwarzer, and John "Dutch" Schwarzer; (third row) Andrew Noble, Glenn Schwarzer, and George Noble.

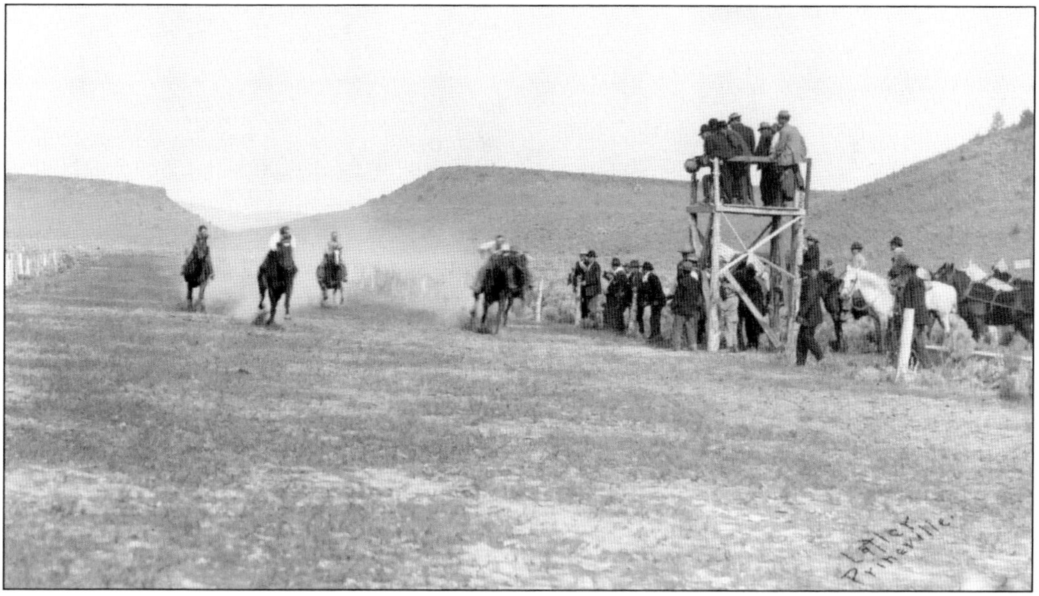

Pictured here is a horse race at Paulina in 1910. Horse racing was a very popular sport, and races were held in most small communities with wagers placed on competing horses. Local men owned the racehorses and entered them in various races, which were always well attended.

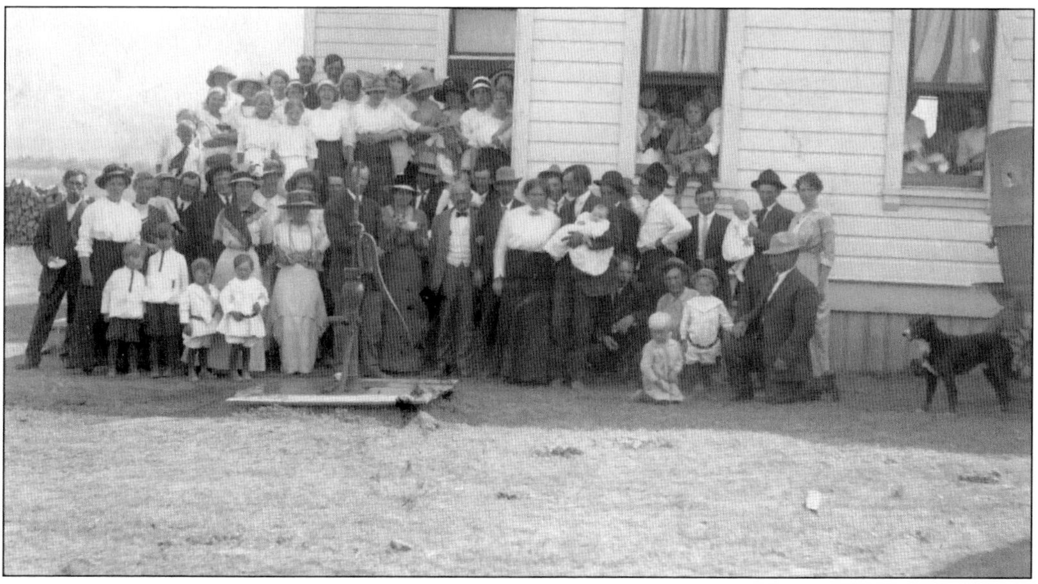

Church services in outlying communities and regions in the early settlement era were often held at rural schools, as the school building was a common meeting site. This is a church service at the Paulina School in 1913 with a large gathering for the Sunday sermon. Later, the Beaver Creek School was moved into town, and it currently serves as the church building in Paulina.

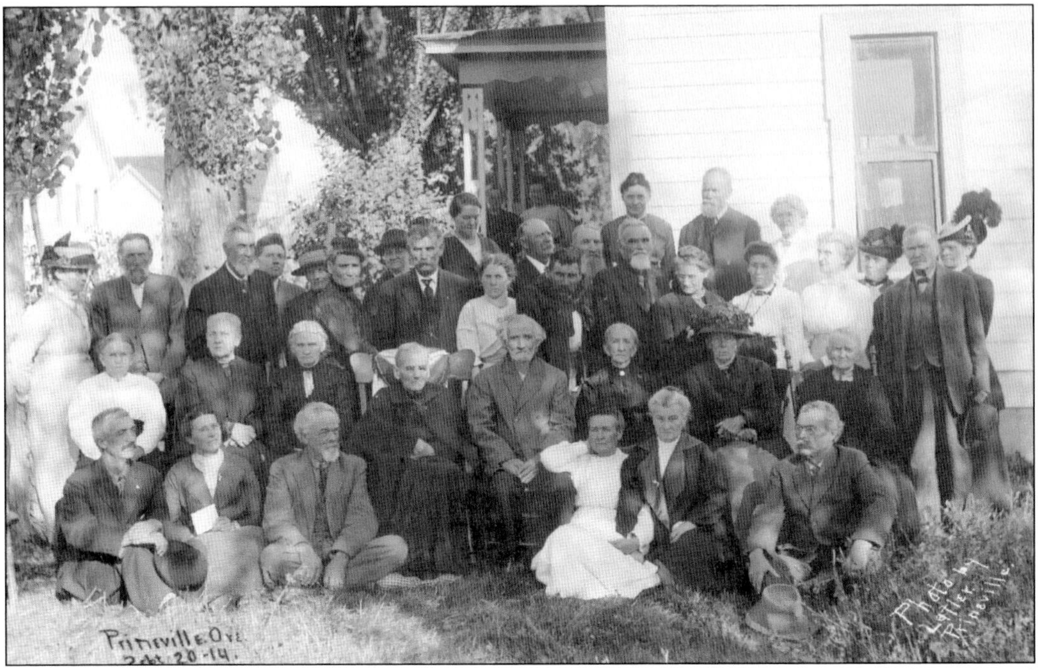

Early pioneers held periodic reunions to share memories and reminisce about the difficult and pleasant times of taming one of the last frontiers of Oregon. This is a pioneer reunion held at the Ewen Johnson home in Prineville in 1914. Those pictured are, from left to right, (first row) Oliver Powell, Ella Powell, Mark Powell, Aver Powell, Emma Street, and Jim Street; (second row) Thurza Belknap, Nancy Snodelry, Jane Powell, Nancy Johnson, Ewen Johnson, Elizabeth Bell, Lottie Elliott, and Sylvania Johnson; (third row) Libby Zell, Abe Zell, Straud Price, Tine Miller, Jake Johnson, Jennie Johnson, Jehu Johnson, Isaac Ketchum, Sarah Ketchum, Martha Dodson, America Crooks, and Joe Crooks; (fourth row) Pete Zell, Sarah Zell, Jack Summers, Ollie Stewart, Charles Elkins, W.A. Booth, Lucy Booth, George Millican, Ada Millican, Margaret LaFollette, and Emma Prose. Standing on the porch are Frances Stearns and Elvira Cyrus.

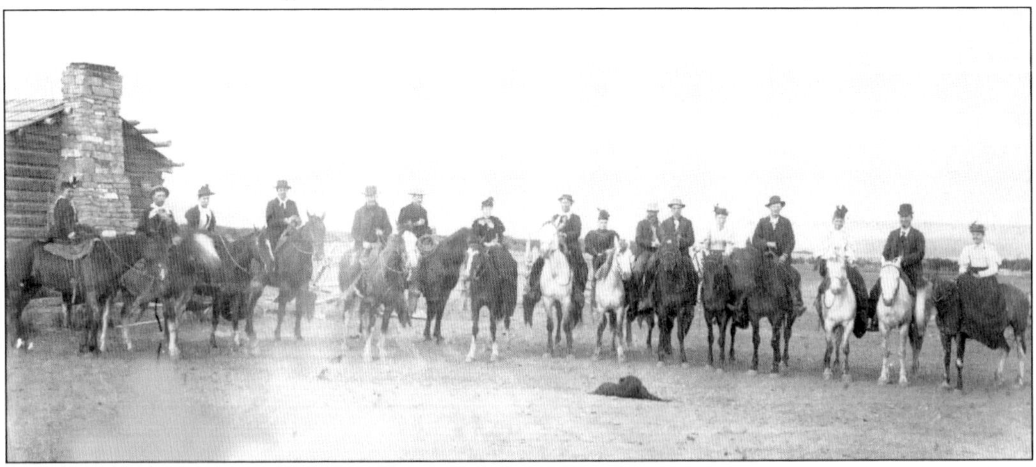

This is a gathering of local ranchers at the old Glenn Place between Post and Paulina about 1896. From left to right are Orla Faulkner, Grant Miller, Sally Hinton, Chester Claypool, Sam Clemmons, Billie Foster, T.D. Belcher, Henry Faulkner, Minnie Howe, Joe Lister, Fred Mauzey, Josie Brown, Ed Rannells, Eva Brown, Warren Brown, and Ollie Brown.

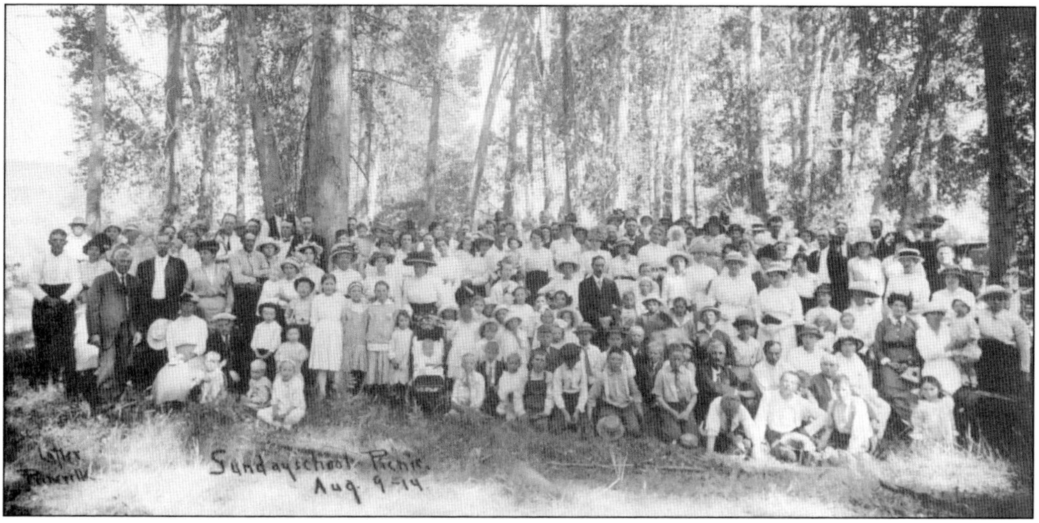

This is a gathering of local settlers on McKay Creek at a site known as Gulliford Grove in 1914. It is a Sunday school picnic. The site is a stand of cottonwood trees, at which a gazebo with a dance floor was constructed. Settlers from the surrounding area and from farther distances traveled to share good times. There is still a yearly gathering held at Gulliford Grove by descendants of early pioneer families.

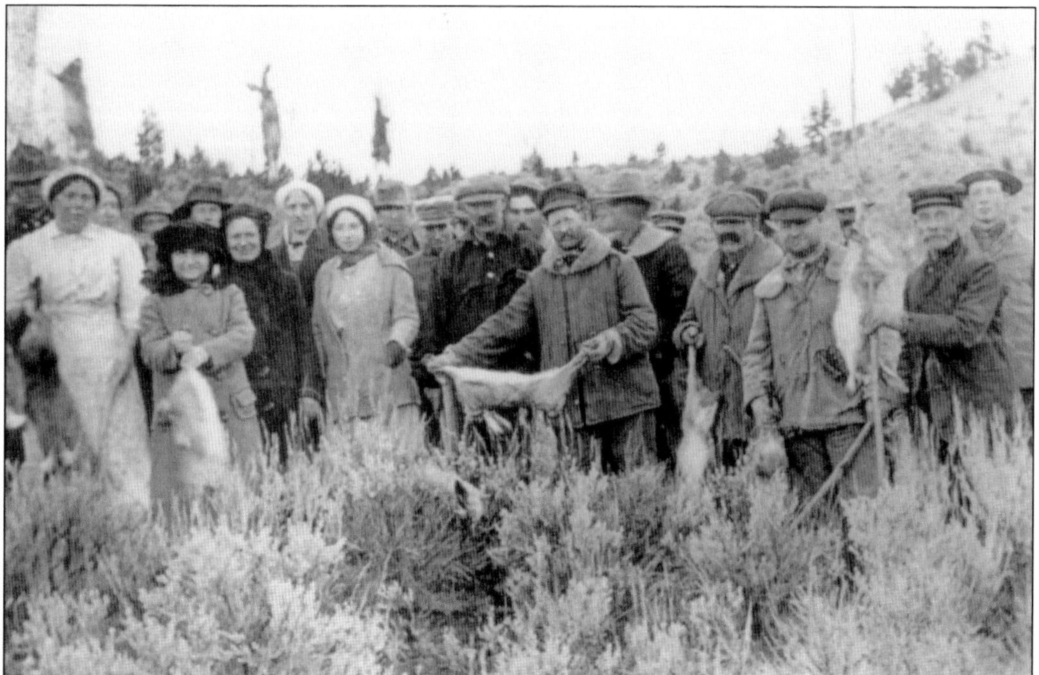

This is a group of Paulina homesteaders at a jackrabbit drive in 1910. Early settlers were concerned about coyotes killing livestock, so they waged a campaign to remove the predators. Unfortunately, in the process they reduced the main predator of rabbits. As a result, rabbits devastated crops as the population boomed. Locals would hold drives that involved using nets. They would beat the brush, herding the rabbits to the nets, and then beat them or shoot them. It was not uncommon to kill over 1,000 rabbits in a single rabbit drive.

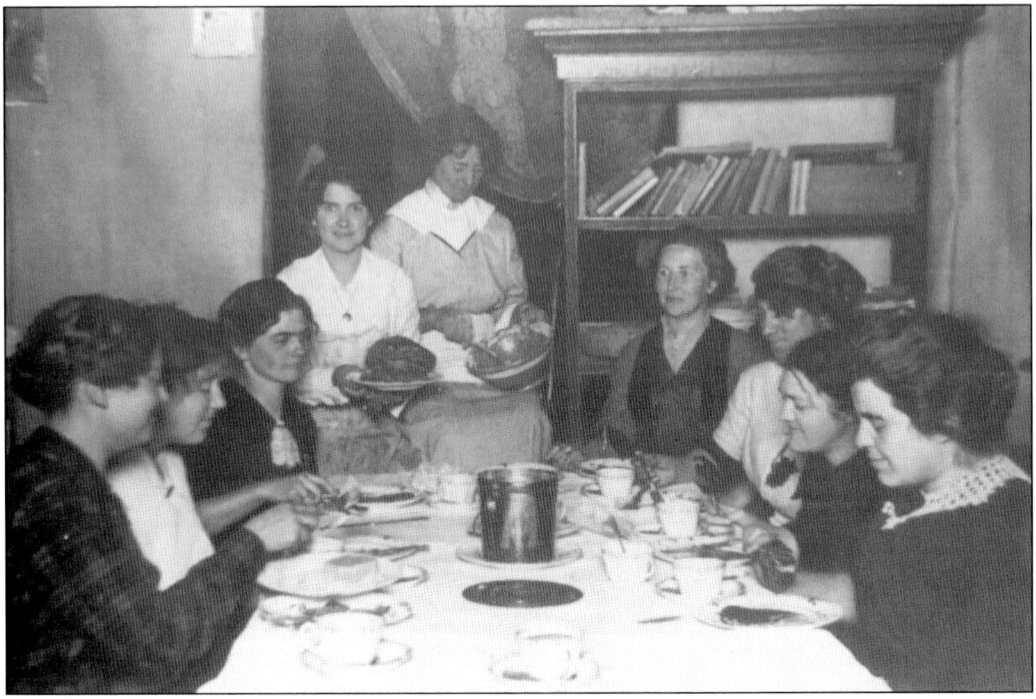

This is a pancake supper held at Alice Day Pratt's cabin about 1914. It is a gathering of teachers. They are, from left to right, Miss Jeffries, Miss Herman, Miss Cassidy, Miss Hubbard, Miss Pratt, Miss Hewes, Miss Engdall, Miss Evans, and Miss Hodges.

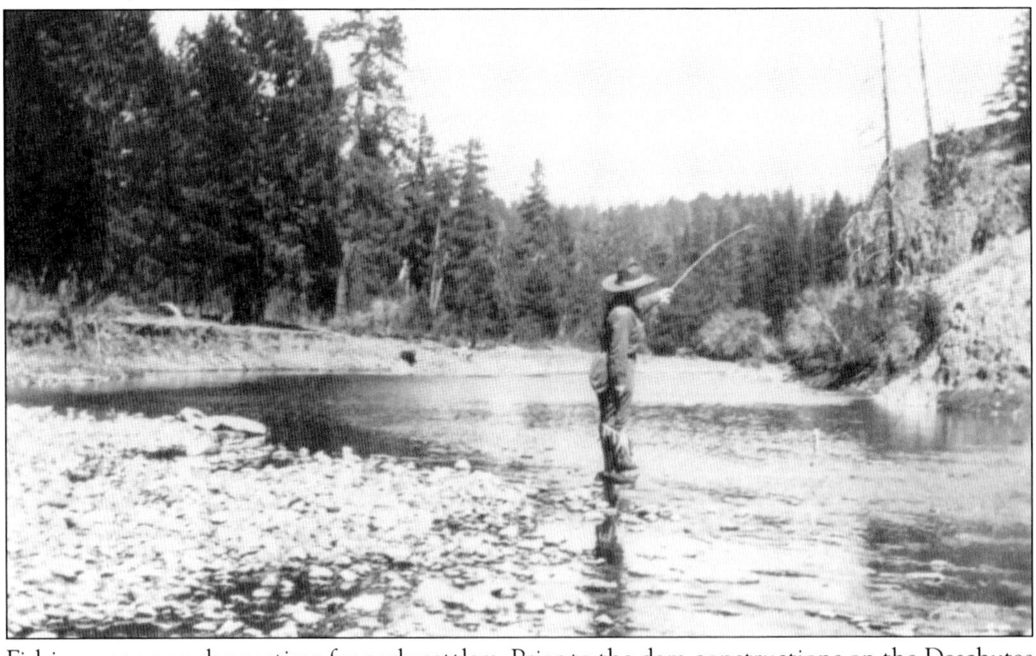

Fishing was a popular pastime for early settlers. Prior to the dam constructions on the Deschutes and Crooked Rivers, salmon made runs up the streams. Ruby Roba Barkshire is fishing on the North Fork of the Crooked River about 1920. Ruby was the daughter of George and Mary Roba, who owned a ranch in Paulina Valley. Ruby later took over operations of the ranch.

Sarah Thompson (left) and Marie Spinning (right) are displaying shooting skills on the range near Prineville. They appear to be dressed for a social event rather than a hunting trip.

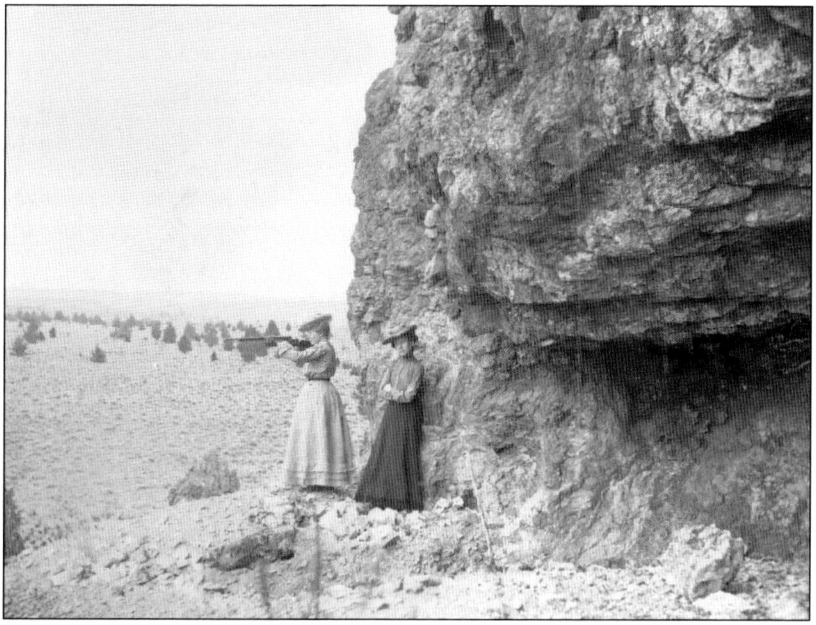

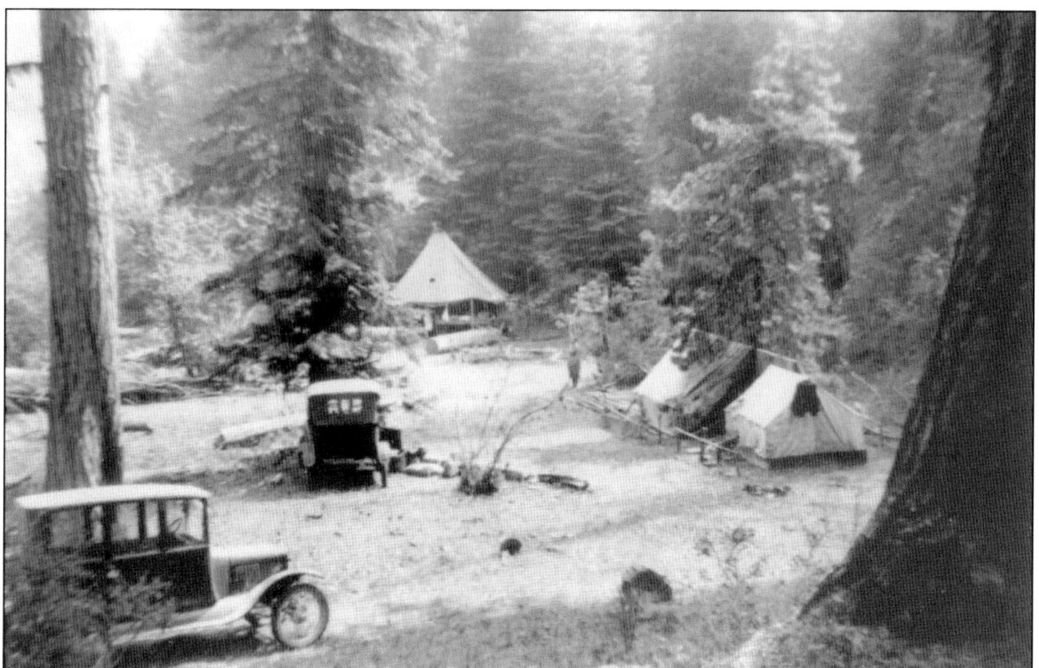

Camping was a very popular pastime for early settlers, and the use of automobiles provided increased opportunities in the remote regions of the county. This is a c. 1914 forest camp on the West Fork of Mill Creek near present Wildcat Campground.

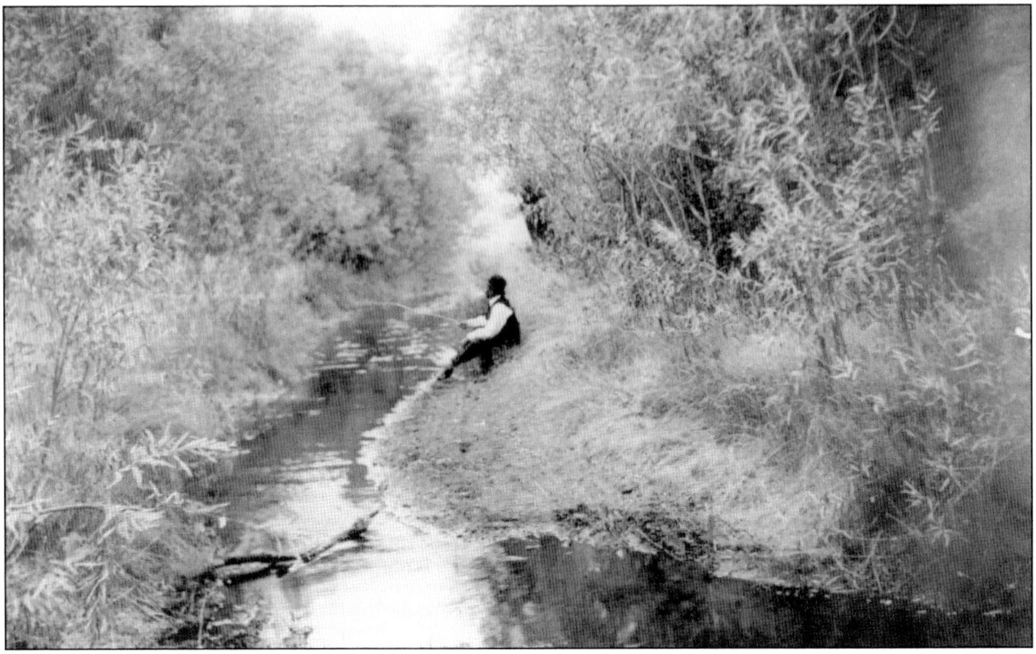

John "Jack" Cadle is fishing on Ochoco Creek near the present Keystone Ranch about 10 miles east of Prineville about 1900. Note the lush riparian vegetation along the stream bank. Heavy livestock grazing near the turn of the 20th century resulted in much of the riparian vegetation deteriorating, and stream banks were often exposed. Recently, efforts have been made to restore riparian zones throughout the region.

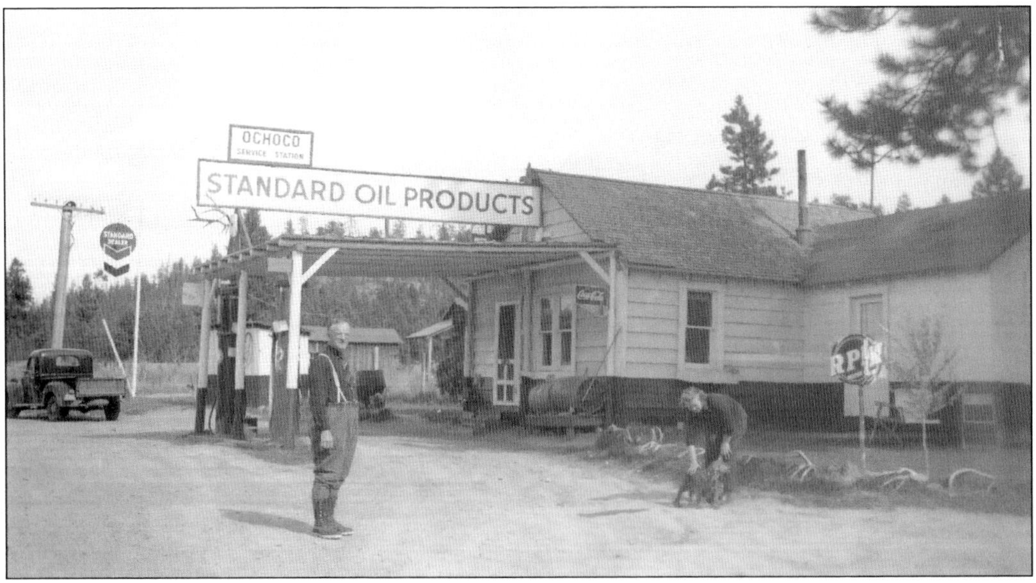

The increased use of automobiles and construction of the old Ochoco Highway in the 1920s from Prineville to Mitchell and points east created the need for fuel stations and rest stops along the route. Bert Tolliday established the Ochoco Service Station on the old Ochoco Highway about 20 miles east of Prineville and operated it for several years. He is standing at center. The woman is unidentified. Today, the structure is no longer standing.

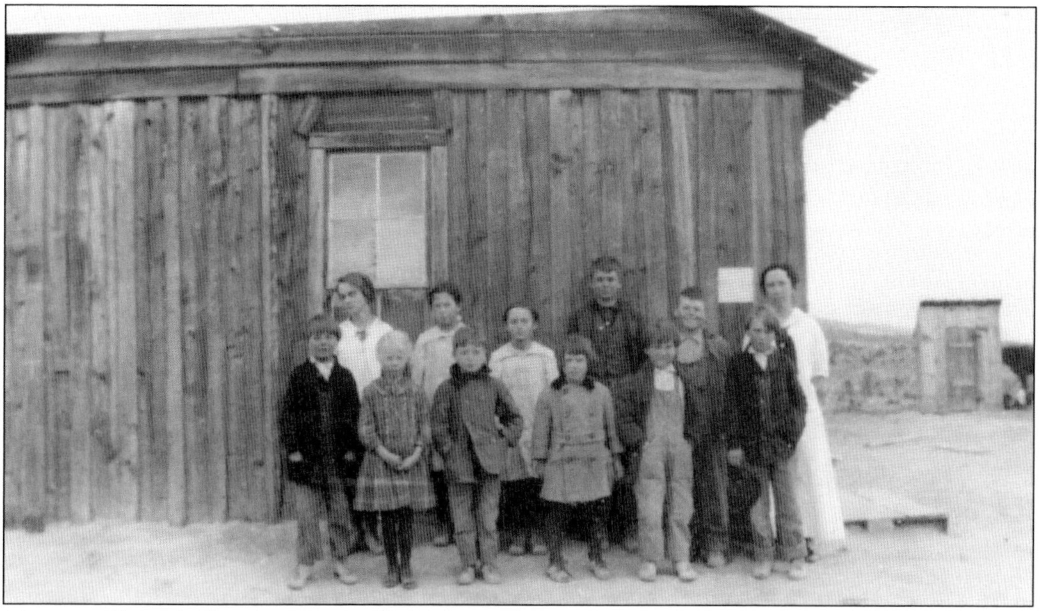

Many small rural schools were established in early Crook County. The schools were often located within a few miles of each other to reduce the distance that children had to travel. This is the Camp Creek School in 1917. Students are, from left to right, (first row) Loren Parrish, Beulah Demaris, Howard Batea, Frances Saunders, Babe Parrish, and Gail Parrish; (second row) Dorothy Hackleman, Ruth Saunders, Edith Saunders, Abe Hackleman, Walter Fallen, and Leatha Evert Morris, teacher.

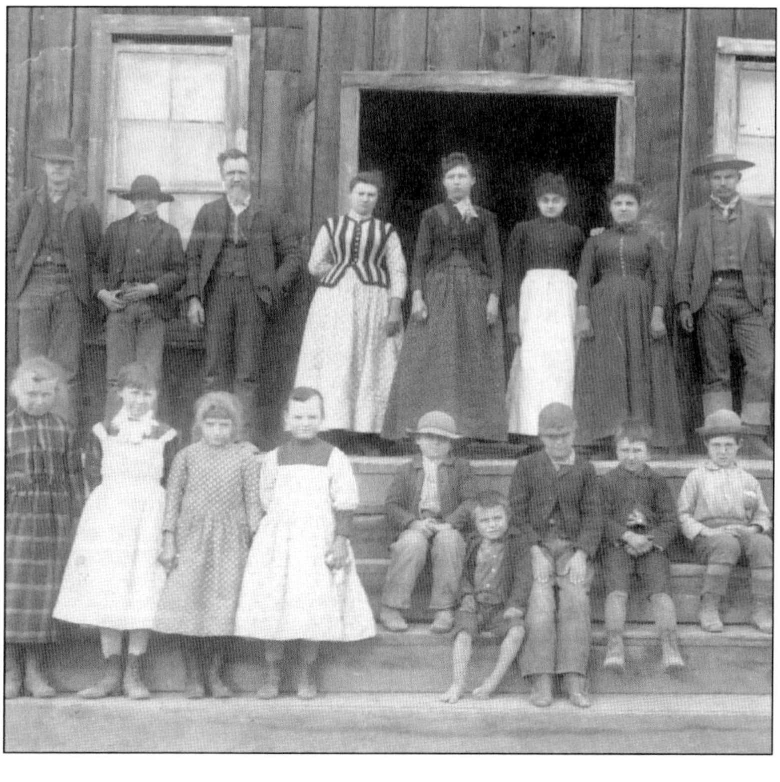

Students, teachers, and some parents are seen at the Claypool School around 1895. The people are unidentified, but the photograph demonstrates the large cross-section of ages for students. The Claypool School was at the David Wayne Claypool homestead near the confluence of Mill Creek and Ochoco Creek, about eight miles east of Prineville. Most schools were one-room facilities, and several grade levels were taught at the same time.

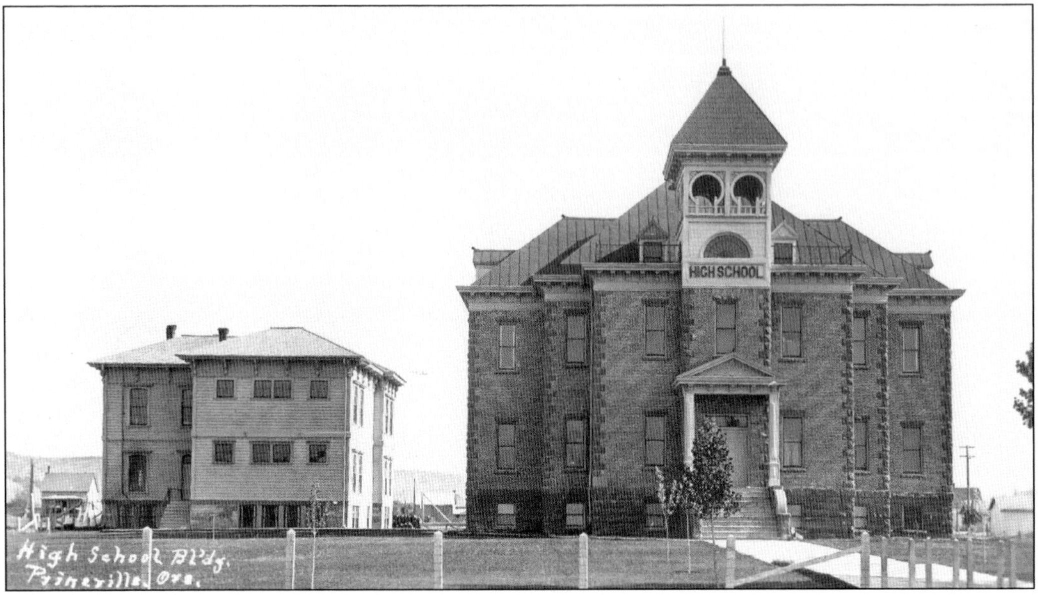

A high school was constructed in Prineville in 1904, one of the first built in the state of Oregon. It was located at the corner of Fairview and Third Streets. It was a three-story brick building. Students from Bend, Redmond, Madras, and outlying portions of the county had to board in Prineville to attend until the other communities established high schools. To the left of the school is Crook County's old courthouse, which was moved to the site to be used as an annex. The buildings were torn down in 1939. Crooked River Elementary School is now located at the site.

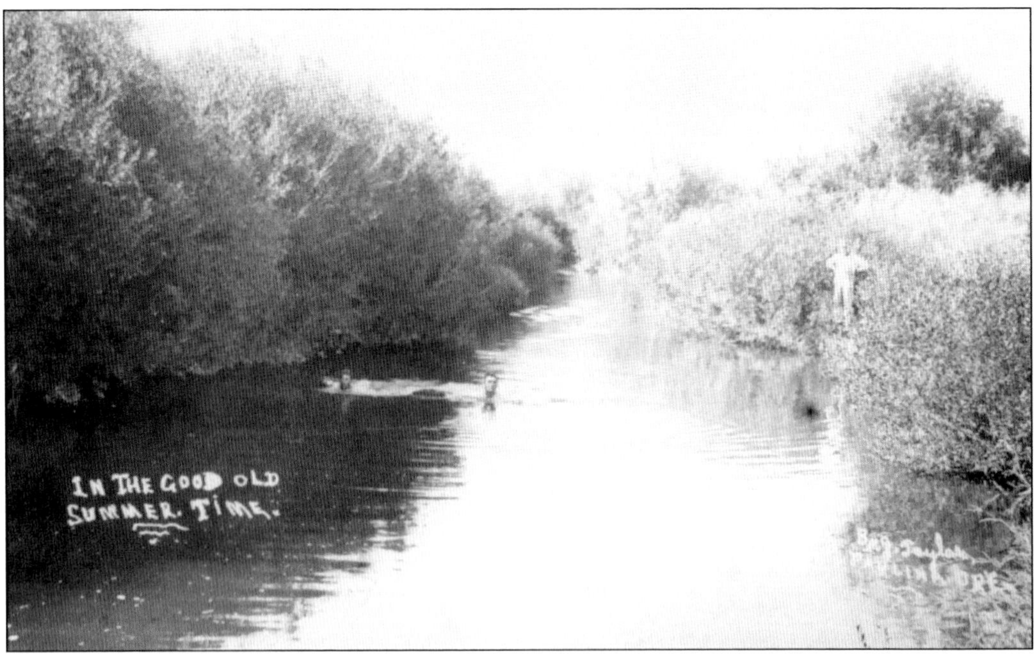

These young men are swimming in upper Beaver Creek about 10 miles northeast of Paulina in 1910. Note the lush riparian vegetation along the stream. Although the stream does not appear to be deep, it does look inviting to be used as a swimming hole. Beaver Creek is one of the major tributaries of Crooked River.

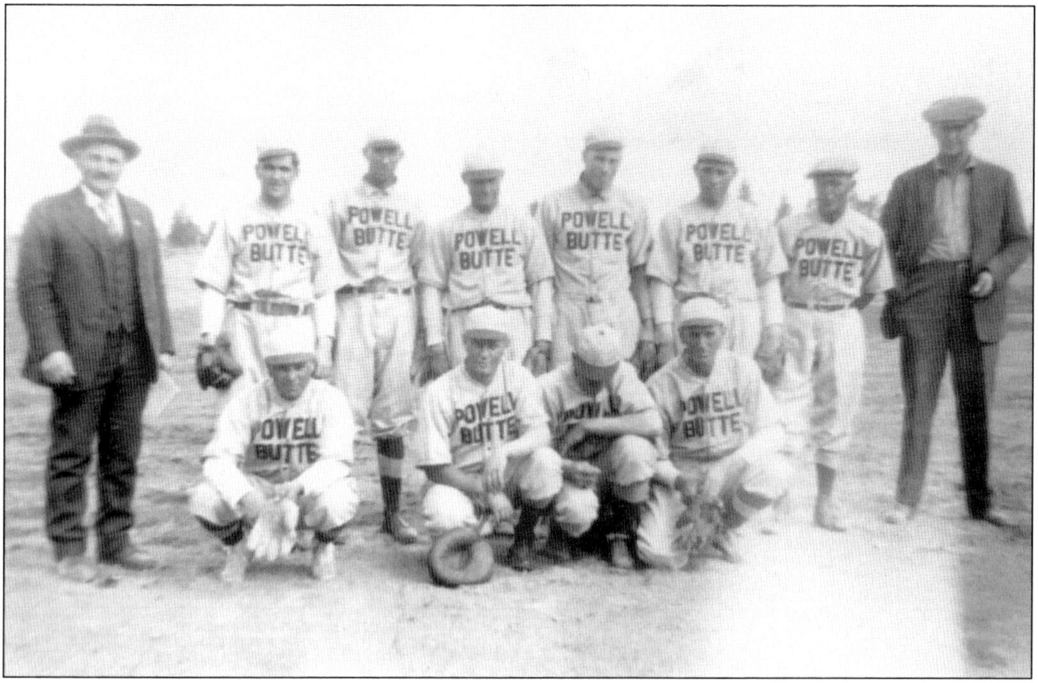

Baseball was an extremely popular sport in central Oregon. Any community that could field a full team of nine players established a community team to play neighboring communities. Often large crowds traveled to see the games, and it was a big social event. This is the Powell Butte baseball team in 1926. Players are unidentified, but the team was mostly farmhands and farmers.

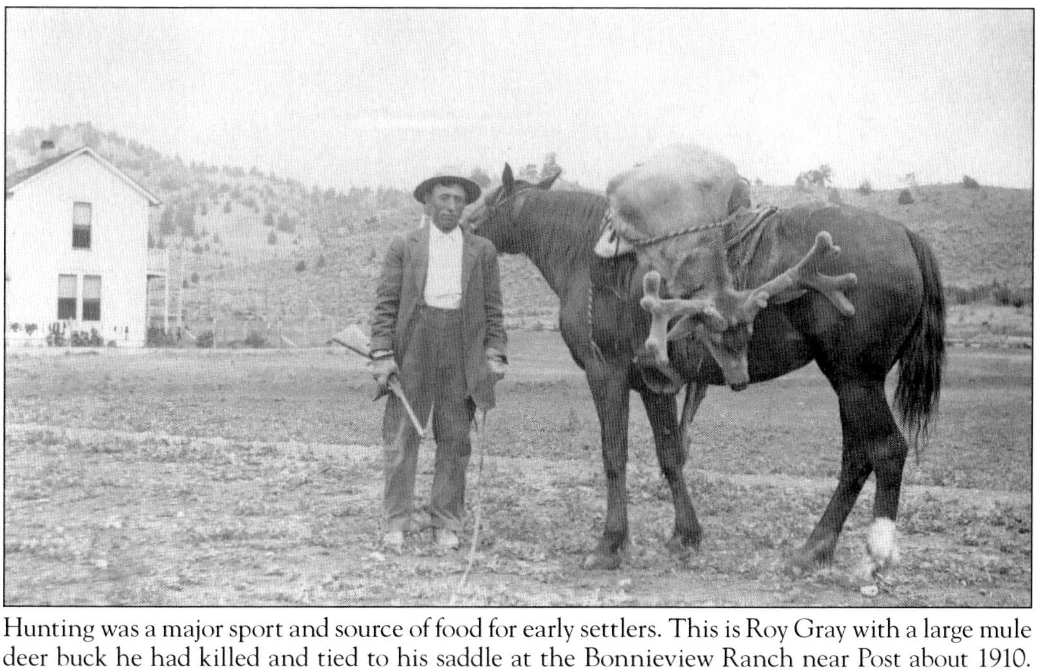

Hunting was a major sport and source of food for early settlers. This is Roy Gray with a large mule deer buck he had killed and tied to his saddle at the Bonnieview Ranch near Post about 1910. Hunting continues to be one of the most popular annual activities in the county.

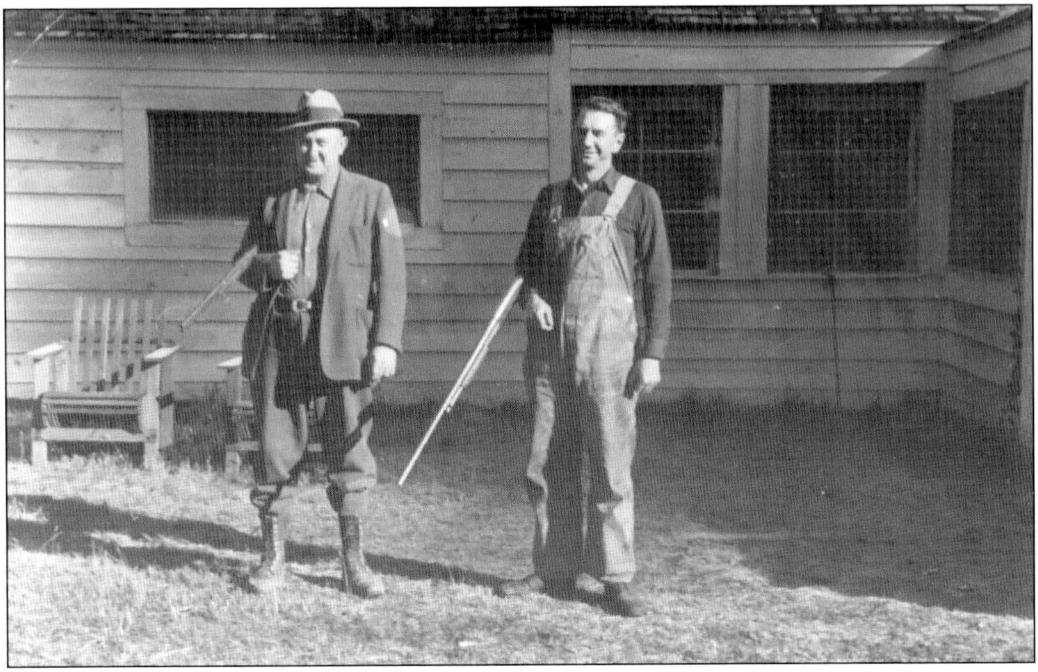

Local hardware store owner Hugh Lakin (right) owned a ranch on upper Mill Creek near the Ochoco National Forest boundary. He had connections with relatively famous individuals who came to hunt and fish on his ranch. The gentleman to the left is Hall of Fame baseball player Ty Cobb, a frequent guest at the Lakin Ranch. Another famous guest was Dean Witter, who established a national investment firm. This photograph was taken about 1930.

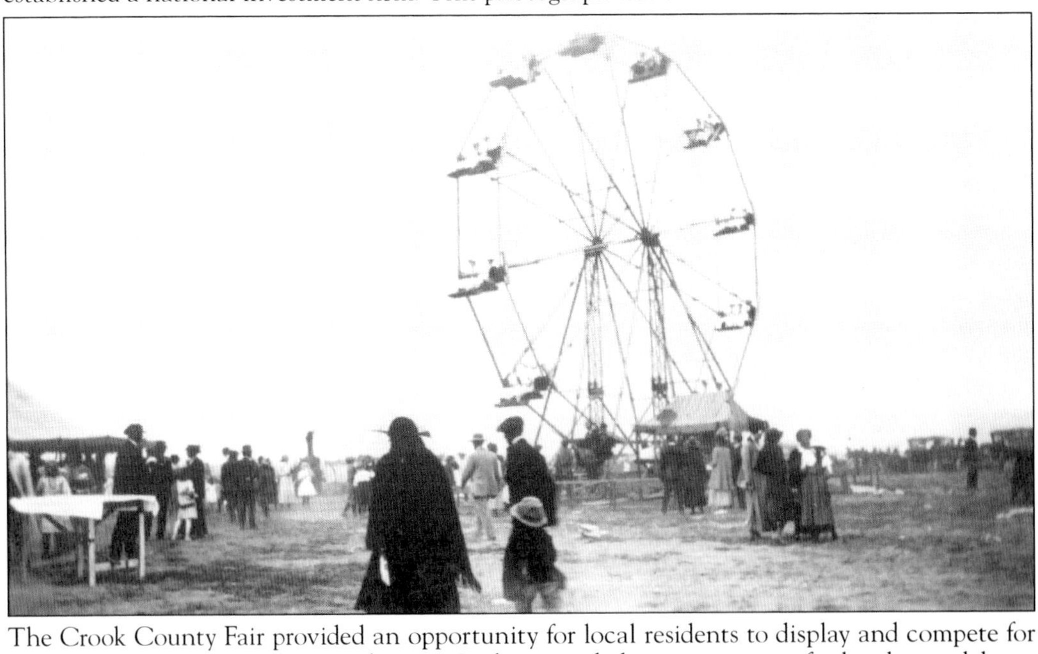

The Crook County Fair provided an opportunity for local residents to display and compete for awards on farm and domestic production. It also provided an opportunity for locals to celebrate and have a good time. This is one of the first Ferris wheels to arrive in the community for the 1917 fair, and it attracted a large crowd.

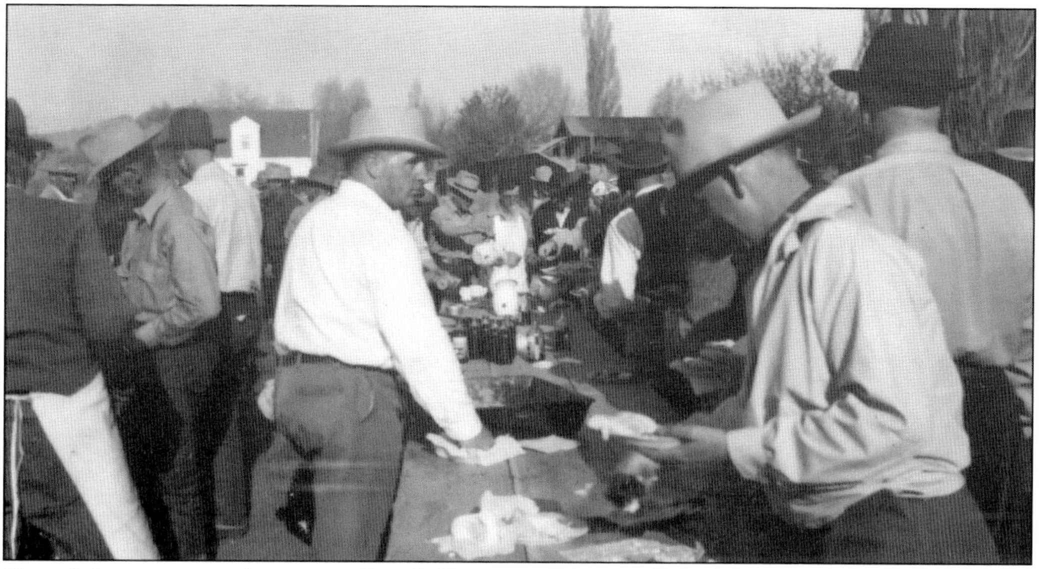

One of the major social events in Crook County is the annual Lords Acre Sale held at the Powell Butte Church the first week in November. Pastor D.L. "Penny" Penhollow and members of the Vice, Minson, Carter, Thompson, and Musick families established the event in 1947 as a means to raise funds for church expansion and projects. Farmers were encouraged to donate the profits from crops grown on one acre of their farms. As crowds arrive from all over the country to eat a country barbecue and purchase a variety of products produced locally, the event has grown to be a large fundraiser for the church.

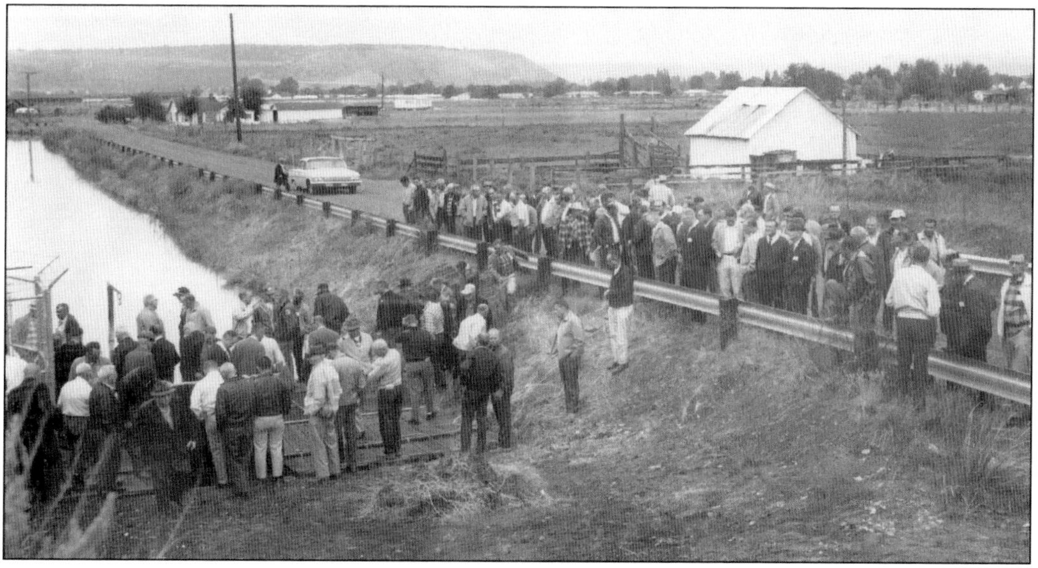

One of the significant irrigation and flood control projects in Crook County was the development of Bowman Dam on the Crooked River about 20 miles southeast of Prineville. The dam was completed in 1964, and this is part of the dedication ceremony as water first arrived through the irrigation canal system. The Crooked River Project provides flood control on the Crooked River and a water supply for local farms, and is one of the most popular recreation sites in central Oregon. The dam was named for Arthur Bowman, who lobbied to have it constructed; Prineville Reservoir (behind the dam) is named for the community.